Schizophrenia: The Positive Perspective

This fully revised second edition of *Schizophrenia: The Positive Perspective* uses biographical sketches and essays to discuss schizophrenia and related conditions, providing advice on methods of coping, routes to growth, recovery and well-being, and how schizophrenia can be viewed in a positive light. It also explores the insights of R.D. Laing and discusses how they can be applied to contemporary ideas and research.

In this expanded edition Peter Chadwick, a previous sufferer, builds on his earlier edition and introduces new topics including:

- Cannabis smoking and schizophrenia.
- Psychoanalytic approaches to psychosis and their extension into the spiritual domain.
- Using cognitive behaviour therapy in the treatment of profound existential distress.
- How experiences on the edge of madness can be relevant to understanding reality.

Schizophrenia: The Positive Perspective encourages hope, confidence and increased self-esteem in schizophrenia sufferers and raises new questions about how schizophrenia should be evaluated. It is important reading for anyone working with schizophrenic people including psychologists, psychiatrists, social workers, and other mental health professionals.

Peter K. Chadwick has lectured in psychology for the universities of Liverpool, Strathclyde, Birkbeck and Goldsmiths Colleges, London, and also for the Open University. He was Professor of Community Psychology at Boston University from 1991 to 1994. He retired from teaching in 2006 and was awarded the DSc by the University of Bristol in 2007 for his research over the past four decades.

Schizophrenia: The Positive Perspective

Explorations at the outer reaches of
human experience

Second edition

Peter K. Chadwick

With contributions by
Travis Parker and
Terry Hammond

Routledge
Taylor & Francis Group

LONDON AND NEW YORK

First edition published 1997
by Routledge

Second edition published 2009
by Routledge
27 Church Road, Hove, East Sussex BN3 2FA

Simultaneously published in the USA and Canada
by Routledge
270 Madison Ave, New York, NY 10016

Routledge is an imprint of the Taylor & Francis Group,
an informa business

© 2009 Peter K. Chadwick

Typeset in Times by
RefineCatch Ltd, Bungay, Suffolk
Printed and bound in Great Britain by
TJ International Ltd, Padstow, Cornwall
Paperback cover design by Andy Ward

This publication has been produced with paper manufactured to
strict environmental standards and with pulp derived from
sustainable forests.

British Library Cataloguing in Publication Data
A catalogue record for this book is available from the British Library

Library of Congress Cataloging-in-Publication Data
Chadwick, Peter K. (Peter Kenneth), 1946–
   Schizophrenia: the positive perspective : explorations at the outer
reaches of human experience / Peter K. Chadwick. – 2nd ed.
      p. ; cm.
   Includes bibliographical references and indexes.
   1. Schizophrenia.   2. Gifted persons.   3. Schizophrenics.
4. Creative ability.   I. Title.
   [DNLM: 1. Schizophrenia.   2. Creativeness.   3. Marijuana
Smoking – psychology.   4. Schizophrenic Psychology. WM 203
C432s 2009]
   RC514.C44 2009
   616.89′8 – dc22   2008018507

ISBN: 978–0–415–45907–5 (hbk)
ISBN: 978–0–415–45908–2 (pbk)

All science is poetry
Percy Bysshe Shelley

This book is dedicated to Oscar Wilde
and R.D. Laing, both men whose
ideas were buried before their time

Contents

Preface

In each of us there is a little of all of us.

Georg Christoph Lichtenberg (1742–1799)

Schizophrenia is a uniquely human disorder and therefore studying it does not so much tell us about a set of aberrant processes in a small, categorically different group of people, it tells us about our very humanity. To suffer from schizophrenia is to be human. This is partly because vulnerability to it is associated also with the workings of the creative process, with language, high sensitivity and imaginativeness generally and in many instances with enhanced spiritual sensitivity and empathy. We could not eliminate schizophrenia as we can eliminate smallpox without doing serious and irreversible damage to our species. Sadly it tends to be psychiatric and residential social workers, day centre staff, nurses and community workers who see this vital positive side to the schizophrenia sufferer rather than professionals and laboratory-based researchers in psychiatry and abnormal psychology. When the former speak, as they do, of sufferers' 'uncanny sensitivity', 'frightening empathy' and of how sometimes it is possible to have relationships with schizophrenia sufferers that are far deeper than those they have with so-called 'normal' people, we are dealing with things that are usually outside of the beam cast by investigators in empirical science.

In this short preface I wish briefly to outline the broad conceptual basis of my approach to this issue and show the theoretical foundations of this text. This preface also will give me a chance to reveal my attitude and stance, to show in which general direction my *will* is oriented and how I feel emotionally towards this domain of human life.

The research I have pursued on this topic over the last three decades has been done largely within the tradition begun by Meehl (1962, 1973) which argues for a genetic predisposition in the sufferers ('schizotaxia') producing the so-called 'schizotaxic brain' and which in life and development eventuates in a certain personality organisation, the most common usually referred to as 'schizotypal personality'. This tradition in Britain (Claridge, 1988, 1990,

1997) sees schizophrenia, like hypertension, as a systemic problem with a genetic basis that eventuates in illness under stress and the stresses induced by a certain lifestyle. The genetic basis for schizophrenia, although complex, is now a field of increasing optimism (Cardno and Gottesman, 2000; Arranz *et al.*, 2000; Riley *et al.*, 2003; Kalidindi and Murray, 2004) and there is no evidence that environmental factors alone can cause the illness in a person genetically unrelated to a schizophrenia sufferer. However, there also is no doubt that nurture contributes to the emergence of this illness (Tienari, 1991; Tienari *et al.*, 1994; Cullberg, 2001) and that modifying the environment to which a sufferer returns is vitally important in preventing relapse (Goldstein *et al.*, 1978; Hogarty and Anderson, 1986; Tarrier *et al.*, 1994). Early intervention with people who are showing signs of the disorder is an integral area of research in which education of families and the public, in what to look for, is important (Birchwood *et al.*, 1992; Birchwood, 2000).

There is now no justification for a return to 1960s attitudes to the effect that 'families cause schizophrenia'. I suffered a schizoaffective psychotic crisis myself in 1979 and the most critical abusive stresses and experiences that brought this about occurred at the state secondary school I went to and in three of the neighbourhoods where I lived. Although my mother and brother were both highly disturbed, my mother was also a very warm person who, 'when push came to shove' as we say in England, was always on my side. Had it not been for abuse at school and in the community I definitely would never have suffered psychosis.

Having said this, however, it does seem that adverse childhood and later experiences in a person genetically hard-wired to be highly sensitive to stresses such as criticism and scolding, disrespect, being unwanted, angry outbursts and so on can eventuate the schizotaxic vulnerability to this illness (Myhrman *et al.*, 1994; Tienari *et al.*, 1994). Life inevitably involves abuse from time to time, but only about 1 per cent of people become schizophrenic; clearly something more than the vicissitudes of living is required.

In the light of the fact that the pendulum in research internationally has swung first from environmentalism ('mind with no brain') to biochemical reductionism ('brain with no mind'), it now rests pretty well between these misguided earlier extremes and both genetic and constitutional vulnerability as well as environmental and cognitive, emotional and motivational factors are recognised as important in explanation and recovery (Corr, 2006).

The particular approach I therefore am using in this book is the so-called vulnerability-stress-coping model (see also Anthony and Liberman, 1986 and Levin, 2006 on this) within a bio-psycho-social-spiritual rationale. I am taking it that the genetic vulnerability involves many genes, usually of small to moderate effect ('polygenic theory') and that these genes are widely distributed in the population. Some 'vulnerability' genes may actually be involved in such things as pattern detection, remote associative thinking, perceptual sensitivity and creative and linguistic imaginativeness and meaning seeking generally. Hence we are all 'a little schizophrenic', it is part and parcel of the human condition and may indeed *be* why we are such an imaginative and creative, inventive species (and such a talkative species) as we are. Tim Crow has argued (Crow *et al.*, 1989) that the asymmetry of the human brain, and hence the emergence of language skills, was a speciation event in human evolution and that psychosis is the uniquely human condition that it is because of this. Again, this approach argues that we have schizophrenia because we are human. The particular gene combinations and interactions that make a person seriously vulnerable to actual schizophrenic illness – where, as I found myself, the brain–mind system goes tonically out of control in a kind of positive feedback spiral and the agentic sense of Self as being in control of one's own mind is completely lost – seem to be a threat only to about 10 per cent of the population. Nonetheless, the distribution is graded and to some degree psychosis-proneness is part of what we are as human beings and can be seen as an actual dimension of personality along which we all sit at various points (Eysenck and Eysenck, 1976) (although the Eysencks do not focus on schizotypy). A genetic model compatible with a dimensional view of psychosis has been proposed by Roberts and Claridge (1991). This so-called 'normalisation' perspective I am adopting here also is used by Kingdon and Turkington (1994).

This conceptualisation of schizophrenia sees sufferers as kith and kin with the rest of humanity, sees madness as not essentially an alien state experientially but something that everybody, because of their humanity, has at least a slight inkling of at some time in their lives. Schizophrenia, in my view, and as a sufferer who has known it from the inside, is essentially an exaggeration of normal processes that interweave with toxic results for one's well-being and, on many occasions, for one's very willingness to stay alive at all.

Despite the portentousness of this illness and the severe distress associated with it, the general climate in the research community is clearly optimistic (Harrison *et al.*, 2001; Hirsch and Weinberger, 2003). The real pessimism is about the gap between the actual technology and procedures that truly are available to help schizophrenia sufferers (and to prevent the exacerbation of distress into illness) and the actual provision of services to patients (Craig *et al.*, 2003). The plight of many schizophrenia sufferers and indeed the attitudes of the public towards them is a disgrace to the Western world. We see here how ignorance is the fuel of fear and prejudice. Also, because sufferers can so easily be assessed as less capable than they are, real physical illnesses can be very easily missed and misdiagnosed as 'depression' or 'demoralisation'. Mistakes like these can be fatal.

This book tries to reflect the optimism which we researchers do nonetheless feel about our attempts to understand and to help but, more than this, also talks in addition about the positive qualities of the schizophrenia-prone mind. It is now clear that personality dimensions other than the schizotypal, such as paranoid, schizoid and hypomanic personality styles (O'Flynn *et al.*,

2003) lie on a dimension where schizophrenia and schizoaffective illness are the extremes. The picture, however, now is complicated by the fact of the *normality* of the personalities of many people who go on to suffer schizophrenia (Peralta *et al.*, 1991). Clearly this condition can, and does, eventuate from our 'humanness', it is as heterogeneous as is the species and it can strike in very unpredictable ways. It is in no sense a sign of the character weakness of the victim. In this text I will present material on schizophrenia induced toxically by cannabis smoking (Chapter 4), an issue, of course, of great public concern these days; on the paths in and out of my own 1979 schizoaffective episode (Chapters 5 and 6); on schizotypy and paranoia (personality styles particularly at risk) (Chapters 8 and 10); and on the experience of 'psychotic phenomena', such as hallucinations, in a person who in no other way is above the threshold of psychiatric morbidity (Chapter 9). This latter instance is an issue first raised by Romme and Escher (1993). The book centrally is a study in experiential and phenomenological psychology and psychiatry and is critically concerned with ways of coping, ways of preventing illness and paths to recovery. In talking of recovery to a good and worthwhile quality of life with meaning and purpose (Anthony *et al.*, 2003; Ramon *et al.*, 2007), I am stressing here the value also of understanding the *causes* of the illness to the prevention of its reoccurrence and to inner nourishment, self-enlightenment and personal growth. In my own case my approach was that if I could understand and explain how my illness happened, I could make things so that it would never happen again – and it worked. I also tried to see meaning in the illness and related it to my spiritual life. Patients do involve themselves in causal thinking about their illness and the attributions they make have a major impact on stigma and recovery (Charles *et al.*, 2007 and references therein).

In the later parts of the text (Chapters 12 and 13) I talk more of issues such as peer support (see also Lawn *et al.*, 2007 on this) and psychotherapeutic interventions in psychosis with a positive slant being put on the insights of R.D. Laing, whose contribution (e.g. Laing, 1990/1960) I feel was marred by, and underestimated in its value by, his adoption of too extreme a stance on therapy. This part of the book also calls for still more integration in therapy approaches and also outlines a basis for mutual dialogue between therapists concerned with spiritual, existential, psychoanalytic and cognitive issues. The issue of the 'schizophrenia' label itself, given how dreadfully stigmatising for sufferers it has become (May, 2000; Dickerson *et al.*, 2002), is addressed in Chapter 2, where I argue that 'neuro-integrative disorder' or perhaps 'neuro-integrative relatedness disorder' probably would be better and far more accurate terms (see also Levin, 2006 on this).

Although I do not believe that many things for which psychiatry has diagnostic categories are illnesses, I have no doubt that psychosis is an illness, though it can, of course, take many forms. There is a group of researchers, chiefly in psychology and psychotherapy, who challenge this view (see Boyle,

2002; Sanders, 2007) but my own experience and research does not lead me to ally myself with them (Chadwick, 2007a). I admit, however, that current forms of chemotherapy are not satisfactory, by any means, for all patients and that psychological, psychosocial and spiritual interventions, as I have found myself, are of enormous benefit to recovery (see P.D.J. Chadwick and Lowe, 1990; Garety *et al.*, 1998; Martindale *et al.*, 2003; Morrison *et al.*, 2004; Mosher, 2004; P.D.J. Chadwick, 2006). I do, however, believe that in the future better, individually targeted medication, based on individual DNA analyses, will massively brighten the future for schizophrenia sufferers. In my case the drug haloperidol, actually quite an old, typical neuroleptic invented by Paul Janssen in 1958 and first marketed in 1961, accidentally was, for me, the nearest thing one could ever have to a perfectly individually targeted medication for schizophrenia. I was transferred to it from chlorpromazine in November 1981 and the moment the drug 'hit' in my brain I thought to myself (reflecting on the agonies of my past), 'It's all over'. I have never looked back since that moment in my life. I went on to obtain a second PhD, in psychology, stayed in work for 25 years and eventually was awarded the DSc for my research. I married in 1983 and my wife and I own a lovely bungalow in the countryside. We love each other unthinkingly and have been together for over 25 years. My life was completely revolutionised by that medication, which far from reducing me to a societally conforming zombie has enabled me to feel more true to myself than I was before – and has not damaged my creativity. The possibility, and indeed the actuality, that psychosis can lead on to one becoming better than one was before, of course very much a Laingian dream, has been addressed by a number of authors (Silverman, 1980; Chadwick, 2002a; Attwood, 2007). For this reason I believe that the research, in genetics and psychopharmacology, for better – and eventually individually – targeted medications is a research thrust of enormous promise. It has my full support. I have no enthusiasm whatsoever for movements, which do exist, towards 'drug-free psychiatry'. Were they to become successful, people like me would very quickly be in the graveyard.

Sadly, in the present state of our knowledge, medication, including haloperidol, is not helpful for everybody. In the end, medication or no medication, everyone has to find their own path to peace and to quality in their lives. Sometimes, as in my own case, this may require a total revision in almost every aspect of the way one lives, the work one does and the people with whom one mixes. Even with well-targeted medication, there are no easy ways of getting out of schizophrenic illness. This book tries to show the other side of the coin from a focus on deficit and dysfunction and I hope will be encouraging to all people in any way touched by schizophrenia and related conditions. After all, if there is no 'other side to the coin' all one can do is 'make the best of a bad job', as we say in England. But this is not how I see schizophrenia or indeed psychosis in general. Hence this text.

In closing I would like to thank certain colleagues who have, in one way or another, supported and encouraged my research over the decades. I would particularly like to thank David Carless, Isabel Clarke, Gordon Claridge, Philip Corr, Tim Crow, Kevin Dutton, Steven Hirsch, Guy Holmes, Areti Karytopoulou, Craig Newnes, Emmanuelle Peters and John Wilding. My great thanks also go out to Sylvia Ross, who typed this work with incredible speed and efficiency, as well as excellent compassionate understanding of its contents, and of course to my wife Jill – who has always accepted me for what I am, not for what I ought to be or should be. The one-liners at the chapter heads, in the body of the text, are my own ideas and opinions and are really an outgrowth of my relationship with Jill.

The book could not exist without the support of the people in its pages who volunteered to expose their 'psychological innards' and experiences to the world. I am especially grateful to Travis Parker and Terry Hammond for their excellent pemanship in Chapters 3 and 4 but also to the other members of The Borderliners Group, formed by Desmond Marshall and myself in March 1992: Simon Blair, Geoff Garfield, Jonathan Smith and Ivo Wiesner. Their support of myself and my research over the years has been invaluable.

Finally I also would like to thank my many thousands of students in psychology that I have taught, at various institutes during my nomadic life, since October 1975. They have educated me as much as, if not more than, I have educated them. Joanne Forshaw, who suggested this project of a second edition to me in the spring of 2007, has been an excellently understanding and efficient editor, almost always accessible and speedy in reply. For a writer such things are *so* important.

Though I speak well of medication in this preface, hope is as important as any pill. This book tries centrally to write about people's humanity, about 'the taste of the soup', as Einstein would put it, rather than 'the formula of the soup'. In doing so I am trying to bring the people in its pages alive to the reader as flesh and blood human beings, not as organic machines. This book then is essentially a person-oriented approach rather than a reduction-istic one. Perhaps recognising how schizophrenia (or neuro-integrative relatedness disorder) is an emergent phenomenon from our very humanity will help people to see that only by working together, rather than by stigma-tising sufferers as alien freaks, can we minimise the cost of this illness in human suffering and move on to a position where sufferers have meaningful, purposeful lives.

Peter K. Chadwick
Birkbeck College (FCE)
University of London
Winter 2007/08

Acknowledgements

Chapter 12 is based substantially on two previous publications:

Chadwick, P.K. (2006) Coping with the positive and negative experiences of psychosis: Hints from patients, *Clinical Psychology Forum*, No. 163, July, pp. 5–8.
Chadwick, P.K. (2007) 'Is this letter a telephone?' On the acceptance and emotional understanding of psychotic thought, *Clinical Psychology Forum*, No. 171, March, pp. 3–7.

This material is published with the permission of the Clinical Psychology Division of The British Psychological Society.

The excerpt from Desmond Marshall's book, *Journal of an Urban Robinson Crusoe*, in Chapter 8 is reproduced with the permission of Desmond Marshall and Saxon Books.

Chapter 1

Introduction

In defence of spirituality, mysticism and madness

> It is not so much the cognition that is important but the music to the cognition that is important. People do not follow logic, they follow magic.

In the early 1960s, when I first started reading psychology and thinking psychologically, I'd be about 16 at the time, it really did look as if psychology could change the world. In those days Skinner, Eysenck, Broadbent and Rogers were soaring to prominence. The ambience was upbeat and bullish. We genuinely felt that we could 'crack the code' of the human mind, shape human behaviour, understand people's deepest fears and aspirations and bring harmony and peace to the planet. The future was not physics, it was psychology!

I write now in 2007/8, in my seventh decade. I am a student-battered, script-battered, seminar-battered old-timer. I no longer believe it. At least I no longer believe it of psychology as it *is*. What psychology could be is another matter and there my hopes are greater.

In this first chapter I am trying to say that psychology needs to embrace, not scorn, the insights of the spiritually minded, the mystical, the pre-psychotic and even be prepared to listen to 'The Impossible' from the psychotic (and indeed from the Surrealist artist) if it is fully to understand mind and person and our place in the general scheme of things.

The problem of psychology's relevance as an endeavour is that the positivistic attitude of the mainstream of the subject simply doesn't have the breadth and scope to embrace the world's problems. It has become yet another intellectual box fighting, in the epistemological evolutionary game of things, for supremacy in its physics-imitating perspective. 'Give us power!' the establishment seems implicitly to shout, 'We're like physics!' This is in a world of Christians, Jews, Muslims, Buddhists and Hindus in their hundreds of millions. What, one might ask, does a white middle class or upper middle class Western psychologist, steeped in (so-called) Enlightenment rationalism, evidence-based practice and a leafy suburb ideology of scientific humanism know of the mindsets and mind contents of the warring factions of the

Middle East? What do they really know of *any* spiritually guided large communities such as those of India, Pakistan, Uganda, Nigeria or southern United States? Telling these peoples, whose cultures greatly value intuition and revelation, to 'wise up to the truths of materialistic science', forget their 'silly, vacuous, mystical ideas' and embrace the (supposed) certainties of reason, fact and evidence (itself a rather nineteenth-century view of science) is psychologically not a viable proposition. Assuming that secularism is 'The Truth' and that religion will 'just have to move over' is simply not how people and the world work. To think like that is intellectually childish – and the twentieth century has shown us anyway that laboratory focused, analytical reasoning based ideologies do not give us the certainty that positivists so prize as central.

One has to ask, 'What *is* a human mind that it can have spiritual – and indeed schizophrenic – experiences?' One needs to know why such experiences of feeling open as if to forces from beyond ourselves are so compelling, why they can be both dangerous and personally nourishing and what value they have for us as a group of communities here on this earth. Rather than spiritual experiences being merely a secondary functional product of our capacity to believe, might they – and some of the insights of the borderline psychotic and psychotic – not be a primary capacity that enables us to resonate to or 'tune in' to forces or dimensions at present beyond our understanding? As some would put it, do they enable us to see 'the other side of the carpet'?

A hostile critic might say, as indeed such people do, 'This is not science!' or 'You are moving away from science!' However, as my own ideas have settled over the decades, I cannot agree with such accusations. The word 'science' derives from the Latin word *scientia* which means 'knowledge'. As a scientist I am a knowledge-seeker and any science must use methods appropriate to its subject matter, not merely copy physics. It is not the job of a psychologist merely to find facts – where a fact is what a true theory states – but to enhance our understanding of mind and person in the cosmic scheme of things. It must recognise our capacities as symbol and metaphor users, as seekers of that which is *beyond* rationality and logic and also facilitate the possibilities of person.

Of course, as we move away from the materialistic to mentalism, to art, to the multicoloured world of madness, to spirituality, our language runs the risk of becoming less precise and exact. Perhaps Wittgenstein would warn us not to speak at all but remain silent? However, the root word of both 'experiment' and 'experience' is the Latin *experiri* which means 'try'. I think we should at least *try* and that it would be intellectually unadventurous not to do so.

The admittedly ambitious integrative discourse I am proposing for such an understanding, in trying to make psychology relevant and valuable to everybody, is that of a blend of the rational side of science with art and with spirituality. This 'scientia' (science–art–spirituality) discourse has, as its aim, the seeking of *knowledge*, using both experience and experiment, in the service of broadening the actual attitude of psychology out from its current fetish with positivism, materialism and atheism.

Seeking generalised facts about human nature from very large samples, the 'nomothetic' way, ignores the nuance and subtlety of evidence at the level of the individual person. Therefore in this book findings will be referred to both from nomothetic and from idiographic sources. It may indeed be that it is only at the level of the single case, the idiographic level, that we can see how different levels of description interact and interweave to produce the thoughts, feelings and behaviours that they do.

All of the great mathematicians and scientists have prized the value of intuition and revelation – as if it is possible for knowledge to come in 'on another channel' than that of narrowly focused analytical reasoning. These might be said to be insights had in 'altered states', however transient or long-lasting they might be. How, in the general business of life, do we assess such insights as laying claim to knowledge? Some truths, such as, 'You reap what you sow', 'Time waiteth for no man' and 'A man on tiptoe is bound to fall over' we seem to accept as self-evident. On other occasions insights that have the quality of being *reversals* have a knack of commanding people's respect. 'Love your enemies' (Jesus); 'She who hesitates is won' (Wilde) . . . statements like that somehow don't propel us to seek the evidence of science for their acceptance as valuable to the general conduct of human affairs. They are fresh, different, clever and in a sense shock us by their novelty in comparison to the tired old platitudes to which we are used.

Also statements from highly esteemed authorities, such as Einstein's 'Imagination is more important than knowledge' or Churchill's 'The optimist looks for opportunities in every difficulty, the pessimist looks for difficulties in every opportunity', carry weight as people infer their value via the very success-in-life of the people who utter them. In this sense the statements have been 'tested by life' in a kind of 'I got where I am today by thinking like *this*' fashion. The very success also of a spiritual teacher may be taken as a sign of the truth of what they say, as of course some in the humanities and social sciences say in addition of Freud and Jung. Ideas tested by millions in life over decades can override those tested on thousands in snapshot laboratory studies.

Obviously when faced with claims to knowledge and truth we must think but also feel carefully. Coherence; generalisibility; plausibility; explanatory power; testability; novelty; the insight it brings to matters previously puzzling; relevance to current concerns; ideational beauty and elegance; practical value; clarity; accessibility, all in different measure in different circumstances are important.

Like psychoanalysis, the insights of the spiritual quester, the mystic and the psychotic access and inhabit such an intimate and precious realm of the human psyche that the usual, rather impatient methods of impersonal science are often crass in their evaluation. However, just as psychoanalysis has moved on and is not, as some would have us believe, still chained to 1890s thinking (see Stern, 1985; Tyson and Tyson, 1990; Milton *et al.*, 2004) it is perfectly legitimate for insights that span, in their claims, the breadth of mind and life, to be assessed by the relevant 'interest community'. Such insights cannot be shot down by a singular experiment but over the decades they are put to work and assessed in the complex engine room of life.

Spiritual insights and those had on the edges of madness tend to have a status, growth and movement in life that is amoeba-like. They are not targets for 'do or die' critical experiments as utterances such as 'The Universe is one Great Thought' (Sir Arthur Eddington) or that from a psychotic patient I know: 'Don't try and climb rain or sweep sun off the pavement', are often at a metalevel that does not give access to such things. In the end we move forward in the knowledge quest as best we can, always adjusting methods and approaches to the subject matter. It may be somewhat messy but it is all we can do. It is just life.

In the chapters that follow, writ large will be experiences in altered states of consciousness from the drug-induced to the psychotic. We will explore to the limits of human phenomenology but in saying this I have to confess that qualitative investigations of this kind that I have conducted over the decades have provided me personally with at least as much nourishment for the con- . duct of life and for the apprehension of mind and reality as all the thousands of papers I have read in empirical science these last 47 years (since beginning science A level study) that were essentially predicated on (what is often taken to be) the Pythagorean belief that 'all is number'. One must wonder at the outset that there is some important truth to be derived from this.

Chapter 2

Demystifying madness and mystifying sanity

In dreaming, aspects of reality are incorporated into the dream; in delusion, aspects of one's past, and of fantasy, are incorporated into the reality.

Although it is a mistake to believe that R.D. Laing thought the sane to be mad and the mad sane, Laing did try to show that insanity was at least intelligible and hence that schizophrenia sufferers are kith and kin with the rest of humanity and not a categorically different group of people.

In this book I am taking the Laingian argument (see Laing, 1990/1960, 1990/1967, 1970) a step further by arguing that the processes involved in schizophrenia are in themselves quite normal processes but that a concatenation of them, in a person in a certain catalytic situation, will produce what we see as psychosis. They are like chemicals, harmless in themselves, that are toxic or explosive when combined together. This, in itself, is, I think, one particular way in which one can put a positive and less stigmatising slant or perspective on schizophrenia. But there are others.

'DEEP TRUTH'

Another aspect of the thinking of Laing and also of Carl Jung – although neither of them articulated it very fully or clearly – is that psychosis, or at least the very edges of psychosis, where one might be said to be 'supersane' rather than insane, can give one a profound insight into the nature of reality. This is a very fragile state on the penumbra of madness where the boundary between within and without is dissolved or partially dissolved and the state of consciousness changes such that the uncanny becomes the rule rather than the exception. I call this 'The Borderline' (one might also refer to it as 'Tertiary Process') and I had first-hand knowledge of it myself, independently of Laing and Jung, on my way to a schizoaffective psychotic episode in London in 1979. Although Jung has written on these matters (see Chapter 7), his colleague, quantum physicist Wolfgang Pauli (see Jung and Pauli, 1955), was concerned that Jung did not really understand his own discovery nor that he had got it particularly clear in his mind (Laurikainen, 1988). In Chapter 7 I try to unpack the experience at The Borderline as I remember it myself to present the case for this, admittedly very controversial, view as clearly as I can manage. This very precious state of consciousness is more akin to 'superphrenia' (Karlsson, 1972) than schizophrenia but is one also with its own dangers. Indeed most who venture there either do not return or return at a heavy price (Greenberg *et al.*, 1992).

'RECOVERABILITY'

A third perspective on schizophrenia of a generally more positive tone is one that focuses on the educability and 'recoverability' of the person. It is quite wrong, and indeed counter-therapeutic, to regard this disorder as inevitably a life-destroying phenomenon. Psychotic illness can at times be a creative illness, as it was for Freud and Jung (Ellenberger, 1994/1970) and there are occasions when patients not only get well, they go on to become better still with time such that they become better than they were before (Silverman, 1980; Chadwick 2002a and Chapter 6 this volume). Harding *et al.* (1987a, 1987b, 1988) have shown that schizophrenia does not have to have a deteriorating course and found that about 50 per cent of schizophrenic patients were classifiable as 'cured' or only slightly disabled. Patients treated in certain therapeutic communities where the philosophy has been that the illness offers possibilities for growth and integration tend to have markedly better capacities for independent living than those treated only by medication (see Mosher and Menn, 1978; Bola and Mosher, 2003; Mosher, 2004).

The tractability of psychotic symptoms to psychological and psychosocial interventions is now becoming very apparent (see Chapter 13) and education of both families and patients about psychosis is extremely helpful (Atkinson *et al.*, 1996; Freeman *et al.*, 2006). It also is not therapeutically damaging for patients to increase, by private reading, their own knowledge about schizophrenic illness (MacPherson *et al.*, 1996). It is quite wrong to assume that reading about psychosis will itself cause problems for those closely involved.

THE BENEFITS OF PSYCHOSIS-PRONENESS

A fourth positive perspective on schizophrenia relates more directly to the positive capacities there imbricated into the very proneness to the illness itself. A delusional episode may be a release of a fiction-making capacity and betray considerable imaginative inventiveness (Chadwick, 2005c) as well as giving an individual the feeling that they are at least a person of consequence (Storr, 1958). Patients often report that a delusion made life exciting and spectacular and took them away from a boring existence (Chadwick, 1992, 2006a) while others have 'successful' delusions which protect them chronically against unbearable intrapsychic anguish. Such chronically successful delusions also can protect against depression and give the person a feeling of considerable purpose and meaning in life (Roberts, 1991). At the physical level Brüne (2004) discusses work that shows also that schizophrenia sufferers have a greater activity of killer cells that could give them a greater resistance against infectious diseases. This advantage also seems to be possessed by their relatives.

Individuals who score higher than normal people on psychometrically assessed paranoia also score higher than them on empathy (Chadwick, 1988, 1997a, p. 140) and diagnosed paranoid patients are better than normal controls at the detection of lying (La Russo, 1978). Schizotypal individuals have generally been found to be higher (than non-schizotypals) in creative fluency and flexibility of thought (Schuldberg et al., 1988; Poreh et al., 1993; Chadwick, 1997a) as have non-paranoid schizophrenic patients (Keefe and Magaro, 1980), and the number of outstanding creative individuals over the course of history who have been thought to possess a paranoid, schizoid, schizotypal or schizophrenic disposition is huge (see Post, 1994, 1996; Chadwick, 1997a, p. 16). John Nash, Ludwig Wittgenstein and James Joyce are those most frequently mentioned in the psychological and psychoanalytic literature although Einstein also had schizophrenia in his family. John Nash himself said (ABI, 2007):

> I would not dare to say that there is a direct relation between mathematics and madness, but there is no doubt that great mathematicians suffer from maniacal characteristics, delirium and symptoms of schizophrenia.

It is important to note that although Nash suffered schizophrenia from 1959, his ability to produce mathematics of the highest quality did *not* leave him (ABI, 2007). He made a recovery in the 1990s, was awarded the Nobel Prize in 1994, with Harsanyi and Selten, for his work on game theory and did say of himself that he wouldn't consider himself recovered if he could not still produce good things in his work (ABI, 2007, p. ccxci).

James Joyce, whose daughter Lucia does seem to have suffered the illness, was a man of phenomenal linguistic ability generally but of singularly unstable temperament – though he was supported, emotionally, a great deal by his brother. Certainly as the publication of *Ulysses* approached, Joyce's paranoid fears about people he had mentioned scornfully in the book, with only thinly veiled identities, were reaching near-psychotic intensity (Ellmann, 1982/1959, pp. 516–18; Chadwick, 2001a, p. 50). Interestingly Wittgenstein, a man of the most extreme intellectual intensity and rigour, was also a man who was said to have about him a somewhat distant, other-worldly, mystical ambience (Edmonds and Eidinow, 2002). When a person says, as Wittgenstein did, that it is very difficult, when confronted with great art, to say anything that is better than saying nothing at all, one knows that this is someone who is far more than a rationality machine.

Jung, a man who seems to have had more acquaintance with psychotic experience than he was comfortable in admitting, also of course was prepared to confront the uncanny and the ineffable to a degree far beyond that dared by traditionally minded scientists.

The enhanced spiritual sensitivity of schizophrenia-prone people has, since the work of Buckley (1981; Buckley and Galanter, 1979), been a topic of considerable recent research (Chadwick, 1992, 1997a, 1997b, 2001c, 2002b; Jackson, 1997, 2001; Clarke, 2001, 2002). It is in fact becoming apparent that having a personality organisation that has a high loading on a dimension conferring vulnerability to psychosis in no way means that the person has a dysfunctional existence. Their lives may indeed be enhanced in quality over those of their more sober peers (McCreery and Claridge, 1995; Jackson, 1997).

Even people right 'on the edge' do not *have* to be seen as a mass of deficits, dysfunctions and disorders (see also Gergen, 1990 on this). The artist Andy Warhol once said:

> Sometimes people having nervous breakdown problems can look very beautiful because they have that fragile something to the way they walk or move. They put out a mood that makes them more beautiful.
>
> (Warhol, 2007/1975, p. 64)

In this book we are exploring out to the very edges of the phenomenology of person, to the edges – as did the Surrealists (see Short, 1994) – of what it is possible for a person to think and experience at all. I feel, therefore, that it is valuable for us to see, in the sense of 'grounding' us in the here and now, how the processes involved in such a venture relate to those operative in everyday life. This takes us back to the first perspective mentioned at the beginning of this chapter.

THE NORMAL INGREDIENTS OF MADNESS

One of the processes that goes awry in psychosis is so-called confirmation bias (Wason, 1960; Chadwick, 1992). This is the seeking of evidence and ideas that confirm a belief while relatively neglecting that which discredits it. It is doubtful that any scientific theory or indeed religion, political stance, business plan or rationale for anything in life could be created without con-firmation bias. I even have suggested (Chadwick, 1992) that it could be itself an anti-entropic force in nature working against the relentless drift physically to disorder. In a way it is an aspect of pattern detection and feeds on confirming inferences and imaginings and on 'going beyond the information given'. All of these things are part of the repertoire of cognitive skills needed for creativity – but in madness they seem to go into some kind of overdrive such that the person finds 'fitting' confirmations relentlessly.

As Bertrand Russell once said, 'When a scientist has his [*sic*] theory that's alright, but when the theory has him the door is open to madness'. This feeling of being the vehicle, puppet or pawn of a belief correlates with the amplification of confirmation bias and can take a person careering to destruction or self-destruction (see Chapter 5).

Under feelings of terrible threat, as sufferers of paranoid forms of delusion often are, the person may have the arousal level and hypervigilance of a threatened beast. Imagine being a pro-democracy suspect in Saddam Hussein's Iraq. How would you feel? Given the nature of their beliefs it is not surprising that deluded subjects often jump to conclusions (see Garety and Freeman, 1999) and are generally cognitively impulsive, prone to 'fear the worst' in the face of actual threat (Chadwick, 1992) and prone to overgeneralising from singular instances – confirmation bias again manifesting itself in a different guise.

There is a kind of normality in the frenetic cognitive style of delusional psychosis understandable given what pressure they think they are under. These biases (rather than deficits (Bentall, 1994)) in style can be retained, if to a reduced degree, when they are empirically tested after their episode. This is the operation of a kind of 'hangover effect' (Chadwick, 2006a).

People on the margins of, or in, psychotic states often hear things that have not been said or occasionally see things that are not there. In an intriguing experiment by Skinner (1957) a tape of random speech sounds ('phonemes') was played to normal people from behind a partition. Participants nonetheless 'heard' meaningful sentences and phrases in the essentially random input. If one takes out a speech sound (for example 'to') in a tape and replaces it with a cough, then on playing the tape including the phrase 'go – the shop', people will nonetheless 'hear' the excised sound (Warren, 1970). It is in our natures as human beings to try to make sense out of the stimulation we receive (Gregory, 1970). We do this by adding to and even rearranging that stimulation, particularly in unclear or noisy conditions. None of these so-called 'top-down' processes is abnormal. It even is possible, though the effect is slight and comes through, to the extent it does, under suboptimal conditions, for normal people to 'see' that which they imagine (Perky, 1910).

Some degree of hallucinatory capacity is there in normal people and we would be perceptually incapacitated without it (Sekuler and Blake, 1985). We use it to fill gaps in the data we receive and make confusing data more understandable to us. Context and expectancy effects can enhance these tendencies in normal people and patients alike. The processes are particularly likely to be amplified and exaggerated, however, in those who, for one reason or another, are in a minority or stigmatised group. Such people feel under threat and hence have to anticipate danger and second-guess potential enemies. This can easily lead to overactive imaginations. Blaming other people also is, in itself, a very convenient way of protecting self-esteem and this perfectly under-standable process has been found to be operative in paranoid patients (Kaney and Bentall, 1989; Kinderman, 1994).

Readers who have never suffered psychosis would benefit in their under-standing if they empathised with the kind of situation in which patients find themselves. For example: imagine that you are a spy and you have obtained information that MI6 are 'onto you' and intend to find, arrest and detain you that day. It is instructive to try to live the day with that belief in mind. Alternatively, if that is too stressful, try a 'delusion' that 'people can hear my thoughts' and see how much confirmation you can pick up for that idea in one, preferably busy, day. It is hardly surprising that patients, psychologically hurt by confirmations, often eventually decide *not* to seek out further evi-dence but to withdraw into the isolation of their room or flat – a so-called 'safety behaviour' (Freeman and Garety, 2004a, 2004b). One might say 'anybody would'. There is no doubt that, often, knowing more and more about the context of a person's psychosis tends to make it seem much less crazy. 'Craziness' is an inference we make when we don't really understand.

Others who have written positively of psychosis (e.g. Curtis *et al.*, 2001) have celebrated the enhancement of creativity and imaginative and emotional vitality as insanity approached. Martyn (2002) also stresses in research on self-management of schizophrenia that patients greatly value having a posi-tive perspective on their capacities and experiences rather than indwelling within a disease and degeneration discourse. Clearly the discourse that professionals encapsulate a patient or service user's problems within can sometimes make that person's difficulties worse.

Though researchers may scorn psychotic people's tendency to see meaning in coincidences, they should reflect on how discovering a coincidence in conversation with someone can emotionally 'lift' that conversation. We all naturally see meaning and magic in coincidences. It is one of the many things that make life worth living.

It seems unlikely that the actual content of psychotic thoughts is relevant to their assessment *as* psychotic. Science fiction and fantasy writers, writers of espionage novels and Hollywood screen writers all have ideas as wild or indeed wilder than any psychotic patient. The writer, however, is the agent of his or her ideas and takes them as constructed fiction not detected fact. In psychosis, by way of contrast, you don't 'think a delusion', the delusion 'thinks you' and hence it is not the belief but the *manner* in which the belief is held that is critical to the 'psychosis' assessment (Chadwick, 1992, p. 3, 2007a; see also Bennett, 1964; Toulmin, 1972 and Moor and Tucker, 1979 on this). It would be wrong, however, to assume that patients hold to their beliefs and 'that's that'. Firstly they do not necessarily hold them with complete and sustained conviction (Garety, 1985; Garety and Hemsley, 1994) and secondly it does seem, following early work by Beck (1952), Watts *et al.* (1973), Alford *et al.* (1982) and Rudden *et al.* (1982), that delusions are indeed amenable and open to challenge, discussion and even refutation – after careful examination of the evidence for them (see Chapter 13). In addition there are many people who suffer hallucinations who show no other sign of psychiatric morbidity (Romme and Escher, 1993) and hallucinations, even in psychosis sufferers, need not always be pre-emptively negative (Morrison *et al.*, 2004, p. 136).

JETTISONING THE SCHIZOPHRENIA LABEL

A final positive perspective on schizophrenia is one which sees the end of the 'schizophrenia' label itself as being in sight (Van Os, 2006). At Bath in 2007 the ISPS did indeed decide to *drop* the term 'schizophrenia' from its title. It is true that a general distinction is possible between those who suffer psychosis more as a mood disorder (manic depression, hypomania etc.) and those who suffer it more as a disorder of perception, cognition and organisation of the Self (schizophrenia). It also has been known for some time that subtypes of schizophrenia map onto equivalent subtypes in schizotypy (Liddle, 1987; Venables and Bailes, 1994) and research into fundamental processes such as latent inhibition (inhibition of attention to a stimulus that has no consequences) gives powerful support to a continuum from control subjects to schizotypy to schizophrenia (see Gray *et al.*, 2002, especially p. 273 and references therein and studies in O'Flynn *et al.*, 2003). However, the actual term has become so stigmatising for those involved that it has become a burden of crippling proportions (Dickerson *et al.*, 2002). The diagnosis as a description of a disease entity is far less successful as a guide to therapy than a focus on symptoms (Persons, 1986; Bentall *et al.*, 1988; Morrison, 2002; Morrison *et al.*, 2004) and seems therefore to have more legal and political relevance and relevance to the insurance industry than appropriateness as a guide to prognosis, help, coordination of services and intervention (Sanders, 2007; ISPS Newsletter, June 2007). The separation of cognitive and mood elements also is in practice extremely difficult to make and, as in my own case, a catch-all diagnosis of 'schizoaffective psychosis' often captures the clinical picture more accurately. This is particularly so in view of research that suggests emotional problems may underlie seemingly purely 'cognitive' disturbances (e.g. Zigler and Glick, 1988; Kinderman, 1994; Kinderman and Bentall, 1996). This is consistent with much research that shows the importance of socio-emotional factors on cognitive development and self-reflective capacities (e.g. Fonaghy and Target, 1997; Scheidt *et al.*, 1999).

    The general concept of psychosis itself (as a failure to discriminate reality from fantasy), *einpsychose* (unitary psychosis) or perhaps 'neuro-integrative' or 'neuro-integrative relatedness disorder' all seem to me to have more survival value as terms and would be less socially discriminating. There also is less chance of such categories being confused with dissociative identity disorder. Difficulties in integration and relatedness are central features of the processes underlying schizophrenic illness, which indeed is more 'loose mindedness' than 'split mindedness'. It is particularly because of such problems that the mystic and creative are seen as 'swimming' while the psychotic is 'drowning'. While it is likely true that lower inhibition in semantic networks can allow psychosis-prone individuals to often emit compellingly original remote associative ideas (Duchene *et al.*, 1998), for effective creative work these ideas need synthesising and organising into an integrative framework. Here is where arts therapies can be so useful, and as well, via the relationship with the therapist, useful in enhancing relatedness (see Thomson, 1989; Learmonth, 2003; Rooney, 2003).

Though I say that madness is the result of a concatenation of essentially normal processes, this does not at all mean that madness, any more than the phenomenon of chemical explosion, does not exist. However, the evidence for a continuum existing from normality to psychosis (Strauss, 1969; Van Os *et al.*, 2000; Van Os, 2006), and the present-day focus on component processes, does indicate that a label originating as a categorisation of a disease entity which is supposedly trauma-independent and to be treated only by physical methods is one that is rapidly outliving its usefulness given the inappropriateness of the disease concept to schizophrenia (Morrison *et al.*, 2004) and the highly negatively charged and misleading associations that have come to be attached to the diagnosis (see also discussion in Levin, 2006). The emphasis on neuro-integrative difficulties also presents a diagnosis less reducible to insulting terms such as 'schizo' and 'psycho'. In practice this is far from a trivial consideration (Antoniou, 2007).

In view of the way this book will often discuss the engagement (and disengagement) of mystical and psychotic thought, it is sobering, in light of the above, to find that mystico-religious beliefs, many of which psychiatrists might routinely classify as 'psychotic', are also widespread in non-clinical populations (Peters *et al.*, 1999; Peters, 2001). It also is now well known (Cox and Cowling, 1989) that belief in the paranormal and supernatural is widespread in such populations. It is sad that the professions of psychiatry and psychology are not, as a rule, at all sympathetic to 'atmospheric' thinking of that kind and tend to pathologise it, much to the disgruntlement of patients and their families. In terms of the ancient Oriental distinction between Yin and Yang, the feminine and the masculine, the general ambience of these endeavours is one of Yangian 'intellectual machismo' (Chadwick 2007b and Appendix II in this volume) such that work that dares to stray away from the safe valley of human experience, where Freud's 'secondary process' of clear, rational, analytical thought dominates, is often classified as 'occult'. It is interesting, and again rather sad, that many important thinkers of basically mystical underlying orientation, such as Fechner, Kepler, Newton, Pauli and Schrödinger, have been engorged by our culture and only their 'Yangian' products digested. Eventually they are presented to students as far-seeing pioneers of the Yang way when in reality they were nothing of the kind. This is one of the many 'delusions' transmitted by routine science education.

THE PATHOLOGY OF THE NORMAL

We are living at a time when any form of off-centre behaviour, thought or feeling is in danger of having a label, implying a mental health problem, attached to it. This began of course in psychiatry but has now spread to the popular media with such terms as 'shopaholism', 'kitchen performance anxiety' and 'crammed diary syndrome' (doubtless joggers have 'endorphin addiction'). This really is a trend to the total pathologisation of life – the cost of which is not only stigma but 'self-stigma' (Fung *et al.*, 2007). It is frustrating the way psychiatry and psychology undervalue mental states away from the label-free centre – as this chapter has tried to demonstrate – and undervalue qualities necessary for artists and spiritual questers. In closing it is rather refreshing to consider what labels *could* be put on people who feel safely away from psychopathologists' spotlight – which means basically that they are no trouble to themselves or anybody else. Are these people suffering from 'pathologically middle-of-the-road personality disorder'? Or perhaps 'reality obsession', 'rationality fixation', 'pathological blandness', 'non-existent personality syndrome', 'insufficiently diverse sexual fantasy life', 'mania logica', 'mania psychoanalytica' or 'aspiritual personality'? Clearly two can play at the game of label sticking but this does show, when we end up, via taking a different perspective, with *everybody* labelled (and thereby everybody stigmatised and stigmatising themselves), that the way things are going is rendering the whole deviance categorising process utterly meaningless (see Chadwick, 2003a, for more on this). This book and this chapter have been written more in the spirit of acceptance and de-pathologisation, a reverse trend to that currently in operation. Perhaps one day we might even accept one another for who we are?

Cannabis and altered states – a positive view

Travis Parker

> Temptations that have to be half whispered always promise Dionysiac ecstasy.

SHORT NOTE FROM PETER CHADWICK

Should one smoke cannabis or not? Does one *want* to? The cannabis legalisation website: www.ukcia.org certainly is a forum for people to air their views. The viewpoints are many but in this book I am presenting those of two experts-by-experience: Travis Parker here in Chapter 3 who puts forward a positive case for cannabis smoking and Terry Hammond, in Chapter 4, whose son Steve developed schizophrenia after cannabis use. An informed debate is what is required and these two chapters set out the upsides and downsides of this enigmatic drug as well as anyone could ask in the space available. Personally I am neither pro nor anti though I do not smoke cannabis myself. These two chapters, however, certainly take the reader on a roller coaster ride through the territory created by this tortuously difficult issue of our day. With no further delay I now hand you over to Travis.

The weed; marijuana; dope; ganja; kif; hashish; Mary Jane; bhang; this famous herb has been in use for centuries, for pleasure, for medicinal purposes, and as part of religious rituals. In some quarters it holds iconic quasi-mythical meaning as either 'the devil's weed', tempting youngsters into a downward spiral of mental deterioration and self-destruction, or alternatively as a 'magic weed' offering changes of consciousness which open dimensions of experience and cognition and forms of excitement, pleasure and insights unavailable elsewhere. Of course, once its distribution and use was criminalised, it also began to attract other associations: as an integral part of a vicious international network of criminal gangs, violent conflict and menacing underworld activity.

Research into cannabis and its effects has grown substantially over the last 20 years. For a while during this period, some of the findings seemed relatively benign, in particular regarding its use in pain control for multiple sclerosis (e.g. Joy *et al.*, 1999; Consroe, 1997), and for glaucoma (Voth and Schwartz, 1997), and also for managing nausea in cancer patients (Schwartz *et al.*, 1997). Its improving reputation culminated in the decision of the British Home Secretary to downgrade the drug from Class B to Class C in 2002. However, since then the tide has been steadily turning and there has been a continuous sequence of negative outcomes reported in the research literature. Its involvement in impaired memory (Heishman *et al.*, 1997; Ilan *et al.*, 2004), road accidents (Laumon *et al.*, 2005) and perhaps most widely reported, as a contributor to psychotic conditions (Johns, 2001; Moore *et al.*, 2007), is undermining the hope of its supporters that it might one day be regarded as equivalent to alcohol in terms of its balance of benefits and costs.

This contribution, however, is not intended as another review of the object-ive, quantitative evidence for or against cannabis, but rather as a reminder of why and how it was ever used and enjoyed over the many centuries since its effects were first discovered . . . what is, we might say, all the fuss about? To answer that question we shall be taking a more qualitative approach and looking at the history of its use both in a long-term sense, exploring its use in religious ritual over the centuries, and more recently since its rediscovery in the West in the 1960s when the 'counter culture' took root and the generation of baby boomers determined to explore the limits of both social and psycho-logical structures: hippies, communes, free love, encounter groups, beat poetry, the Beatles . . . all invited us in one way or another to experiment with different ways of living and thinking. Many of these experiments proved short-lived, but the presence and use of cannabis as well as other substances, with their mind-altering powers, could be found almost as a kind of linking thread in all these movements and groups. Forty years on, following the Thatcher revolution in the 1980s and the resurgence of a rampant market mentality, we now regard with general disdain any activity or thinking which does not promote long, obedient hours in the workplace and a commitment to economic productivity and money-making above all else. The cultural tide has well and truly turned and the enjoyment of the weed has become regarded at least in some quarters with the same general contempt often directed at those 1960s phenomena in general. The growing medical evidence for its harmful effects combines therefore with its failure to match the new cultural/social ethic to render it highly suspect indeed.

MARIJUANA USE THROUGH HISTORY

Abel (1982) has reviewed the history of cannabis and helps us to remember how culturally relative our current thinking inevitably is. References to hemp can be found in China and Japan albeit as a source of rope and bow strings.

Early Indian records show the first real signs of an appreciation of its psychoactive properties. The earliest reference to bhang's psychoactive effects is in the fourth books of the *Vedas*, written before 2000 and 1400 BC. Here it is named as one of the herbs that can release us from anxiety. Another document from the fifteenth century refers to it in terms such as 'light-hearted', 'joyful', and 'rejoices', and claims that among its virtues are 'astringency', 'heat', 'speech-giving', 'inspiration of mental powers', 'excitability', and the capacity to 'remove wind and phlegm'. However, apart from its use for relaxation and enjoyment, it was also used by fakirs and holy men as an enhancement of their communication with God.

To the Hindu the hemp plant is holy. A guardian lives in the bhang leaf. To see in a dream the leaves, plant or water of bhang is lucky. No good thing can come to the man who treads underfoot the holy bhang leaf. Besides being a cure for fever, bhang was seen as having many medicinal virtues; it 'cures dysentery and sunstroke, clears phlegm, quickens digestion, sharpens appetite, makes the tongue of the lisper plain, freshens the intellect, and gives alertness to the body and gaiety to the mind. Such are the useful and needful ends to which, in his goodness, the Almighty made bhang. In the ecstasy of bhang the spark of the Eternal in man turns into light the murkiness of matter. Bhang is the Joygiver, the Skyflier, the Heavenly-guide, the Poor Man's Heaven, the Soother of Grief. No god or man is as good as the religious drinker of bhang.' The supporting power of bhang has brought many a Hindu family safe through the miseries of famine. To forbid or even seriously to restrict the use of so holy and gracious a herb as the hemp would cause widespread suffering and annoyance and to large bands of worshipped ascetics, deep-seated anger (Abel, 1982).

In Europe hemp has been used in rope making for centuries, but its uses for other purposes had been noted already by the fifteenth century. In 1484, Pope Innocent VIII issued a papal fiat condemning witchcraft and the use of hemp in the Satanic mass. In 1615, an Italian physician and demonologist, Giovanni de Ninault, listed hemp as the main ingredient in the ointments and unguents used by the devil's followers. Hemp, along with opium, belladonna, henbane and hemlock, the demonologists believed, was commonly resorted to during the Witches' Sabbath to produce the hunger, ecstasy, intoxication and aphrodisia responsible for the gluttonous banquets, the frenzied dancing, and the orgies that characterized the celebration of the Black Mass (Abel, 1982).

Ganja in India generated revenue for the British Crown during the days of the Empire but its intoxicating effects did bother the authorities. 'The ganja menace' caught the attention of the Temperance League, and a commission, on 16 March 1893, was ordered to determine whether cannabis should be prohibited in India. The commission met on 3 August 1893 and remained in session until 6 August 1894. After hearing statements from numerous witnesses it concluded: (1) Moderate use of cannabis had no appreciable physical effects on the body. (2) Moderate use of cannabis had no adverse effects on the brain, except possibly for individuals predisposed to act abnormally. Excessive use could lead to mental instability and ultimately to insanity 'in individuals predisposed by heredity to mental disorders'. (3) Moderate use of cannabis had no adverse influence on morality. Excessive usage could result in moral degradation. Cannabis intoxication could result in violence, but 'such cases were few and far between'.

The Egyptians taught the French troops to use hashish and although Napoleon issued an ordinance banning it, the psychiatrist Dr Jacques-Joseph Moreau (1804–84) decided to study hashish. After trying it on himself, he enlisted volunteers. Thus it was that Moreau became drug dispenser to the Hashish Club (Club des Hachichins), a coterie of France's leading writers, poets and artists. The club met on a monthly basis in the elegant Hotel Lauzun in Paris's Latin Quarter. Visitors or members included Alexandre Dumas, Gerard de Nerval, Victor Hugo, Ferdinand Boissard, Eugene Delacroix and Gautier himself. Charles Baudelaire and Honoré de Balzac also attended but were said not to use it often, although R. Blondel, who was Baudelaire's doctor, once said: 'Each one who takes hashish has the dream that he deserves'.

In England, Thomas De Quincey announced that he would try some 'bang' and report on it, but this never materialised. He did write that:

> one farmer in Midlothian was mentioned to me eight months ago as having taken it, and ever since annoyed his neighbours by immoderate fits of laughter; so that in January it was agreed to present him to the sheriff as a nuisance. But for some reason the plan was laid aside and now, eight months later, I hear that the farmer is laughing more rapturously than ever, continues in the happiest frame of mind, the kindest creature and the general torment of his neighbourhood.
>
> (De Quincey, 1998/1822)

During the twentieth century, the reputation of cannabis largely waned as governments in Europe and America started from the opening decades of the century to introduce legislation controlling and outlawing its use. During the 1930s and 1940s in the USA governmental warnings about the dangers of the weed grew in intensity, including the making and distribution of the notorious film *Reefer Madness* portraying the alleged homicidal effects of smoking dope. (This film was a favourite on college campuses during the 1960s and 1970s.) During this period it also began to be associated with blacks and jazz musicians, and negative propaganda about cannabis took on what would now be regarded as distinctly racist overtones. Harry Anslinger, 1930s Head of the US Federal Bureau of Narcotics, was said to have put more jazz bands in jail than he could count. Famous musicians were observed and some sentenced for possession of cannabis. In front of the 1937 US Congress,

Anslinger talked about 'satanic voodoo jazz' and those 'reefer smokers' that would make white women want to have 'sex with Negroes' (Fachner, 2003).

The beatniks in the 1950s paved the way for the explosion of interest and experimentation again amongst musicians but also poets and some academics in the 1960s, where the connections between the cannabis experience and certain Eastern religious teachings began to be commented on once again. By and large the 'establishment' took a pretty dim view although from the 1970s some more favourable voices began to be heard once again, albeit this time owing to the medicinal effects which were beginning to be noted.

THE EXPERIENCE OF BEING STONED

So what does it do to you? And why does it retain its appeal? Several papers have described the subjective effects of cannabis as reported by users (e.g. Green et al., 2003; Eisenman, 2003; Hammersley and Leon, 2006). Green et al. (2003), for example, discuss empirical research into the experiences of and motives for smoking marijuana and conclude that it shares with alcohol the capacity to reduce tension and induce relaxation; it enhances mood and social bonding, but includes some motives not found for alcohol such as enhancement of perceptual and cognitive experience and experienced creativity.

An early collection of views and commentaries on the nature of the cannabis experience, *The Book of Grass*, edited by Andrews (1967) collated the writings of some of the earlier participant-observers such as Aldous Huxley and William Burroughs. We shall draw on these descriptions and combine them with the recollections of the author and his companions to highlight some of the pleasures available at least to some cannabis users, albeit not all. (Why some people seem immune to its influence remains unexplained. We recognise the individual variation in people's reaction to alcohol so we should not perhaps be too surprised. Whether the variation is best seen as a function of personality or of neurological differences, or both, we cannot say at present.)

Talking to users and consumers, there are a number of themes which recur when enthusiasts get started on the delights of 'wacky baccy'.

Cocking a snook

Its illegal status undoubtedly adds to its appeal for adolescents and young adults. It offers a vehicle for that rebelliousness which for many adolescents is a necessary part of defining their independence from parents: 'I know you've still got to be careful who you mention it to; not everyone will approve'.

Smoking dope can appear to claim a bit of bold individuality for myself: 'I'm *not* going to join in with the consensus view that it's a dangerous and bad thing to do; I'm going to judge that *myself*, and not accept the hand-me-down views of politicians and policemen without question'.

Social bonding

Two kinds of bond are available to the stoner: firstly there's the feeling of belonging to a semi-secret and moderately marginal club; coming across another enthusiast offers an instant buzz of recognition for the cannabis connoisseur. Yet this is a recognition we must be careful not to acknowledge too publicly; you and I know that we sharing something in common but, 'wink wink', we mustn't let everyone see that we do. A more respectable version of this feeling may be familiar to Freemasons.

And yet, someone could object, so what? You could get the same claims to boldness, risk taking, individuality and club membership from being house-breakers or boy racers . . . these people too sail close to the wind and probably feel at least as much exhilaration as the dope smoker, so what is it particularly about dope smoking which provides the pleasure and satisfaction? What is its intrinsic attraction? Can we present an account of the behaviour and experience of the drug itself which captures its appeal . . . what does it do to the mind?

Intimate bonding

There's a second kind of bonding many smokers know, which comes more from the intrinsic qualities of the drug experience itself, which is the sense of deep sharing, a feeling of intimate mutuality that sometimes can happen when two or more are gathered together and sharing a joint, while listening to music or telling a story. You can really feel you know deeply what the other(s) are experiencing at the same time. You're really in the middle of the stoned space together. Those moments of experienced bonding provide their own intrinsic and powerful reward.

Meeting up with an old friend

Its effects when smoked creep up quite quickly. Within ten/fifteen minutes alterations in consciousness can be detected, although it's often helpful (and fun!) to have a smoking partner to check against: 'are you stoned yet?' 'Can you notice anything yet?' If this question is followed by a momentary pause and the beginnings of a smile of welcome recognition, you know your partner is beginning to get it, and that welcome, that recognition as the dope begins to infuse and embed itself in your being (mind and body . . . we'll come on to that later), is also part of the deal. One user I know who was offered a smoke a few years after he'd last used it, took one puff, held it in, paused and then exclaimed, 'Hello again!', like he was meeting up again with an old friend, whose character and energy he had forgotten about, forgotten what it felt like to be with. And for those who know how to appreciate the encounter, 'it's a pleasure to meet you again indeed'.

Not everyone who consumes necessarily likes (or knows how to?) introspect as the effects take hold. In many ways a meditative detached attitude is helpful to the appreciation of the weed and those who are more used to looking at their own experience and identifying the structures and contents of experience may more likely turn into connoisseurs than others, who just like to get on with living and are not in the habit of exploring their interior lives.

Being in the moment

Being stoned can be called 'a lived philosophical state'. The structure of the stoned state seems to imply or highlight certain ways of being, ways of look-ing at the world that are related to the perspectives and attitudes one can find in Buddhist writings and teachings. For many, including the author, the cen-tral feature of being stoned is a deeper immersion in the present moment, but the caveat is: whatever that moment may contain. Thus, it affects every stoner uniquely, all depending on how she/he is at the time. Mellow becomes blissed out but uneasy becomes paranoid. (Remember Baudelaire's 'Each one who takes hashish has the dream that he deserves'.)

Deep and meaningful

Meaning is exaggerated, everything takes on enhanced significance; it all gets to be so much more important. Thus ideas, phrases, become inherently more profound, more pregnant with value, more potentially world-shattering; they will amaze and revolutionise everyone's understanding of life.

Tastes and flavours

Tastes and flavours hit you with a new freshness, new depths and are absolutely a million times more delicious, and contrasts and variety of flavours can seem quite kaleidoscopic; savoury, sweet, followed by another savoury; then more sweeties, the appetite grows and can become gluttonous; one has to have more, often much much more. These are the famous 'munchies'.

The slowing of time

The passage of time changes when one is immersed in the present. There is a feeling of time being stretched or expanded or perceived as slowed down or sped up. Ninety-five per cent of 151 participants of Charles Tart's study *On Being Stoned* agreed with the following statement:

> Time passes very slowly; things go on for the longest time (e.g. One side of a record seems to play for hours).
>
> (Tart, 1971)

In experiments on time perception, stoned subjects failed to estimate time intervals correctly, and tended to expand the estimated interval. Jones reported that a 15-second time interval was expanded to a mean of 16.7 seconds, estimated under the influence of oral THC (tetrahydrocannabinol), while being counted correctly in the normal state (Jones and Stone, 1970).

Seconds and minutes pass by in slower motion, allowing you to dwell and linger in the passing moment as it passes, sometimes barely perceptibly, almost hanging in space/time like a still photo. One savours the moment luxuriously, as it enlarges and opens up the texture of sensuality; pleasure in all its forms takes on a new definition; sexual foreplay and intercourse benefit from the slowing of time, each small shift in body sensation available to be appreciated. Moving through an hour, especially if one goes out of the house for a walk or a takeaway, is like moving through a tunnel; when you're in one section of it, the section you've left behind quickly becomes ancient history; standing on the pavement, in the cold afternoon air, becomes your whole world, and can be quite daunting: so much going on; so many people; so many sights and sounds, movement; bustle; traffic; you have to concentrate on where you are and which direction you want to head in. What did you come out for again? And then you remember back to the room where the decision was taken to head out for a take-away curry; that warm, quiet, smoke-filled room; lying about and dreaming and imagining what foods you could possibly buy. That place suddenly seems a long while ago, a long way away.

Spatial discontinuity

Spatial continuity falls away. Physically moving one's position in space can offer a quite new perspective on the world. Even getting up and moving to a different part of the room is like going on holiday; you're suddenly in a different world which looks and feels different from where you were a minute ago. There are faint reminders of a childhood state of mind when the various rooms in the house each had their distinctive character, and it was something of an adventure to move from the kitchen to the living room. The world then was a much bigger and impressive place; cannabis can sometimes re-evoke that sense of wonder.

Michael Pickering (in *The Book of Grass* by George Andrews, 1967) comments:

The effects, usually coming on after two or three or four pipefuls, are different for each person, but several general characteristics are usually common to everybody. First of all, you suddenly notice as if for the first time in your life, how fantastically beautiful everything in the world is – even little things you hardly thought worth looking at before . . . all colours become incredibly bright and intense, and sounds and touches full of beauty. When I first got high on kif, I was in a filthy youth hostel in Casablanca – but lying on a table was a small alcohol heater someone was using for cooking; it was dark and the heater was shooting out a long bright blue flame. Suddenly this flame was to me the most beautiful object in the world – the only thing worth looking at – it was full of exquisite wisps of orange and red – it was swirling round and round in the air, always emitting a lovely hissing noise that filled the whole room. But there is much more than just the heightening of the senses. You begin to think think think. More profoundly and more interestingly than ever before. You have fantastic ideas thrown up by your imagination which knows no bounds or restraints. And you feel an intense physical exhilaration – that makes you want to leap around. Everything in the world suddenly becomes true and real – you can see deep into people's minds by just looking at their eyes – you can tell everything about them, their thoughts, characters, dreams and secrets. You can see what people are really like – their 'image' is shattered – and so is yours – you start behaving as you really are. Politeness for the sake of politeness is impossible, or if tried, it is completely unconvincing. You become obsessed with the beauty of everything around you. To any observer you appear crazy – but this is nothing to you – you are in your own lovely world creating thoughts and visions and sounds and sights – creating whatever you like – doing whatever you like – you have woken up at last and start seeing the world as it really is for the first time – the kif has drawn the veil from your eyes and there is only life and growth and creation.

(p. 164)

Lawrence Lipton writes in the same volume:

The euphoria that the beats who use marijuana are sensing is not the wholly passive, sedative, pacifying experience that the users of commercial tranquillizers want. On the contrary, they are looking for a greater sense of aliveness, a heightened sense of awareness. Of all the euphoric, hypnotic and hallucinogenic drugs, marijuana is the mildest and also the most conductive to social usage. The joint is passed around the pad and shared, not for reasons of economy but as a social ritual. Once the group is high, the magic circle is complete. Confidences are exchanged, personal problems are discussed – with a frankness that is difficult to achieve under normal circumstances – music is listened to with rapt concentration, poetry is read aloud and its images, visual and acoustical, communicated with maximum effect. The Eros is felt in the magic circle of marijuana with far greater force, as a unifying principle in human relationships, than at any other time except, perhaps, in the mutual metaphysical orgasm. The magic circle is, in fact, a symbol of and a preparation for the metaphysical orgasm. While marijuana does not give the user the sense of timelessness to the same degree that peyote does, or LSD or other drugs, it does so sufficiently to impart a sense of presence, a here-and-nowness that gives the user a heightened sense of awareness and immediacy.

(p. 159)

MUSIC AND CANNABIS

Cannabis invites us into a new relationship with music both as listener and as a player (Fachner, 2003). Listening to music traditionally plays a big part in the stoned experience. There are two ways musical experience can shift: one is in the relationship one develops with the music itself. The band or the orchestra can become three-dimensional; they are around you, spread out in your mental space as you listen; and you really *listen*; every note, chord, phrase and emotional nuance expressed by the musicians you immediately pick up and *enjoy* (just as you did the curry or the chocolate bar). You are *with* the musicians and love what they are doing with their sounds; they're doing it for you after all.

> The music sounded incredibly good. In fact, it was so good and so clear that I thought that it could not be music on a stereo player. The band must be playing in my room!
>
> (Eisenman, 2003)

But there's a second way listening to music can be enhanced, and that stems from the social bonding effect mentioned earlier. If you listen with friends, you somehow know that you are all sharing the same intimacy with the music (and even if you're not, you feel that you are with a great certainty). Especially with tracks that you all know, the feeling that you are all together with that soaring guitar solo, or the lithe sensuous Latin rhythm, only serves to intensify the experience still further.

Playing music too takes on a new dimension when under the influence. Fachner (2003) suggests that certain drugs may lead musicians to certain musical styles and performance because some musicians are more attracted by a specific drug, for example Mezz Mezzrow, a jazz musician from the 1930s who became much more famous for supplying marijuana joints for his friends like Louis Armstrong, Hoagy Carmichael, Tommy Dorsey, than for his playing. Louis Armstrong himself became a life-long fan of the weed, or 'gage' as he preferred to call it (Bergreen, 1998). 'It's a thousand times better than whisky, an assistant, a friend . . . very good for asthma, relaxes your nerves' was one of his pronouncements.

Marijuana seems to help the player really 'enter' the space of the music; you seem to feel the music emerging through you, and it takes your full attention. So much so, however, that you can lose touch with the context of the music: one jazz musician reported to the author an experience of playing at a top London jazz venue some years ago. He was playing a slow ballad, having consumed a little something beforehand; halfway through the piece, he suddenly realised he didn't have a clue which tune he was supposed to be playing; he knew which chord came next but not where the whole thing was heading or where it would end up! (It may or may not be significant that none of the audience had seemed to notice anything wrong when they did finally finish the piece.)

Other jazz players have reported how marijuana can interfere a lot with the sense of time:

> We played the first tune for almost two hours – one tune! We got on the stand and played this one tune, we started at nine o'clock. When we got finished I looked at my watch, it's a quarter to eleven. Almost two hours on one tune. And it didn't seem like anything. I mean, you know, it does that to you. It's like you have much more time or something.
>
> (Becker, 1966, p. 74)

CONCLUSION

Such are some of the effects cannabis can induce. But we should not forget that these effects are not experienced by all. We have already seen that some people remain largely untouched by the drug altogether. Others, while still seemingly having their present experience intensified, find themselves with high anxiety bordering on panic or paranoia. Eisenman (2003) recounts one example of a learned phobia which he attributes to 'state-dependent learning' and he presents this as a reason he never touches the stuff nowadays. A very dear friend of mine hasn't touched the stuff for years since the last time she tried it and had to hide behind the sofa for an hour out of some nameless but deeply unpleasant feeling of dread. Another good friend seems profoundly unaffected in all respects and simply cannot understand what all the fuss is about, positive or negative.

But for those fortunate few who are graced with the right neurological constitution, marijuana offers a delightful garden of altered horizons, enriched tastes and pleasures and a renewed sense of the wonderfulness of the world and life, when the mood and the setting are right. I for one truly hope that however powerful the puritans and the nannies and the political bully boys become there will always be those who will cultivate and honour the experience of this entrancing weed.

Chapter 4

Cannabis and altered states – the dark side

Terry Hammond

> Benign people do benign things, nasty people do nasty things, but to make benign people do nasty things you don't need religion . . . you need drugs and alcohol.

The anecdotal evidence that cannabis is linked to mental illness has been screaming at us for years. In fact the link between them goes back centuries; one of the first references to cannabis as a psychoactive drug was in China during the first century: 'If taken in excess will produce visions of the devil . . . If taken over a long time, it makes one communicate with the spirits and lightens one's body'. Napoleon noticed the adverse effects cannabis had on the Egyptian lower class and declared a total prohibition. During the 1920s the Egyptian government was so concerned about the detrimental effects cannabis was having on the working population that it requested that cannabis be added to the 'Geneva International Convention on Narcotics Control'. In the UK on 28 September 1925 the Dangerous Drugs Act became law and cannabis was made illegal.

There is now increasing epidemiological evidence showing that long-term use of cannabis, particularly if commencing in teenage years, can lead to the development of mental health problems. The Royal College of Psychiatry website shows very succinctly how complex the plant is. The writers point out that there 'are about 60 compounds and 400 chemicals in an average cannabis plant. The four main compounds are called delta-9-tetrahydrocannabinol (delta-9-THC), cannabidiol, delta-8-tetrahydrocannabinol and cannabinol. Apart from cannabidiol (CBD) these compounds are psychoactive, the strongest one being delta-9-tetrahydrocannabinol. The stronger varieties of the plant contain little cannabidiol (CBD), whilst the delta-9-THC content is a lot higher in Skunk.' When cannabis is smoked, its compounds rapidly enter the bloodstream and are transported directly to the brain and other parts of the body. The feeling of being 'stoned' or 'high' is caused mainly by the delta-9-THC binding to cannabinoid receptors in the brain. Curiously, there are also cannabis-like substances produced naturally by the brain itself – these are called endocannabinoids.

> Most of these receptors are found in the parts of the brain that influence pleasure, memory, thought, concentration, sensory and time perception. Cannabis compounds can also affect the eyes, the ears, the skin and the stomach.
>
> (Royal College of Psychiatry, August 2006)

The government does seem to be taking the possibility of cannabis playing a causal role in psychosis more seriously. A spokesman from the Department of Health acknowledged in January 2005 that:

> There is medical clinical evidence now that there is an important causal factor between cannabis use and schizophrenia – not the only factor, but an important causal factor. That is the common consensus among the medical fraternity.

The question for the government is now not whether cannabis is a trigger for mental illness, but how does the government reduce its use?

A CARER'S STORY

Eight years ago my son was taken into hospital following a psychotic break-down – triggered, we believe, by cannabis. This was somewhat ironic at the time as I had been working in mental illness for the National Schizophrenia Fellowship (now Rethink) as their Southern Regional Director. Part of my job was to support and develop carers' self-help groups. Previous to that, in Southampton, I had helped to set up one of the largest supported housing schemes in the country, for people with mental illness, most of whom had a diagnosis of schizophrenia. One would expect that I would have been well equipped to cope. But in fact I was totally pole-axed by Steve's illness.

In this chapter I will be covering:

1   The impact that my son's illness had on me and the rest of the family.
2   What it was like to live with illness.
3   What was involved in the recovery process.
4   The reality of recovery.

I hope that the reader will gain a new insight into what it is like to care for someone with schizophrenia and will understand more why many carers find it hard to let go.

BACKGROUND

It was at six o'clock on a warm summer's evening that my son uttered six words that were to change my life forever. I was watching the BBC News, a woman in black was bent over her dead son, she was wailing pitifully. It was all too depressing, so I reached for the remote. As I did so, my son Steve, who had been studying the floor, slowly raised his head and suddenly demanded to know why I had rung the BBC. 'BBC Steve, what are you talking about?' 'You know' he snapped back, 'don't deny it, you rang the BBC up to tell them that I was a lazy sod – they have been broadcasting it all day'. My heart missed a beat; I went cold and felt sick. I had become a carer.

Several excruciating weeks later, Steve was diagnosed with paranoid schizophrenia and hospitalised. We later discovered that for the previous six months he had been bingeing on cannabis. The psychosis took hold of Steve's mind like some aggressive malignant cancer. We helplessly watched on as his beautiful mind was slowly being mutilated. It was more than I could bear – it was like watching your son being tortured before your eyes and there was nothing you could do to stop it, I felt totally subjugated. I desperately wanted to reach out and rip out what was destroying his mind, I hoped beyond hope that Steve would wake up and it would be all over, that his mind would be clear and that the cannabis haze would have drifted away. Sadly this was not to be.

THE WORST NIGHT OF MY LIFE

It was four weeks later, during the night of Wednesday 11 August 1999, when I experienced the worst night of my life. The following day I had an early start, so I went to bed early; I read a few pages of my book, set the alarm and hit the pillow at just after 11 p.m. Two hours later I was awakened by a terrible crash followed by shouting – it was Steve. I rushed into his bedroom to find him standing in the corner of the room, fear was radiating from every pore of his face – his whole body was trembling. 'Steve, are you alright? What's the matter?' I asked. Steve just stood transfixed, he seemed paralysed with fear. 'Are you my dad?' a quivering voice replied. 'Of course I am Steve.' 'You're not an alien – are you?' 'Of course not Steve, it's me, your dad'. As I approached him to put my arm around him, he flinched and backed off. 'It's me Steve, it's your dad', trying to reassure him. He turned his face away from me and stared out of the window. He started rambling to himself, it was incoherent. I desperately tried to make out what he was saying but it was impossible. I asked him again if he was alright but he told me to go away. I asked him if he wanted a drink, but he told me to go back to bed. I asked him to get back into bed, which to my surprise he did. As I left the room I could see the door frame was badly split where it had been violently slammed.

Chris, my wife, was standing in the hallway, her hands clasping her cheeks; I told her that it was perhaps best to leave him and let him go back to sleep. We both got back into bed and lay discussing the situation. Chris was urging me to get Steve into hospital. We had seen his GP four weeks earlier, who had referred Steve to the local Community Mental Health team. A psychiatrist had visited Steve and had confirmed that Steve was suffering from psychosis – possibly schizophrenia; we were both in a state of shock. The psychiatrist suggested that we wait to see how things developed and that they would try and treat his psychosis at home rather than in hospital.

As we lay discussing what to do, there was a sudden almighty crash and the sound of glass breaking – Steve was screaming at the top of his voice – 'Fuck off! Fuck off! Fuck off!' I jumped out of bed and ran to his bedroom. I entered the darkened room to find Steve silhouetted against the window, he turned and lurched towards me, his six foot frame stood over me – a beam of light from the hallway draped his face revealing eyes that were full of fear and menace. I was frightened. 'It's me Steve, it's your dad'. He studied my face. 'It's alright Steve, it's me', I once again reassured him. He continued to study my face for what seemed ages, he looked totally confused. He suddenly turned away and got back into bed and in a calm voice said, 'Go back to bed dad, it's nothing'. I went to pick up the pieces of the shattered ashtray but he angrily told me to get out. I dearly wanted to talk to him, I wanted to find out what I could do to help him, but the truth was, I was fearful and uncertain what to do. I returned to our bedroom; Chris was crying. 'We have to do something' she sobbed. 'He needs to go to hospital now, I want my son back, I want my son back.' Steve started shouting again. Chris went to go to him, I told her not to and that we should just wait a while to see if he quietened down. She looked at me and said, 'You're frightened, aren't you?' Her words were like a spear piercing through me – little Terry Hammond, the poor kid from the back streets of Tooting, the ducker and diver, the born survivor – never lost for a word – knocked for six. Yes, Chris was right – I was frightened. I sat on the edge of the bed feeling defeated. All that so-called experience working in mental health meant nothing. For the first time in my life I simply didn't know what to do or say – should I cry? – is that what a real man should do? But I don't cry, I have never cried, not once as an adult – not even when grandfather died, who I was very close to, not even when my beloved Sam, the Great Dane, had to be put down. Crying – it's a sign of weakness – isn't it?

The sound of Steve continued to dominate the house. I continued to sit on the edge of the bed, Chris's words still echoing in my head. If I go into his bedroom, would Steve be able to hold himself back this time? Could I defend myself against an attack? He is bigger and far stronger than me; what if he tries to kill me? He is certainly physically capable – who knows what madness lurks inside his head? With a great deal of fear and foreboding I decided to go to Steve's room, I stood outside for a while, listening. Thankfully his shouting

Steve, Victoria, Christine and Terry Hammond.

had abated, he was mumbling away to himself. I opened the door and listened in – he was in bed. I decided that the worst was over and quietly closed the door, relieved that I had not been put to the test. We eventually got Steve into hospital four weeks later – those four weeks were hell!

Several years later I asked Chris about the night she accused me of being frightened. I asked her if she was angry with me and whether she thought I had been a coward. I was somewhat surprised and relieved when she said that she had not been angry with me at all, her anger was with the mental health services for prolonging the dreadful situation we were in and for allowing Steve to suffer for so long. She did not blame any individual professional; indeed, she thought the psychiatrist had done what he thought was right. It was the endemic failure of the 'mental health system' to react to a crisis that concerned her.

WHO WAS A SUITABLE CASE FOR TREATMENT?

Steve's health continued to decline, he became increasingly paranoid and his behaviour became more bizarre and frightening. He made the strangest of wailing noises in the middle of the night; he talked in what seemed like some strange forgotten language – it was totally unintelligible. I started to record him and kept a diary of his actions so I could demonstrate to the mental health team how bad things were getting. I used to follow him on his midnight excursions to the local park. I would duck and dive behind trees and bushes like some demented Inspector Clouseau, just to see what he was up to, only to discover he was having a quiet fag on the park bench.

One night, after having read an article about the high risk of suicide amongst newly diagnosed patients, I went into his room to check that he was still breathing; in a panic I started prodding him – Steve woke in a startle, 'what the fuck you doing dad?' I felt totally embarrassed, made some excuse and left – was I becoming a suitable case for treatment?!

HOSPITALISATION

Steve was finally taken into hospital and there he stayed for three months. When I dropped him off at the hospital, I felt a great sense of relief, as the previous weeks had been a truly dreadful time, but the sense of relief was soon eclipsed by a deep sense of shame. I felt ashamed that I had failed my son, I had let him down. I was abandoning him, at a time when he was in great need. As Steve sat on his hospital bed, passively staring up at the nurse, who gently explained the routine, I felt the same sense of anguish I experienced when I left Steve in the hands of his first teacher – he was frightened then, and he was very frightened now.

As I gave him a hug and we said our goodbyes, Steve stood up. 'I don't want to be here dad, I want to come back with you.' 'You can't Steve', I replied, struggling for a better response. 'But I'm feeling alright now', he said, trying to reassure me. I could see Chris welling up. 'You can't Steve, you just can't.' Those dreadful nights came flashing through my mind – his constant shouting and screaming at his voices, having to wash the blood off the walls and carpet where he had been thumping his head against his bedroom wall. Regularly apologising to the neighbours for Steve's loud music and swearing in the middle of the night.

'Please Steve, give it a try for mum's sake.' For a few desperate seconds I thought, perhaps, just perhaps he was OK; maybe this experience had somehow brought him round, I could feel my paternalistic instincts starting to kick in, my resolve was weakening. The experienced nurse detected that I was struggling and she was clearly concerned that Chris was getting distressed. 'Let your mum and dad get off, Stephen – do you prefer to be called Stephen or Steve?' 'Steve', he instinctively replied. 'Right Steve, what do you want for dinner tonight?', she said, handing him a menu and gently signalling us to leave. I took Chris's hand and left the room. As we did so, Steve shouted out to us, 'You will come tomorrow, won't you?' 'Of course, Steve, of course', I reassured him. The corridor leading from the ward to the main entrance was lined with paintings done by patients; I knew it wouldn't be long before Steve's painting would be exhibited. Tears poured down my face.

THE LONG HAUL BEGUN

When Steve emerged from hospital three months later, he was calmer and his paranoia had subsided, but he was a shadow of his former self. His vibrancy and natural energy had gone – the fun-loving young man who lived for his mates, football and girls had become a ghost-like figure. As the weeks and months went by, Steve's strange and bizarre behaviour continued to manifest. The psychosis seemed to have stripped him of the basic mores and folkways of life; his interaction with people seemed primeval. He avoided all contact. He spent the days pacing around the house, chain smoking and in an unending dialogue with his voices. At night he sat watching the television with no sound, or wandering around the house. He was oblivious to the disruption he was causing: the trail of coffee stains, the putrid smell of nicotine which permeated the house, the loud music and his constant manic giggling and laughing.

THE IMPACT ON US

Steve's illness had dramatically changed our lives and the plans we had for our future years. Before Steve's illness I used to jokingly say to Chris that when the Saga magazine hits the mat, on my fiftieth birthday, we would start to spend everything that Saga can throw at us. We had more disposable income than we had ever had in our lives. Steve and Victoria were carving out their own lives – life was good. Chris and I were really looking forward to being on our own and starting a new phase in our life. But that was not to be, we had become carers, so our plans were on hold for the foreseeable future.

Chris was once asked by a friend what it was like to be Steve's carer. Chris summed it up well. She said that it was like having a young child again – constantly worrying about him. Worrying when he is asleep, when he is awake and when he's not there. 'He's acting different to yesterday, should we tell the doctor? He has a strange look in his eyes – what does that mean? He is starting to go out in the middle of the night – Oh my God! What is he up to?'

In the early years it was hard to leave Steve for any length of time, as we were fearful of what we would find when we got back. Steve had often talked about killing himself; I had visions of finding Steve dead and attending his funeral – and doing the reading. I would then get a flashing thought that Steve's death would be a happy release from the constant fear and terror he was experiencing day in and day out. Almost immediately I would then start to feel a dreadful guilt for thinking such a terrible thing about my own son.

If people visited the house and Steve was downstairs he would rush to his room as if his life depended on it. It would set off bursts of manic laughter – it put us on edge all the time people were in the house. One day the plumber came to fix the boiler. Steve suddenly let out an almighty wolf-like cry. 'What the bleeding hell was that?!' exclaimed the plumber as he dropped his wrench. 'Oh it's alright, it's my son, he does amateur dramatics, he's rehearsing.' The plumber completed his job at breakneck speed and left.

HIS NON-COMPLIANCE

Getting Steve to take his medication and keep appointments with the support team was a nightmare. For the first couple of years the hospital tried various anti-psychotics, which Steve would eventually refuse because of their side effects. While Chris and I fully understood Steve's reasoning, we also had to live with the consequences – his psychosis would burst through and once again Steve's suffering became unbearable.

His shouting at his voices in the night, his head-butting the walls. One night I got up and went to him and found Steve sitting on his bed with his head in his hands, his forehead was covered in blood. I wiped the blood from his forehead, he looked at me and asked me where I thought his voices were coming from. I said to him that I thought they were his inner thoughts, he looked at me incredulously and said, 'No, that's impossible, it's aliens, I'm certain of it'. The psychiatrist once challenged Steve on this and asked Steve how certain he was that it was aliens. Steve replied that he was ninety per cent certain. 'What's the ten per cent?' replied the psychiatrist. Steve thought for a moment and said, 'It could be from within my head I suppose?' That 'ten per cent', that was our beacon of hope. It was that ten per cent that kept us going.

THE SLOW RECOVERY

When he was more settled and on regular medication, he often asked me to stay with him and talk; unfortunately this was usually late at night. He generally talked about his voices and why they say the things they do. I was always mindful of increasing the 'ten per cent beacon'. Sometimes he was happy for me just to sit in the room in silence – I think my presence helped him overcome the fear he was clearly experiencing. The problem for me was that the lack of sleep was causing me problems at work, as on more than one occasion I fell asleep at my desk.

The one thing that seemed to relax Steve was car rides. Very often I would get home from work and the minute I got through the door Steve would ask me to take him out. 'I could really do with going out in the car, my voices have been really bad today.' How could I refuse?! It was a constant juggling act between supporting Steve, finishing that important report from work and spending time with Chris and my daughter Victoria.

THE EFFECTS ON MY DAUGHTER

I was very conscious that I was not giving Victoria the time she deserved. I was also aware of the pressure Steve was putting on her. In the early days when Steve's behaviour was at its most frightening, Victoria stayed at her friend's. When I was away she didn't like leaving her mum alone and slept with her for security. It was difficult for her when she brought friends back, as Steve's manic laughter could always be heard in the background. 'Don't worry, that's just my brother', she would say to her friends. On one occasion, Steve chased one of her boyfriends around the house with a lump of wood. It was like a scene out of the Keystone Cops. Steve was chasing the boyfriend, I was chasing Steve and my wife was chasing me. Steve eventually caught up with the boyfriend, looked him in the eye and then smashed the mirror, which was reflecting the boyfriend's image. Steve calmly turned away, handed me the lump of wood and said, 'My voices have told me he's not a good person'. That relationship did not last; his voices may have been right.

SELF-NEGLECT

There was a point in his illness when Steve started to neglect his appearance, he started to look 'odd'. He wore the same clothes, his hair was unkempt and he was unshaven. One day the local policeman called at our house to say that he had received a complaint – my heart sank. Apparently, Steve had pushed a 14-year-old boy over a wall. I called Steve to talk to the policeman. He told the policeman that the kid was with a gang and they were 'taking the piss' out of him. Steve said 'I had had enough, so I walked over to the ringleader and pushed him over the wall, he was lucky I never decked him!' Luckily I knew the policeman, who was aware of our situation. He gently told Steve not to take the law into his own hands and left – we never heard any more – the kids kept their distance and Steve got the message to tidy himself up. I often think how different that could have been.

THE DRINKING

Steve's situation got worse before it got better. Steve developed a drinking problem – consuming nine pints a session, four or five days a week, plus an unknown amount from our drinks cabinet. When I challenged him over his drinking he said that when he got pissed he felt 'normal'. Unfortunately Steve's excursions back to normality cost us untold problems. It put the whole family under even more strain. Apart from the vomit-stained carpets, beer-soaked bed linen and disrupted sleep, his drinking seemed to accentuate his bizarre behaviour, which he portrayed with less inhibition.

Thankfully, Steve was never aggressive or violent to us, but the disruption and the anguish that followed took its toll. Chris could not hold her anger with Steve; she would demand that if he did not stop drinking he would have to leave the house, which I argued against. But Chris was right, his behaviour was unacceptable and it threatened to undo the work that everyone had put into Steve, let alone the anguish he was causing. Chris's outbursts definitely had an impact on Steve, especially when one day she burst into tears in front of him, in total despair. We eventually made a 'contract' with Steve to limit his drinking to a certain number of pints each week – which over time he kept to. Steve still has the occasional excursion back to 'normality' – but then who wouldn't?

EIGHT YEARS ON

It has been eight years since Steve was in hospital; he still gets his voices, he still gets paranoid and is perpetually plagued by indecision and anxiety. Steve does not work, has no bosom friends other than close family and he still lives at home. But the difference between those first scary years and now is that Steve is in greater control of his psychosis. I asked him recently whether his voices were as bad as they were five years ago. His reply shocked me. 'My voices are as much with me now as the first day I heard them', he said. 'Really Steve?', I replied. 'You surprise me, as you seem to be so much in control these days.' 'I am', he replied. 'It's just that the voices are no longer centre stage any more, they are out there in the wings; they still jabber away, but I have learnt to ignore them – it's only when I get stressed that they come back.'

Steve's recovery continues to progress, he enjoys going to the local day centre once a week, which he has been doing for the last three years. He now comes down the pub with me and occasionally watches Southampton football club at home with a friend. He comes on holiday with us now – providing it's not a hotel. He has just started to use public transport on his own, thanks to the outreach team, and he has signed up to work as a volunteer at a voluntary run horticulture project. He is also now talking seriously about moving on to supported accommodation. So Steve's healing process continues but it has been very slow – it has been like watching a snail cross the Sahara desert, painfully slow, but in the right direction.

WHAT HAS HELPED STEVE?

Steve's steady progress has been a combination of getting the right medication (and steadily reducing the dose), cognitive therapy, anti-depressants (which had a remarkably positive impact on him), social support, especially the day centre and the outreach staff.

One of the biggest contributing factors has been the love and support of family and our friends. I have no doubt that had we 'let go', which some professionals had urged, Steve would have slid into the abyss – he would certainly have developed a drink problem and could well have become homeless. Chris and I have always been mindful of trying to get the balance right between empowering Steve and supporting him. It is not a science and that is why I now get so angry when I hear social workers harping on that carers must learn to let go – it's only those workers who have kids that can truly understand the dilemma carers are in.

For Chris and me, the key help has been the relationship with the psychiatrist, who involved us right from the start. We had regular CPAs (Care Programme Approach), which proved vital to all of us. They helped to reduce our constant anxieties. I believe the CPAs are also a great investment to the mental health team, because if they get the relationship right with the carer then this will have a very positive impact on the person with the illness. It's a 'win win' situation.

Another crucial factor was attending the local carers' group. Even though I had a lot of mental health experience, it was no substitute for talking to other carers – it was the equivalent of going to the Open University each month – the impact it had on both Chris and me was profound. Just knowing that other people understand your problem is a great feeling. The support we gave each other and the advice and tips one picks up are invaluable.

What surprises me is that some professionals, especially GPs, seem to overlook the importance of such groups. I believe it is crucial that those who have any contact with carers should automatically refer them to a local group; it should be part of their job to know the local group and to be in contact with them – it will pay them dividends in the future.

THE LONG RECOVERY

As Steve's painfully slow healing process continues, one begins to realise just how disabling schizophrenia is. You begin to realise how much it has stripped him of his basic function to survive. The positive symptoms are disabling enough – his voices and paranoia; but it is the negative symptoms which have proved to be the most challenging in this fast moving and unforgiving society.

Steve has a chronic lack of confidence – he is plagued by indecision. He is forever changing his mind about the simplest of decisions. If, for example, I ask Steve if he wants to come into town with me, he could change his mind four or five times in the course of ten minutes and then as I get in the car, he will run out and say he's decided to come. He has spent hundreds of pounds on stereos and TVs. He has changed his mind within hours of buying new equipment. 'I think I have made a mistake – I should have got the other model.' 'But Steve we did explore that option and we all agreed that the one you have is the best one', trying to reassure him. 'I know, but what if the *Which* report was wrong?' . . . and so it would go on.

REALITY OF RECOVERY

There is a school of thought that says we must 'empower' people with schizophrenia, we must give them independence and allow them to live independently. Whilst I fully subscribe to this, I am concerned that there is an underestimation of the time that it takes individuals with schizophrenia to become independent. Having worked with people with schizophrenia and lived with the illness for the last eight years, I am convinced the process of 'recovery' is considerably more complex and problematical than some of the more 'naïve' community-based staff believe.

Research by Dr Swaran Singh, which was undertaken at St George's Hospital in London, revealed that the quality of life for people with schizophrenia is *worse* now than it was twenty years ago. Further research from Sweden shows that 43 per cent of people with schizophrenia have no friends, other than close relatives. Other research has shown that 80 per cent are unemployed. Even worse, the Mental Health Foundation estimates that 25 per cent of homeless people have a diagnosis of schizophrenia. There are, according to the Royal College of Psychiatrists, nearly 5,000 people with psychosis in British prisons – primarily schizophrenia.

Whilst I don't want to downplay the impact of other mental illnesses, schizophrenia is profoundly *different*. Most people who develop schizophrenia do not go on to live 'normal' lives. Most are unable to work. Few get married or successfully integrate socially nor do they become prime ministers, spin-doctors, comic geniuses or award-winning actors! As I have said, I do not want to suggest that schizophrenia is worse, because clearly it is not; what I am saying is that the condition is *different* to other mental illnesses and in my view needs to be approached in a more subtle way. The research speaks for itself. Independence for a large proportion of people with schizophrenia is to be condemned to a life of loneliness, isolation and deprivation. What concerns me is that there is a small minority of what I call 'mental health fundamentalist' individuals who are driven by ideology, who naively believe that recovery is all about empowerment. Who believe that day centres are universally bad and that most people with schizophrenia can work. Those with this view may be a minority but they have had an impact on government policy as we see the closure of hundreds of day centres around the country, *often against the wishes of those who use them on a daily basis.* As I have said, I firmly believe that we must always strive for empowerment, but this must be done with realistic optimism.

HAVE THERE BEEN ANY POSITIVES ABOUT BEING A CARER?

The first thing to say is that I didn't want to be a carer, I never chose to be one and I certainly wouldn't recommend it. To talk about the positives of being a carer makes me feel like I am capitalising on my son's dreadful misfortune, but professionally, there have been positives. I suddenly became a 'carer expert' and have been in high demand. I have appeared on countless television programmes and featured in numerous media articles talking about cannabis and the effects on Steve. The opportunity has given me a unique opportunity to highlight the dangers of cannabis. Above all it has helped me to understand the needs of carers more. It has relit my passion to fight the injustices that exist for both carers and those with severe mental illness. My wife set up self-help groups for carers in Southampton and over the last five years these have brought together dozens of families who, according to testimonies, have found a great deal of help and support.

Would we swap all this for our son's health? Of course, both of us would have given our lives if it meant to save Steve from the ravages of schizophrenia – as most mothers and fathers would.

THE FUTURE

The dark days of Steve head-butting the wall are over. Steve is very much more in control of his positive symptoms and indeed is more in control of his life. Chris and I have started to look through the Saga magazine again and have in fact booked a safari. My daughter has produced our first grandchild. So life for us all is settling down and is now looking a lot better. I believe Steve will continue to develop his independence and he will move into his own accommodation. It is also possible that Steve could one day work and I also believe Steve will start to socialise and eventually get married. I have no doubt that Steve is going to require some help and support for a good few years to come, but I do believe he has reached the point that will ensure that he doesn't easily slip back into a relapse. He reads his own mind well and knows how to reduce and avoid stress, which remains the last challenge for Steve to overcome. So now I look back at the day I watched that woman in black grieving over her dead son. At least when I stopped grieving over my own son's misfortune, I could still take him down the pub for a pint.

REFLECTIONS

It is clear that cannabis is a serious problem for a not insignificant number of people. As a civilised society we must try and find a solution to deterring and reducing its use. Current prohibition has not reduced or deterred cannabis use and is at risk of being ignored by the majority of young adult users. More research is clearly required to identify a model that suits the UK and will get public support. For example: even if the rise in cannabis use in the Netherlands has been fairly small with the introduction of coffee shops, that does not mean that a similar policy in the USA or the UK would have a similar impact.

I support the view that cannabis should be a public health issue and not a criminal one, apart from illegal supply and cultivation of cannabis. The government should explore cannabis becoming a civil rather than a criminal penalty issue. It should undertake research to identify the numbers of people who are adversely affected by cannabis and develop a culturally sensitive strategy to support those needing help.

Chapter 5

Getting in to psychosis
The story from the inside

Madness is a confrontation of the poetic mind with The Impossible.

THE NOMADIC LIFE

A nomad is a wanderer. Before I finally settled down, at 35, with my future wife Jill, in West London, I'd had 31 categorically different jobs (counting university teaching as one) and lived in 28 different places. Like most men I'd done my fair share of womanising and for a short period I'd had several affairs with men. In my time at university I'd studied geology, geography, physics, mathematics, rock and fluid mechanics, physiology, philosophy and psychology – whilst ironically at school it was always assumed that I'd go on to be a scholar perhaps in history or maybe English.

A psychoanalyst might say that this, in itself, is the history of a man frenetically *looking* for something, but he doesn't know what it is. Yet it never at all felt like that. In the language we use these days I just didn't want to be 'in a box'. It was just the way I was: itinerant, peripatetic, a man who wanted to live the life of the mind to the full while secretly harbouring the wish, one day, to be a professional psychologist.

Indeed I thought that that way of life, mixing with a lot of different people, living in a lot of different places, would be good training for later being a psychologist. I was surprised, and rather disappointed, when the time did finally come, to find that professional psychologists hadn't themselves lived like that at all. They just came up through the school and university system and were very focused on behaviour in controlled situations. What I'd been doing was 'Mind in Life', what they were doing was 'Mind in Laboratory'. The people who often lived as I'd lived were not psychologists, they were *writers*.

In a way I wanted to sample life widely. Even as a keen sportsman in the 1960s I had done all the athletics events, as well as long distance cycling, rock climbing, football, swimming, weight lifting, boxing, darts, even bowls. After all, so I thought, if a psychologist doesn't somehow 'get in there', savour different aspects of life, how can they function in knowing other people's minds if they don't know their own mind, their own capacities and many different perspectives? It seemed obviously the way for a kind of apprentice psychologist to live.

Because of being a very late child, all my family on both sides were dead or inaccessibly and remotely dispersed by the time I was 25. I was alone with my Labrador dog Penny. My mother (see later), who had been born back in 1902, had sadly never presented the world to me as a very supportive place. 'No one will help you', she'd say. 'They'll slag you off and think they're bloody marvellous while they're doing it but they won't do a damn thing to help you . . . you've only got yourself.' Such was life in the north of England in the 1940s, 1950s and 1960s. She was right. Ironically the only time I ever saw the supposed strong sense of community and camaraderie of socialism there was when a gang had a 'queer' on the run. Then, ironically, their chumminess and brotherly affection for one another was almost homoerotic.

But the trouble with being a wanderer, with no real ties, no family, no bonds to any company, firm or institution, or indeed any town or city is that you don't really feel that you have any identity – or indeed that in any deep sense you are 'bonded with society'. After all there is no consistency to your life, your self, your thoughts and experiences. Where do you belong? Nowhere. What do you believe in? Other than psychology and the study of the processes of the mind I didn't believe in anything. With such fuzzy allegiances I couldn't and wouldn't commit myself to any political party. Like the artist Kandinsky I wanted to remain apolitical and like a poet I didn't like the idea of commitment anyway.

Capitalism, socialism, materialism, the Church, all meant little to me. I wasn't even sure about democracy, majority opinion had never proved its rightness to me, only that at certain times a lot of people can think in the same way because of shared predispositions. I *certainly* didn't believe in 'the ways of north of England life', or 'living for football' or 'living in search of the perfect woman' or 'living for money', etc. The 'ways' I'd been offered or were cryptically on sale in a psychological sense were 'Man for the army' or 'for the brewery, the factory, the building site, the public bar of pubs, the football pitch and terraces'. But I hadn't been offered 'Man for art' or 'Man for poetry, love, sensitivity' and so on. It all looked a product of military and socio-economic history. One had to be 'the kind of man we need' or 'the man who can fit in'. In all those senses I didn't *exist*.

EXISTENTIAL FRAGILITY

During a bullying saga at school (more on this in a moment) I was walking down the corridor in the Sixth Form block and I quietly asked myself, 'Why is this happening? After all what have I actually *done* to deserve all this?!'

Somehow, immediately, the answer came to me. It wasn't an hallucinated voice but it said, as if from beyond, 'You *exist*'. This was in the sense, 'This is all happening to you because you exist *at all*'. The corollary to that of course is, 'It would be better if you didn't exist'. Indeed my mother had always behaved such that if my older brother and I didn't 'behave' she'd walk out the front door and be gone. A lifetime hater of the Chadwick family, she resented deeply, as she often said, 'being left to bring up a pair of bloody Chadwicks!'

Did I go on to live the nomadic life in search of existence itself? Or in search of love, or meaning? To me it just seemed 'the way I was'. It didn't feel like a long identity crisis, just 'identity suspension'.

If you don't really solidly exist, you have rather the behaviour of a spirit. You have to acquire existence rather than assume it. You fear that you may somehow disappear or dissolve. You feel that you don't 'belong' in this world yet somehow you 'long to be'. Perhaps you are a kind of hole in space-time, a 'space in space', not substantial but implodable, permeable, like a sponge, to people and events?

In the summer of 1979 these feelings very much came home to me in a spiritual crisis I had just before going psychotic (see also Chapter 7 and Appendix I on these matters). If one lives 'beyond or outside of identity', beyond the Kellyan (1955) construct system, beyond ego, there is a price to pay, particularly when living in a culture totally incongruent with such a mentality, as of course the 'facts and money' dominated culture of Britain has tended to be. 'Do these ideas make money?', 'Are they of any practical value?' tends to be the British, particularly the English, attitude. This is not the place for 'atmospherics', blurry boundaries and a weak sense of self. British social life and the economy doesn't want these things.

There are even some who would see all this as perhaps rather schizoid, how often I noticed the psychology and the psychotherapy following the demands of socio-economics. 'Be consistent! Be stable! Get an identity! Get a commitment! Love and work needs it!!' Such seemed to be the tacit or implicit 'silent shout' of society.

And of course if one doesn't fit, belongs to no category, is not a type, belongs nowhere, it is a rich source soil for paranoia, at least in a Western context. Because if everybody's bonds with other people are stronger than their bonds with you then, existentially, you are a kind of outcast, you are alone. Your existence is unsafe, there is threat in the air – maybe from everywhere and everyone.

Of course I tried many roles in life. In a way I lived the process life, my life was a whole sequence of roles whilst the real centre of psychological gravity was the very process of creating them. It was the actor's life in a sense as well as the writer's. After all 'I didn't exist' or at least 'shouldn't exist'. What else could I do but act? Wasn't life a mass of clichés, stereotypes, norms and roles anyway? Wasn't it all an act on a stage? I was getting really weary by 1979 of the role playing of everyday life, of people like the bullies at school who 'just did the done thing'. It was as if I was continually 'under cover'. But that too is a rich source soil for paranoia – because your cover could be blown and you could be revealed – but as what? A spirit? A nothing? A skinless vacuum? A hole-in-space? What?

Psychology of a crass kind would just account for all this by supposing 'low boredom threshold', 'strong curiosity drive', perhaps diagnosing 'socio-pathy', but to anyone with any sense it was a lot more than that. In a way I wasn't looking for any one, or any thing, or any job or any particular lifestyle, I was looking for *myself*. And strangely, yet in a very positive way, via the tortuous path of a psychotic episode and the recovery process from it, I found it. Of course R.D. Laing would like this, but Laing never really faced the fact that madness can kill you – and it nearly killed me.

'I'M TOO STRONG TO GO MAD'

People tend to think that deluded individuals believe what they do with utter conviction. It isn't true. Sometimes they do but not always. Who would be daft enough to throw themselves under the wheels of a double decker bus when their rating in the truth of their belief (that they're the Antichrist or possessed by Satan) on a scale from '+7' (belief is absolutely definitely true) to '–7' (belief is absolutely definitely false) was a mere +0.17? Not even +1.7 but +0.17! Sadly I was. How can one *be* that stupid? Perhaps it was because I was about 35 lb underweight at the time? The brain doesn't work properly when you're like that. Perhaps I was cryptically reality testing the belief? Reality testing, like Russian roulette, with my life on the line! But you don't have to be sure of a belief to act on it. Perhaps, somehow . . . it *had* to be done, even if at a cognitive level it was little more than a guess. The script I cryptically was living by was that I had to *pay*. That was basically it. God's banker in the sky had, in a way, told me I was millions in debt on my moral bank balance. Somehow only paying with my very life itself would clear the debt. So strong was *this* script that the evidence for the delusion was 'good enough' to match and sustain it. In psychosis you're not only a victim of aberrant brain functioning, you're a victim of your whole life. 'It's all led up to *this*!', you feel. 'It all fits!' It's a life process getting in to madness, it's a life process getting out of it.

As they say, 'You reap what you sow'. This was my time of reckoning, reckoning for my decadent erotic life, for the hurt and disgust I had caused people. My mother; the girls and women who had loved me and whom I had deserted; even the hurt I had caused people by beating them, in races when I was a sprinter, in exams, in school work. Win, win, win. The competitive urge had been strong in me.

After my father died when I was seven, my mother brought me up to think I was both wonderful (mind you, only because I tended to do well at things when I put my mind to them) but at the same time a 'no good Chadwick rat', a 'Chadwick rotter'. Edie, my mother, was OK to live with when she was in a good mood ('Edie Angel') but when she was in a bad mood ('Edie Witch') it was quite a different proposition. Cognitively she was a stubborn, bipolar thinker. Everything was either this or that – with absolutely *nothing* in between. In herself she was the same: there was no 'Edie Grey'. And of course her two boys, George and me, were either good or bad, and the slightest sign of badness, such as laziness in helping her with housework, then you were 'all bad'. She did on one singular occasion admit to me that, 'Oh no, you're not as black as you're painted' (by her of course) but it was only a one-off admission. I grew up feeling that I was, or could be, successful but under-neath, was emotionally and morally bad and rotten. She said to me later that she did all this 'to make you better'. (Obviously her Edwardian child-rearing ideas hadn't worked.)

'What have I done to be left with a pair of no-good Chadwicks?!', she would wail to God while doing her spring cleaning. 'I must have done something terrible in a former life to be left with a pair of rotters like you two!', she would shout of me and my brother. 'You'll get love and respect when you deserve it!!'

So I was 'no good', 'a rotter', 'a rat'. I went through a period of about a year when I would hit my older brother (the sort of thing 'a rotter' *would* do). Edie never did anything at all to stop or deter me. Never said it was cruel or horrible. Never said it was wrong to do such things. Just stood there while I did it. Years later she said, 'I wanted to make you hard'. Sometimes I'd say sensitive things to her like, 'Isn't love important in life?' She'd always reply with, 'Love?! Ha! Love flies out the window when there's no money!' (a standard Manchester/Cheetham Hill remark I learned much later). She'd say it every time, always the same comeback. Anything like tenderness, compassion, sensitivity or delicacy of feeling she'd scorn with a sneer. Years later she said, 'I tried to knock all that out of yer'. Edie Burghall was so 'Manchester minded' she was completely over the top. Even the bouncers on the club doorways were more tender-minded than she was.

It was a totally dysfunctional, personality deforming upbringing. Edie, to be blunt about it, was 'off her head', she really needed help – but she'd been brought up in the asylum age when anything 'mental' was absolutely terrify-ing. She never had the courage to go to a therapist. If she'd admitted there was anything *at all* wrong with her, she behaved as if the whole world would cave in around her.

When I lay in the gutter on New King's Road in Fulham with the bus beside me, blood dripping from me, it was as if Edie Burghall and the bullies at school were there on the pavement looking down on me saying, 'Job done!' Burghall had even said such things as 'I'll stick a bloody *knife* in yer yer bloody swine!!' and 'It'd be good to kill a Chadwick!' She and my father had *had* to get married back in 1918 at a time, of course, when such things were topics of deep shame. The Chadwicks seemed to have blamed her and 'lorded it over her' (as the wronged party) ever since. It had been very unfair. Edie Burghall took out her revenge on her own ('Chadwick') children. My father had also felt trapped into marriage, I never got the impression, from things she said, that he did actually love her.

The bullies at school were almost entirely football people. Socially they ruled the roost. 'The power of football', as we say these days. They, the First XI soccer team and the First XV rugby team, thought (stupidly) because of my ornate hairstyle that I was 'queer' (homosexual) and a big-head (win, win, win). Cartoons on the board, poems circulating (poetry was OK as long as it was in the service of ridicule and humiliation), gossip spread around the district where I lived, shopkeepers and particularly hairdressers questioned, old contacts 'interviewed' so as to dig up any relevant 'information'. It went on for two years, 1963–64. Football may be 'the beautiful game' but it certainly isn't played by 'the beautiful people'. Being thought to be a poof and a big-head were the two worst things you could be in the north in those days. Edie, 'I won't tolerate weakness!' Edie, had also hardly helped me to cultivate a warm, trusting, cuddly personality. That must have put people off. 'You've gotta be as hard as *nails* in this wuuuurld!', she would sneer time and again with this mad, sick, evil expression on her face. I can tell you the woman was sick with the hate and pain of early twentieth-century Manchester life.

I remember when we were sat at dinner at school and this lad across the table from me, Mark Radnan, said, 'Hey Chad, you've got thick lips, you must be kind'. Immediately I came back with, 'Kind?! Ha! I'm not kind! I'm a rotter, a no-good rotter, I'm not kind at all!' It was life at home coming through at school. Radnan sat there with a shocked expression on his face. I was 14.

Transvestism was my sexual orientation when I was young. Apparently I'd been fetishistic ever since I was an infant and only a few days old. The vast bulk of transvestites and transsexuals think the sun shines out of their mothers but my feelings for mine were incredibly conflicted. Really I obtained all my positive attitudes to women and to femininity from all the girls I knew as a teenager in Manchester. They were really nice, made me think well of women. But Manchester *men* in those days were revolting. It was obviously the radicalising effects of industry and two world wars but they were cold, aggressive, extremely cruel, very easily angered, arrogant, nasty, disloyal, abusive, they gave me an absolutely obnoxious image of 'Man'. No wonder I was a transvestite, who'd want to be a man? The identity was awful.

In 1974, when I was studying psychology as an undergraduate, we were doing Laing and Cooper's work on schizophrenia. In my room in digs I remember thinking, 'I wonder if *I* could go schizophrenic?' But I thought to myself, 'no, my mind is too strong'. God, how many times have I heard people say that of themselves?! Ha!

What you have to do is take your deepest, darkest fear, that's, as service users say, your 'button'. Then imagine life pressing on it over and over and over again with a ten tonne weight. How 'strong' is your mind now? Are you *that* sure you 'couldn't go mad'? Think about it. Maybe, so far, you've just been lucky.

My button, after Manchester and school, was that my transvestism would be discovered by a very 'unsafe' person – such as an aggressive, macho, slanderous betraying *man*. Echoes of school and the macho football bullying ring. The ornate hairstyle probably was the decorative urge in my transvestism 'leaking' into my male behaviour. I'd wondered if they *knew* about my transvestism, they seemed so bullish and cocksure and in those days the culture of the time had got it all wrong and thought people in drag were homosexual. Now we know it's not like that at all but back then we didn't. So I'd felt completely demoralised by my own guilt. I learned years later that the bullies hadn't known – though I had told a couple of friends about it. They hadn't betrayed me though I'd worried that they had.

Alas in 1974 my transvestism was rumbled by a broken-nosed tough guy and his girlfriend in a very poorly soundproofed house where I lived in Bristol; they were in the flat below. Both were big club people with lots of contacts. It was the beginning of the end for my sanity. After all, what was I? A no-good Chadwick, a rat, a rotter, a queer, a poof, a big-head and now 'a known pervert'. As was her way, my mother had always made very clear her extremely low opinion of me as a person (so as 'to make me better'). The bullies at school had nothing but amused scorn for me. What resources did I have to call upon to stand tall within to counter all this moralistic persecution?

My girlfriend of those days, whom the neighbours of course informed, thought what I did was 'vile and despicable'. I had to stop it or we were finished (I didn't). The male friends I had (also informed) were similarly disgusted. I was veritably swimming in a sea of moralistic self-righteous people. It was a very very lonely scenario.

After I moved to another place I used to go back hammering on the downstairs door of the people who had outed me so as to confront them. But it was never opened. I heard that the man and his buddies were 'going to take photographs' of me in the male role to warn people because people 'deserved to know' about this 'vile and despicable' pervert. Such were the attitudes in the culture towards transvestism in 1974. I might just as well have been a Nazi war criminal. So now, not only was gossip circulating, as it was, it would be *illustrated* so people who didn't even know me could recognise me! And since I was always to be seen with Penny, my dog, I did stand out. It was a really spooky, evil feeling.

The reader can probably imagine that this was a very toxic situation for paranoia and self-consciousness. After five years of feeling 'recognised' and hearing that I was being talked about, I was ripe for insanity. If Manchester had been 'the lock', the outing in the West Country was the key that turned that lock and opened the door to paranoid insanity. In psychotic paranoia you do have to believe that people *really will* go to extreme lengths to discredit, humiliate and destroy you. At school and in Manchester I learned that if you, as a male, were off-centre in sexuality and gender role behaviour, they would. The bullying saga of 1963–64 was a *rehearsal* for psychotic paranoia. It taught me how to think like a paranoid psychotic.

In 1979, while living in Hackney, in East London and, by then, cross-dressing openly and going out cross-dressed to pubs, clubs, restaurants etc. (after all, what was the point, now, of concealing it?), I wrote to some colleagues in psychology about the 'terrible and unfair persecution' the people in the West Country had brought upon me. But, catastrophically, when their willingness to reply quickly dried up, some of the phrases I had used in my letters were echoed by DJs a few days later, in their talk on the radio. Of course, used as I was in Manchester to total disloyalty and betrayal of 'sissies' I assumed, wrongly, that the letters had been passed on to the media for amusement. A so-called 'bridging inference'. After all it would be a good way to put a 'known pervert' in his place. Manchester people, after all, had always spread rumours about poofs like wildfire, they loved it. With this single bridging inference: 'They've passed the letters on to the media "for a laugh"' (itself a very 'Manchester' way to think) I 'lost the plot' of daily life. Bridging inferences themselves are perfectly normal processes but this one took me from a quite reasonable state of threat sensitivity, reasonable in the circumstances, to psychotic paranoia. The media now were persecuting me! Now I was insane. It was only five years on and my mind had not been 'too strong' after all. (Perhaps the very mystical ideas I had had before this event (see Appendix I and Chadwick, 2001c) had blurred the boundary between within and without and made such an 'invasive' style of thinking more available to me?)

One might say, of course, what's *that* crazy about going from feeling the talk of the district (which with my decadent ways I was) to feeling the talk of the radio? Insanity is not that inaccessible, not that difficult a state to get into. This indeed is why, when I did go mad, I had no idea at all that I was psychotic. It had all happened via perfectly normal processes and in small increments. When the critical bridging inference did occur ('the letters have been passed on' etc.) it was no different from thousands upon thousands of other bridging inferences that I, like everybody, had made in my life that had been perfectly accurate – including dozens of inferences of disloyalty and gossip-spreading at school during the bullying saga that had almost all been proved true. Why shouldn't this one be accurate? Qualitatively the *kind* of thinking I did was quite normal, I had no reason at all to think I was deluded. As the psychologist the late Ivor Pleydell-Pearce said to me a couple of years later, 'Well Peter, if we'd been in just the same situation as you, we might have done exactly the same thing'.

IS THERE ANY *HOPE?!*

The story here on in through madness to the suicide attempt on New King's Road in Fulham, subsequent hospital admission and the administration of medication to bring me back to sanity, is basically a story of how seemingly confirmatory things – snatches of conversation overheard in the street; things said by newsreaders and DJs; headlines on newspapers; out of context comments made by people in the workplace – all these things jolted and jogged me towards a terminus both dreaded and yet longed for. In confrontation with one's destiny is peace.

The delusion I constructed after hails of astonishing coincidences was that a group of people I called 'The Organisation' were persecuting me via all means possible with the basic (rather Edie Burghall-style) message, 'Change or die!' I decided, again prompted by streams of uncanny coincidences, that this was because I must be possessed by Satan or be the Antichrist. After all, Burghall had always said I was 'all bad', a rotter, a no-good, a rat. It all seemed to fit the script of my life and the narrative or story I had been given about myself, perfectly.

I wailed to the local vicar who had come to see me in casualty after the suicide attempt, 'Is there any HOPE?!' Rottenness within, rottenness without, God a savage God, callous, disloyal people one could never trust, a hateful extended family that had deserted us like gazelles jumping over a fence to get away after my father died. At the time of all this I also had no job, no secure home, no money, no love, nothing. The delusion was the *only* meaning I had in my life and it was driving me to kill myself!

The only thing left to do was to 'cast Satan out of myself' by having my head and brain crushed by the wheels of a ten ton double decker bus. I would then be cast, with Satan, out into 'Outer Darkness' but nonetheless on 'New King's Road'. The road of 'the new king' so Jesus would then come into the world to reign. I believed it, as I said earlier in this chapter, with a rating of +0.17. But it was so important, it was worth dying for. Die at least doing *one* good, really really good thing. At the 'Divine' age of 33 I had, like Jesus, hit the buffers, but from the opposite direction.

With two buses on an otherwise totally deserted road at nine o'clock in the morning (!) it looked as if they were waiting for me – indeed I assumed they were. The situation (as usual) had obviously been 'set up' by The Organisation. Wasn't everything by now, in my life, set up by The Organisation? Of course it was. But having been told years earlier that I tended to get things right 'the second time', I chose the second bus for my dive into oblivion.

With brakes screaming and passengers doubtless lurching and tumbling, the left nearside wheel of the bus crushed my right hand, as I lay on the road, like an egg under a brick hammer. It squeezed hard against my right shoulder and upper arm, rotating my body round as it did so and grazed and scoured up the right hand side of my face and head, effectively rolling my cranium out of the way rather than crushing it. Far from this being a cry for help I was virtually speechless with shock and disappointment at having survived!

As I lay in the gutter blood dripping from me onto the tar of the road – reversed in my 'Satanic' mind, of course, to 'blood dripping on the *rat*' (Edie Burghall would like that). It all fitted. Everything did. This was no delusion, this was *real*. Once I'd been virtually scraped off the road and put in the ambulance I found that the relentless flow of confirming coincidences I'd suffered for the last couple of months still kept coming. Even the vicar who was to see me in casualty had, the previous night, when I had spoken to him in distress, misheard my name as 'Peter Channel' – exactly what I felt I was for spiritual forces to come into the world. Things like that had been virtually firing at me for months. The two ambulance men I now found were called Peter and Paul. I was taken to Charing Cross Hospital (to me 'the hospital of the charring cross'). Portentously I was put in a Ward J for treatment. My consultant was Dr Weller. As I look back on it all now, I really wonder how many coincidences a person can *take* before their sanity is dislodged.

REFLECTIONS

Where is the positive perspective on schizophrenia in such a macabre tale? One might say at the outset that with an upbringing like mine you don't have to be mad to suffer serious mental illness. Doubtless I had vulnerabilities passed on perhaps in my mother's DNA, which led to her terribly disturbed personality and to her bringing latent disturbance out in me. But of course it needn't have been this way. She might have sought therapeutic help; alas in those days one 'just didn't do things like that'. So the macabre tale of her life led on to the macabre tale of mine.

We live in a postmodern world (see Butler and Ford, 2003) and what counts as 'reality' is by no means decided, even by physical scientists. I worked and researched in physical science for many decades, overlapping with my time in psychology, and I can assure the reader that mathematics is not all as cut and dried as practitioners would like the general public to think.

On the other hand there are perspectives on the margins of, and indeed outside of science, that pervade our culture. Students in adult education have been exposed to the details of this episode over the last three decades. I also have given a number of previous accounts of it (Chadwick, 1992, 1993, 1997a, 1997b, 2001b, 2003b, 2007a). People of more spiritual orientation believe I was the victim of evil spiritual forces that were trying to kill me, a view my wife also holds; others who have seen more details than given here of the barrage of coincidences I suffered don't think that this was a psychotic episode at all but a 'paranormal attack'. A few, who think transvestism disgusting, feel I 'deserved all I got'. One kindly lady went to the other extreme and said I was 'converted from the Antichrist to The Christ by the suicide attempt' and that the vicar was right, I *was* 'a channel' for spiritual forces. Still other perspectives have been given but apart from the obvious one of 'psychosis' the one that has repeatedly shone through over the decades is that I am a shamanistic character, a messenger, who has suffered his dark night of the soul but, with luck, survived and returned to then work to help the lives of other people along the way.

On a more conventional note, the very fact that I was forever trying to make sense of things, solve problems and confront my fears shows that I wasn't as disturbed as all that. Those were my attempts, as Bleuler (1955/1911) would understand, to avoid disintegration. But in madness one doesn't 'run away' from anything, a popular way of thinking among psychotherapists, one charges straight into things and faces 'the worst'. It is not an escape but a confrontation. Though I was suffering I was hypersensitively aware of my surroundings, and desperately trying to negotiate a life for myself within them, despite everything. Of course in the end I failed, but at least I was *trying*.

Sometimes people do feel they have a destiny to face. It is good to have stood up to it and come through the other side. A certain amount of courage is needed to do this. After my father died in the early 1950s my own expectations for my future were dim. Indeed when only eight I said to myself, 'I'm finished'.

Over the years the script evolved in my mind that someone had to pay for the mess that was my parents' marriage, that was my mother's awful illness-ridden life, and for the despicable way the Chadwick family deserted us on my father's death – at a time when my mother was recovering from breast cancer and was left a widow with two children. I, the 'no-good Chadwick rat', had to pay, and also had to pay for being a striving, sissy boy among the high-minded virtuous and moral, socialistic, humble, heterosexual people of Manchester. I had to pay, I had to be 'ashamed of myself'. The life script and the personal narrative all fitted, *everything* 'fitted', like hand in glove.

Now I look back on those first 33 years with an attitude of tranquillity and relative indifference. One cannot escape the times during which one is brought up. Though those societal attitudes seem ludicrous to me now, *then* they were all around me. There was no escape from them in a time machine, one simply had to live and get by within it all – with everybody 'doing the done thing'. But these things happen, it's just life, you get on with it. And in a way you have to see it *as* life, it's your personal journey and it's useful to have the mission of trying to carve out the best life you can with the biological and cultural hands of cards you've been dealt. The important thing, however, is to work to transcend your experiences and address more general, even universal, concerns. The following two chapters, which also grew out of my own story, will try to continue to do this.

Chapter 6

Getting out of psychosis

Hints and strategies

> If it is not elemental cognitions that make you depressed, or mad, but your very life itself, then you have to change the narrative, the story.

Obviously the events in Chapter 5 should not have happened. Any admission to a psychiatric unit, a prison, a drug and alcohol rehabilitation centre and perhaps also a divorce court is essentially a failure of prevention. It could have been that in the landscape of pain that seems to have been Manchester life in the first half of the twentieth century (both my parents were born in the first two years of the century) my mother (and the school bullying ring) came to feel that hate and cruelty would always win.

MIRRORING

Having been raised in Edwardian times, Edie had no conception of the emphasis on a child's right to self-actualisation that is so important in the minds of parents and teachers today. To her one 'did as one was told'. This was indeed quite a common attitude for people to hold in the north before the social revolution of the late 1960s and beyond. If there was any single psychological factor that was important for me getting well again, it was finding people in London who mirrored what was within and hence enabled it to be in a sense activated and eventually to blossom. In a way I was, as Laing would understand, the living dead, or at least the living unborn, before I came to live in London. Certainly a life with 'a hard case' like Edie Burghall and years at an all boys state grammar school in the north which, socially, was essentially a training for the army, gave me about as much cultivation of sensitivity as a young butterfly would have for flying practice in the smoke and flames of Hell. For years I was alienated from my Real Self and it was as the latter was able to effloresce over the years after 1979 that I became, in a deep sense, weller and weller. As person-centred therapists always have maintained, continual estrangement from the Real Self is liable to lead to pathology – but it also is true, as psychoanalysts have observed (Winnicott, 1960), that the False Self (that I needed to wear for a long time) can be a caretaker Self until one feels it is *safe* for the Real Self to emerge. Certainly London gave me that feeling of safety to truly be who I am, and as that came about, a healthier personality emerged that functioned perfectly well. The Self twisted and deformed by Burghall and school just gradually dropped away.

CREATIVITY

This efflorescence of the Real Self was helped by thousands of people particularly in West, Central and North London as well as people I came across through reading late nineteenth-century literature. These were in a sense 'friends across time', particularly the clan of Oscar Wilde and his companions in the 1880s and 1890s. In them I also felt 'these are people I could talk to and with whom I could be myself'. This affection I have found for these people and their world has catalysed a number of writings (Chadwick, 1995a, 1997c, 2001a (Chapter 12), 2005a, 2006b, 2006c, 2006e, 2007c) all of which were psychologically refreshing and expressive efforts. In showing also how effective a psychologist Oscar Wilde was, in addition to his many other talents, the work has hopefully also made a small contribution to the secondary literature on this period.

There is no doubt that turning one's pathology round in a productive, creative direction is a path to peace and health. It is a technique in the Churchillian spirit of looking for the opportunities in the difficulty. Since 1979 my own creative writings have focused on Wilde, and of course on psychosis, but also on perception (Chadwick, 1983), on the connections between geology and evolutionary psychology (Chadwick, 1982); on the education of geological perception (Chadwick and Hughes, 1980); on short story writing (Chadwick, 1995b (Chapter 3), 2006d, 2006e, 2007d) and on the paranormal (Chadwick, 2004a, 2005b). It has even proved possible to turn round my actual experience of the delusions themselves into productive scientific writing (Chadwick, 2001b, 2003b). In saying this I carry the flag to advertise the creative potential of psychosis sufferers. I encourage others not to dwell in a morass of self-pity but to turn the creativity implicit in their way of being around to productive advantage. Whether it be in writing, sculpture, painting, dance, fashion, clay modelling, training to be a therapist or counsellor or whatever. You have it in you to do these things.

As in the work of the painter Edward Hopper, the critical achievement in creative work of an expressive kind is to transcend one's personal experience and address more general, even universal concerns. This helps one to create 'beyond the Self' and 'to the world' not merely 'about oneself'. It is necessary to give oneself over to something bigger and more important than oneself. To do otherwise is to risk solipsism, egocentricity and merely narcissistic preoccupation.

PROFESSIONAL HELP

In 1977/78 it was obvious to me that I needed a 'life change' to get out of the corner I was heading towards in my existence. Eventually it was necessary to change my town, my kind of work, my girlfriend, my circle of friends, the kind of research I did, and even, via medication, the chemical state of my brain. Between 1977 and 1980 the only things I did not change were my sex and my bank.

To move on to specifics: the medication (haloperidol) I eventually was put on didn't seem to turn me into somebody I wasn't; instead I felt that it removed the barriers that were preventing me from being who I am. Of course this is not the case for every sufferer but it does suggest that the hunt for better targeted medications at the individual level is worthwhile. As I said earlier (p. xiii), my own experience gives me no enthusiasm whatever for campaigns for 'drug-free psychiatry'. In my case well-targeted medication totally revolutionised my life.

Group work I did, Encounter groups and Gestalt groups, coupled with the medication, also helped me to delve more into my feelings life and this also helped me cognitively – something conservatively minded scientists probably would not expect. In fact when I became more at peace with, and accepting of, my feelings, my mind was a lot clearer and cognitive function pretty generally was enhanced. The psychotherapy and the medication combined also helped me to *integrate* thought and feeling a lot better, something I'd found generally ignored in physical science education. Sometimes it is necessary to say and do things as somebody else, and Gestalt therapy does give licence for this. Play writing (e.g. Chadwick, 2007d) also has this facility. As Oscar Wilde knew, sometimes one finds out more clearly what one thinks and feels by putting words in other people's mouths. In Gestalt one also can speak out as if one is an object one chooses in the room, or as an object one imagines. This can add dimensions to one's thoughts and feelings beyond those possible via only speaking as a person.

The activities at the Day Hospital at Charing Cross, though very basic, were valuable in enculturating me back into mixing with people in everyday life, as I had become – as many patients do – extremely reclusive in the months of my illness and just before. The camaraderie and humour in the psychiatric aftercare hostel in Shepherds Bush, where I lived for 18 months, was also extremely strengthening. It took me back, in an atmosphere of trust and safety, into doing vital everyday things, such as going to shops, pubs and sporting events without these activities being accompanied by sinister paranoid thoughts. It is surprising how important and valuable to recovery is the relearning of these everyday things in life. The excellent support and good common sense of my two GPs over the years, Grant Blair and Ian S. Gibson, has also contributed a great deal to my well-being.

My transvestism and bisexual inclinations of those days were not in any way held against me in London. Indeed people seemed to regard them, as I have since found do artists, as adding colour, animation and liveliness to my personality. When I dressed up in the hostel the reaction was usually one of humour and warmth. It simply is not true that cross-dressing in these circumstances is 'abusing other residents'. Attitudes like that are transvestophobic and psychologically damaging. Once these off-centre sexual behaviours were given full expression in a totally accepting atmosphere, my interest in them eventually faded and in September 1980 I went back to straight sex.

In very practical terms: returning (but gradually) into work again, moving into a really nice flat with Jill, who I had started dating in November 1980, and having at least a reasonable income, all these things were highly therapeutic. The 'JAM' triad, job, good accommodation and money, is a vital foundation on which to build.

SUBJECTIVE PERCEPTIONS

From the subjective point of view, my actual perception of the crisis was itself of immense therapeutic moment, whatever the objective genetic and biochemical perspective on it might have been. In the first five years post-episode I accepted that I had had an illness, that my brain had definitely not been working normally at the height of the crisis itself and certainly not when I was admitted as a patient, something my own PhD research confirmed. I also recognised that the medication was wonderfully helpful, which it was, particularly for improving my context and gist processing, for decreasing the 'volume' on my basic affects of anger, fear and sex and for widening my attentional beam (see Chadwick, 2007a for details on these 'cognitive hardware' problems).

My attitude was to regard the illness as an enemy that I had to respect and be very careful about. I was extremely wary of 'being cocky about my illness' because it was evident that it was something that could destroy me and drive me to suicide. As well as the New King's Road suicide attempt I had made three further attempts while in hospital, one involving throwing myself head-long down a flight of stairs. I obviously was in no position to regard this illness in a relaxed, cavalier or intellectual way. This illness, for me, was a potential killer. I had to be VERY wary of it. It was like a powerful bomb that had to be defused and dismantled with great care. I was in a situation where there was no room for error and no room for speculative fancy, the job had to be done *properly*.

As five or six years passed, however, my inner strength genuinely began to return. I started writing for publication again, something that had ceased between 1982 and 1986, and felt that I was also returning to the level of functioning I had had well before the crisis – which probably was optimum in 1970. In effect this helped me to dispense with the 'illness label'. It no longer felt within that I was ill but I decided to stay on a small dose of haloperidol (2.5 mg) anyway. I suffered also from mild symptoms of Gilles de la Tourette's syndrome, which had started at the same time as the psychosis, and halo-peridol (plus tobacco smoking) was a terrifically helpful cocktail for that.

Marrying Jill, getting on to a second PhD programme and into regular work all gave me security, confidence, hope and belief in myself. Having had considerable education before the episode, including a First in psychology, did give me threads in terms of prior qualifications and skills that I could pick up after it. In a practical sense this was terribly important. Things also that are part of the fabric of life, such as good neighbours, eating well (itself not at all to be underestimated), keeping physically active, living in a low crime rate area and having a strong support network of friends and confidantes whom I could talk to about everything and anything, however embarrassing it was, all these things were wonderfully protective and strengthening.

The importance of my relationship with my wife could not be overstated though obviously I cannot go into details. Love, both given and received, does turn one away from a chronically negative mindset such as I was given at home and at school. Acrid cynicism basically destroyed my mother from within; for *life* it was vital to get away from such an attitude.

Keeping a diary-cum-journal, as I have since 1962, was therapeutic although only when it became a medium for self-expression, not just an ideas notebook. A journal really can be like a friend and writing in it therapeutic in itself, even if that writing does not lead to problem solution. Writing, as well as drawing, can help one to work also with metaphors for one's struggle. These may include battling a dangerous enemy, climbing a mountain, climbing out of a pit, treating oneself as a musical instrument that one is fine-tuning, treating one's battling as an attempt to take off into the air like an aeroplane, regarding one's life as a journey from one kind of place to another or as an adventure down a deep pothole or into a diamond mine or up a winding staircase in a mansion, all kinds of images like these and others can be valuable in organising and directing one's thoughts and feelings. There is no reason why one should stick to *one* metaphor, I myself have worked with over half a dozen over the years, all helpful at different times and in different problem situations.

FUNCTIONAL IMPROVEMENTS

It would not have been therapeutically helpful to have simply seen myself as a 'genetic schizophrenic'. I wanted to change, progress, develop and grow, not have my identity stamped on me like branded cattle. Indeed as the years went by, it became clear that my level of functioning was becoming noticeably *higher* than it had been before the illness, not lower. Far from deteriorating or being a 'rutted in schizophrenic' with an illness that would 'forever limit my life', my cognitive, affective, conative, social and spiritual aspects were all, in various ways, better than they had been before and far more integrated. Although my IQ (thanks to university life) had reached 175 on some tests before the episode, it was not consistent there across tests, tending to average and steady at 156 (156 was both the mean and mode on all such tests I took after leaving school but before the illness). However, after the episode it *was* so consistent – a jump of virtually 20 points. This was mildly cheering though not of much relevance to psychological insight skills, which I have always valued far more than logic, and these, of course, are not assessed at all by convergent reasoning instruments. Such tests also have no relevance at all to one's ability to integrate thought and feeling – something one sees so beauti- fully in Tennyson (Byatt, 2004). It seemed, however, that well after the crisis I did reach a level of general functioning I could only occasionally savour before it. So in effect the whole debacle had brought out the best in me (as I also felt was the case with the effects of the medication). It seemed that this level of functioning had been clouded previously by such things as distracting worrying thoughts, attentional problems and self-doubt. I was also a lot happier. The only decrement was in my ability to take a good photograph. Before the crisis I had been quite a talented photographer, with many photographs published, but the medication fractionally numbed my visual sensitivity and capacity to grasp an aesthetically beautiful angle in an instant. The damage to my right hand in the suicide attempt also ruined me as a darts player. Those were the only costs of the crisis. Journalists who think mental health problems make a person 'non-functional' should take note.

CAUSAL THINKING

My life was better, however, only by attending to every aspect of mental life from the biochemical and physiological to the emotional, motivational and cognitive through to the social and spiritual. Admittedly this meant often blending rationales and ideologies in an intellectually uncomfortable way. Every single relevant aspect of my life nonetheless was changed by me to make sure that such a disaster did not happen again. Indeed I suffered no relapses. Such changes also meant enquiring deeply into the *causes* of the illness, not simply working out how to get out of it. If you know the reticular pattern of causal antecedents of the episode you can avoid going down similar kinds of paths in your life again and you become aware of your vulnerabilities. Emphasising just 'recovery and rehabilitation' is not enough. One has to be mindful of secondary prevention and hence of not making the same mistakes in thought, feeling and also in one's behaviour and social life again. Finding where a delusion came from psychologically helps you to emotionally uproot it, not merely reality test it or dismantle it cognitively. This is likely to reduce, as I found myself, the probability of reoccurrence.

Researching the essential normality of the mental process that led to 'the abnormality of crisis' was itself therapeutic. Seeing oneself, however, as categorically different from the rest of humanity was ostracising, depressing, alienating and even pathogenic. Realising the unfairness of abuse also was reducing of guilt and shame – and enhancing of self-forgiveness. Abusers do tend to protect their consciences and self-esteem with statements such as 'you deserved it!' and 'you're to blame!'. These are always useful statements for a sadist to hide behind. It is vital to rid oneself of such self-perceptions and create a different story or narrative about oneself to that provided by the abusers. Indeed one of the Oxbridge boys said to me of the bullies, 'Ignore them Pete, they're pathetic'. Personally I didn't want any contact with their 'world' and their army and football terraces mentality. To interface with them was like mixing with people from another planet. But then I had to go off and find *myself* not just copy them.

Catalysing one's own motivation and regaining one's self-esteem and ego resilience after the trauma of psychosis are among the hardest problems of all. Again the metaphors one uses are critical. These need to be activating and confidence building not demoralising. One has to *want* to get well and be motivated to get *away* from the psychotic state. I saw it as 'a bastard' or as 'a Satanic threat' that I had to beat within myself. Seeing madness in a rather Laingian way as a pretty well understandable reaction to a dreadful situation was esteem-lifting and self-protective but seeing it as a failure or as running away from reality or as a sign of poor character or as a stupid mistake were all weakening and depressing ways of construing. All were of no value. One needs positive 'self-talk' such as 'I'm gonna beat this swine!' not language that undermines hope and resolve.

Taking the recovery process slowly, not panicking if one has any 'blips', not rushing things and not demanding too much from oneself too early are all vital strategies. Psychosis is a serious illness; it should not be regarded lightly or lightheartedly nor its power to destroy underestimated. Overconfidence about one's capacity to contain psychosis is very dangerous. Seeing it, or one's vulnerability to it, as having a positive side in enhanced creativity, sensitivity and empathy is nonetheless encouraging – and helps one to feel that one can 'turn the coin over' into something productive and useful.

At a cognitive level one has to be mindful of how biases such as confirmation bias, jumping to conclusions, jumping to more spectacular and portentous interpretations and the retrieval of only negative, not positive, autobiographical memories can send one's thinking skidding. Guilt feelings, expectancies and context effects, as well as noisy surroundings, can also trigger or exacerbate hallucinations and delusional perceptions. One has to be mindful of how one's mental processes can be tricked into moving in dangerous directions. Once you've had the wheel of a double decker bus looming one inch away from your face or found yourself soaring through mid-air down a long flight of stairs because of psychosis, you don't take its causative and exacerbative factors lightly (nor do you just treat it as 'an interesting intellectual problem').

Because of this, insight itself and the gradual gain of insight over time is a strengthening process. Certainly reading the professional literature on psychosis I found strengthening, illuminating and protective not weakening in any way.

SPIRITUAL AWAKENINGS

The reader can probably obtain an inkling from the previous chapter that the life and personal situation I was in in 1979 was a scenario that closed around me and engulfed me. I could find no way out and so, like a man stuck underwater with no air, I lost an agentic sense of Self, a sense in other words that I was in the active driving seat of my own life. This is how one can become so much more passive and have one's locus of control (Rotter, 1966) pass from within to without. This catalyses one to give oneself over to forces from outside oneself and, of course, the door is hence opened to both the spiritual and the psychotic (see Chapter 7). It is particularly self-doubt that can switch the experience from the numinous and hierophantic to the infernal and the paranoid but nonetheless the glimpses of the sacred that one does obtain can plant a valuable seed that one can cultivate later when one feels stronger and more self-loving.

It was vital to me in my recovery therefore to capitalise on positive spiritual experiences I had just before I went psychotic in 1979 as they opened up to me a different way of experiencing 'that which is beyond' and in a sense tuned my mind to think and feel differently about God and about my (previously dreadful) relationship with God (see Appendix I). This was critical in later years and shows that no-one should downgrade experiences of this kind simply because they predate psychosis.

PSYCHODYNAMIC WORK

Psychoanalytic work I did on myself was at first very stressful and often prompted the need to take extra medication to reduce stress and arousal. I could not have participated in psychoanalytic work of any kind at the same time as coming off medication, it would have been disastrous and probably would have made me relapse. Psychoanalytic therapy was never designed in the first place for recovering psychotics and often the ego strength of such people is too low and fragile to withstand the stress of such interventions. However, as the years went by, self-analysis of this kind proved a less stressful way of working and more rewarding. It was particularly useful to see how cognitive processes had been slave systems to deeper emotional and motivational problems – and also how thereby my social behaviour had also been warped by these factors. Eventually by seeing the whole hierarchy (or perhaps it would be more truthful to say: heterarchy) of reticular causal factors it was possible to see how they dovetailed together and mutually energised each other as a flexible totality. I admit, however, that some people do prefer – and find it less confusing – to work only at one level, say the cognitive, but therapists of this genre do generally show how the processes focused upon have consequences for the individual's general psychic economy. The advantage of a blended psychodynamic and cognitive approach is that one is dealing with material that is either in or available to consciousness, unlike the unseen processes of physiology, pharmacotherapy and physical interventions such as ECT. There people may feel better but have no idea why. This obviously is disempowering to some degree.

Having said this, however, it is nonetheless true that medication, for me, through increasing clarity of thought, reducing emotional volatility, improving context apprehension and generally strengthening ego processes (such as impulse control, organisation of thought and gratification delay), actually made insight work of a psychoanalytic kind more, not less, productive. Certainly the anxiety-reducing effects of both medication and psychodynamic insight work had considerable 'knock-on' effects for general happiness and enhancing my behaviour socially. In recursive fashion this made it less likely that paranoid ideas could take seed or grow to any degree if they did.

THE BLEND OF BIOCHEMISTRY AND PSYCHOLOGY

Obviously one cannot simply rely on medication to 'do the job'. It is true that it does change one as a person, but then one has to put that changed personality 'on the road', so to speak, and experience different reactions to it over the years to gradually change one's perceptions and expectations about people and life. That takes time and needs patience. Fortunately medication helps one to 'surf' the stressful waves of life rather than being in a state where one is hit hard by every ripple. Then one's behaviour itself becomes more consistent, one's feelings are steadier and hence the reactions of people to one become more reliable and positive and less confusing and disturbing. These more positive consequences also enable one to construct a more strengthening narrative about oneself back to oneself. In my case I had to completely throw the story or thumbnail sketch I had been given of myself in my first 18 years into the dustbin of life. Clearly a full understanding of all the processes that lead in and out of psychosis needs a biological, an intra-psychic *and* an interpersonal perspective taking subjective factors into account. Metaphors, narratives, self-talk and insight are just as important as genes and neural pathways. It is not enough only to explain psychosis and recovery from it via a model based exclusively on the physical sciences.

Chapter 7

Thinking at The Borderline
The 'Deep Music' theory of reality

> If you have no interest in The Impossible, you never know what the boundaries are of The Possible.

THE REALITY OF THE SYMBOL

It is the conventional wisdom in science that psychotic thought, and even thought prior to madness or at 'The Borderline' as I would put it, has only personal, subjective significance. It does not relate to 'The World', only to the inner life of the thinker. Because of this, mainstream research in psychiatry, abnormal psychology and psychopharmacology has no real interest in schizophrenia other than as an endeavour for finding things wrong with the people they study so as to 'correct' them. In this chapter I wish to capitalise on, and unpack, my own thinking at 'The Borderline' in 1979 in order to create a radical reinterpretation of the way we look at altered states of consciousness of this kind.

The thinking articulated here I'm sure involves me treading in some steps also made by quantum physicist Wolfgang Pauli and it does take us from physics, which I studied for many years in the context of its relevance to geology, into psychology. This clearly is a step that physicists themselves, since psychology is not their subject, are apprehensive about taking. In this chapter we move into these dangerous and forbidden waters.

The Measurement Problem in physics, where at the microlevel, reality is not instantiated (i.e. a particle does not actually come into existence) unless an observation is made, shows that the problem of the nature of the micro-world (Niels Bohr's 'Deep Truth') and that of the nature of consciousness are not separate issues. One is dependent on the other. For there to *be* material reality there simultaneously has to be consciousness as a primary aspect of the 'stuff' of the world. For there to be reality at all, the mentalistic is, and has to be, imbricated into it, giving it its very existence as a co-dependent partner in the orchestration of 'what is the case'.

All conscious entities, however, relate to the world via searching for things of 'significance', from food to God. The qualities of experience are structured by the search for meaning and the effort to make sense out of the information provided by the senses. It seems unavoidable to infer that this meaning-seeking quality to consciousness – which indeed is the very essence of consciousness itself – is what transduces the 'potential' nature of a particle into an 'actual' particle that we can then record and assess in numerical ways. In a very direct sense, number and the constituents of matter eventuate from meaning seeking.

There is, however, no state of consciousness more intensely, obsessively meaning seeking than that of the deluded psychotic mind. Does this intense 'meaning feeling' or semiotic arousal have tangible physical effects for the psychotic in their trade with the world? Consciousness naturally involves thought, feeling and will; cognition, affect and conation. Materialists will probably not want feeling and will brought into the picture. They see cognition as of the essence of the world, not affect and conation. But if meaning seeking is a co-partner in the creation of what is, then all three qualities are of the essence of reality.

In all areas of human questing, from geology to forensic science, the *surface* always has clues to what is beneath, to what is hidden. The meaning seeking of human consciousness I see as only resembling a small granite knoll, an outcrop of a giant underlying batholith. I call this underlying batholith, like a barely thinkable ocean of meaning, the 'Deep Music'.

After my own crisis in 1979, some of the uncanny coincidences during which are given in Chapter 4 of *Borderline* (Chadwick, 1992), I was not prepared to scoff at Pauli's belief (derived from lines of thinking similar to the above in the context of The Measurement Problem) in 'the reality of the symbol' (see Laurikainen, 1988). Pauli was himself often a witness to the uncanny. If there was anyone who could make a quantum mechanical experiment *not work* just by being in the room it was Pauli, a phenomenon that physicists, far from sneering at, took very seriously (Pagels, 1982) and termed 'the Pauli effect'. Clearly mind and matter could not be entirely separate. Not only could consciousness bring particles into existence, there were reliable instances here, perhaps because of Pauli's hypercritical mentality, where quantum predictions could be negated by an attitude of mind. Pauli's weakness was that, whereas he would always spot when a wrong theory *was* wrong, he had a distinct tendency to knock down good ideas as well (Pagels, 1982). In signal detection terms, he avoided all 'false alarms' by paying the price of making 'misses'. When he was in the laboratory, he would also make quantum mechanical experiments 'miss'.

Perhaps it is possible, in abnormally intense states of mind, to influence or access a deep symbolic process in reality in which 'actual' events can be orchestrated. Events seem to be brought into synchrony with thought (synchronicity) and match thought symbolically since the zone of reality accessed is intrinsically psychophysical – Jung's 'psychoid' level (see Jung,

1969, pp. 176–7, 183–4, 215–16, 436, 515). I referred to this at the time, in the summer of 1979, essentially oblivious to Jung and to Pauli, as 'The Borderline' or The Zone of Potential to Kinetic conversion. This referred to the transition from the ocean of Potential, the Deep Music, to The Zone of Actuality, the hustle and bustle, movement and events, of ordinary material reality.

Traditional scientists will, of course, scorn such reasoning as 'preposterous' and some may even infer that I am 'still ill' even to suggest it. There are, however, a number of clues that do point to the likelihood that Niels Bohr's Deep Truth to reality is symbolic and not material.

SOUND AND SYMBOL

In Ward J of what was then the orthopaedics department at Charing Cross, quite specific confirmation of these ideas occurred. Taps and clicks synchronised with thoughts I feared were true (one tap) or feared were false (two taps) started to happen. Medication eliminated this phenomenon but it reappeared about five months later in the psychiatric aftercare hostel where other people could hear them (Chadwick, 1997a, pp. 162–3). When a particularly disturbing tirade of rappings occurred much later in the kitchen of a flat I shared with my future wife Jill in Perham Road, West Kensington (in September 1981), and which she also was able to hear, I was only able to defeat them and stop their occurrence by reading intensely the first four or five pages of the New Testament (see Chadwick, 1997a, p. 48).

These rappings, with their symbolic code, one tap for 'Yes', two for 'No', though at the time totally novel to me, have happened to other patients in the middle of psychotic episodes (see Chadwick, 1992, pp. 64–5) and, I now find, are extremely well known as a phenomenon to researchers in the field of the paranormal. To a much lesser extent than in 1979–81 they do still happen to me. My wife can always hear them and even our two cats can be distracted by them. They obviously are not hallucinations. Their symbolic code, however, does show how sound energy can code thought for, in this case, an upsetting and distressing purpose. The rappings always synchronise with thoughts of a self-doubting nature. They clearly are a negative manifestation of the paranormal, what I call The Negative Borderline.

The possibility, as I said above, that events can symbolically match with thought does indicate that in certain brain states the disconnection we usually assume between mind and matter can disappear and mind and matter may reveal an underlying identity. The rappings, it should be noted, always synchronised perfectly with the onset of thoughts *in consciousness* not with brain events, which occur fractionally earlier in a temporal sense (Libet, 1993).

During the terrible Perham Road incident, hundreds of audible rappings a day were going on for several days in the kitchen where I was working and

often tapped once ('Yes' or 'True') to the thought, 'So I must kill myself?'
Even more terrifying, however, were sequences such as:

'So I am a lost soul?'
'Tap'
'I must face my Destiny?'
'Tap'
'But I can be forgiven?'
'Tap, tap'
'I am finished?'
'Tap'
'I am better dead?'
(No tap but *ball* kicked *once* against a garage door outside by a young lad.)
'So I must kill myself?'
'Tap'.

The intrusion of events from *outside*, such as the bang of a ball against the garage door, was utterly *terrifying* as how on earth could this happen unless the very symbolic structure of reality itself were not in some way 'entrained' with my thoughts? It seemed reasonable to infer that in some extreme mental states one could indeed 'access' the deep symbolic structure to reality, but later I realised that this could be on either the Negative *or* the Positive side.

At the time these remarkable events were occurring to me certainly a sceptic would have had no idea at all what to do. Jill would flee the kitchen when bursts of rappings were very intense. Had a Bible not been available to read, a present from my mother on 23 September 1957, I could very easily now be dead. The rappings were particularly keen that I rush out and throw myself under a lorry.

So horrific was the event that I tore the pages of my journal, referring to it and describing it, out – and made papier mâché of them to flush them down the toilet. I assumed that the events were evil and that the lavatory was the proper place for them. Jill thought of the event, 'It sounds as if evil spirits want you dead'. When I did flush the mash of paper down the pan, two flecks of paper came to the surface after the very final flush had been completed. The first and smaller one read 'be', the second 'attentive'. This of course (though obviously meaningless to materialists) is a statement in the Bible to the effect that we should be alert to the appearance of Christ in the world. In my paranoid state of mind I took this to be a deliberate mockery of me, as when very deluded I had thought I was the Antichrist. I gave a V sign to the 'mocking' shreds of paper and finally flushed them away. It could have been a message demanding of me more humility.

THE POSITIVE AND NEGATIVE BORDERLINES

A highly negative emotional state, perhaps as Christians would expect, does seem involved in accessing The Negative Borderline but even the latter has perhaps a glint of the positive as shown in the denouement of the episode above, obviously an example of a 'paranormal attack'.

But the uncanny also occurs, in a much less spectacular and showy way, in positive states. This I call The Positive Borderline (see Table 7.1 for the intentional character of these two realms). There the uncanny *facilitates* one's life and helps one to grow rather than tormenting and distracting one and driving one to destruction.

Both states are altered states of consciousness but they have certain thematic relations between them, one however being the reverse of the other. (Herman Lenz (1979) has argued that slivers of the negative can also occur in the positive.) In The Negative Borderline a certain style of very self-doubting, low confidence and low self-esteem inference (with self-as-victim) seems to dominate. The inferences are 'World to Self' (Peters, 2001) but negative (see Table 7.2). In the actual content of The Positive Borderline, inferences are more wholesome, positive and 'Self to World' (Peters, 2001, p. 205).

Table 7.1 The intentional character of the Positive and Negative Borderline realms

The Positive Borderline	The Negative Borderline
Events feel sincere	Events feel like Satanic tricks
Events happen so that one has time to use them and learn from them	Events happen too fast to keep up with
Events are of humble solidity	Events are spectacular and showy
Events enable one to grow and thrive	Events lead one downhill to destruction
Realm nurtures, calms and rests	Realm terrifies
Realm clarifies and illuminates	Realm confuses and bewilders
Realm strengthens will	Realm paralyses or weakens will
Realm turns one into an agent	Realm turns one into a puppet
Realm enables one to consolidate	Realm presents transient, evanescent shocks on which one cannot build
Realm protects and shields	Realm induces one to think every raw nerve is exposed
Realm gives 'direction' that leaves room for choice, decision and manoeuvre	Realm gives 'signs' and 'directions' that enslave and lead relentlessly down into a trap
Realm takes one into life and leads one to build solid bonds	Realm takes one out of life and leads one to trust no one
Realm enables one to build relationships	Realm destroys bonds
Realm is slow, rounded, sincere, humble and full	Realm is fast, sharp, tricky, impressive and empty
One is a *part* of existence, in place, yet utterly indispensable	One is at the centre of existence yet totally expendable

Table 7.2 The experiential contents of The Positive and Negative Borderlines

Experiences at The Positive Borderline	*Experiences at The Negative Borderline*
I am in touch with everyone	Everyone can hear my thoughts
The world is not as it is commonly seen	The world has changed, there's a war on
There is a great harmony and oneness between all things	People and the world are all together against me
Nothing is trivial	Everything means something, even street signs and car number plates
No one is a stranger	Everyone knows me and is plotting against me
I am both supreme and insignificant	I am The Christ and The Devil
I am passive, floating, at one with the universe, open to all	I am dissolving, decaying, penetrated by rays, penises
Meaning is everywhere/All is meaning	Everything I do or that happens has double, triple or quadruple meanings
I do not think, I am thought	I do not think, thoughts are planted in my head by computers/ hypnotherapy at a distance
I am not of this world	I am an outcast, an alien, a hated freak
I see the universe in a grain of sand	The totality of my torment is in this little dead leaf
I must suffer to see God	Only by killing myself can I save my very soul
There is a universe of love in a stranger's smile	The whole of my life is summed up in that policeman's stare
There is a purpose to all things	There is a reason for all this persecution
My mind is not of space-time	I have terrible premonitions
There is a great Presence we cannot see	My privacy is gone! I'm being observed by a powerful organisation
The silence of the cosmos overwhelms me, envelops me	What is this deafening silence?! What are MI5 planning?!
Even birdsong has a celestial ring to it	Traffic going by seems to damn me by its thunder
Will, trust, faith and meaning are the bases of all things. The world is alive!	My will is powerless, I trust no one, believe nothing anyone says to me. The world is a dead thing
The world is one great thought	The whole world is thinking about me and planning to destroy me
God and Consciousness pervade all things	There is a force in the world, a presence, intent on humiliating me

After Chadwick (1992, p. 93 and 1997d, p. 10). (See also Lukoff, 1985 and Kemp, 2000 for more general discussions of the relations between the mystical and the psychotic.)

It is clear that the thinking of the mystic and that of the psychotic person have some thematic similarities in being concerned with meaning, with issues of great emotional and cognitive power and scope and with fundamental questions of Man's place in, and the nature of, the cosmos. Psychosis usually, if not entirely, biases to the negative but borderline psychotic or pre-psychotic and mystical states give an apprehension of the positive.

Previous parapsychological research (Lee, 1991, 1994) on the clairvoyant capacities of acutely ill schizophrenic patients produced remarkably positive results. Interestingly the patients' performance only dropped to chance level when medication was administered, though their psychiatric condition was then much improved. These research results are in line with expectations to be derived from what I have written above. It would indeed be predicted from Deep Music theory that manifestations of what one might call 'mind–matter coalescence' such as clairvoyance and psychokinesis will be enhanced in near-psychotic and psychotic states. It would therefore be quite wrong to say that all thinking of an interpretive kind on The Measurement Problem is bereft of predictions.

In altered states of this kind (see also Rogo, 1990, pp. 69–74) the threshold of consciousness is lowered (Evans, 1997) and the previously inaccessible becomes accessible and realisable. Perhaps capacities and insights previously clouded by or to consciousness also become available? Table 7.2 certainly suggests this. Lee's work, however, depends on extremely sensitive timing, rapport with participants and experimental subtlety and has as yet proved difficult to replicate. Research of this kind can also be frightening for disturbed people (Greyson, 1977) and hence faces ethical problems in its conduct.

REALITY *AS* SYMBOLIC

Much could be said of course of this reorientation from materialism to symbolism. Indeed the views of mind, life and reality in the two perspectives are quite different. I summarise them in Table 7.3. This kind of thinking puts a much more positive, if portentous and disturbing, perspective on schizophrenia and related psychotic and near-psychotic conditions and encourages us to blend reductionistic and holistic thinking in the understanding of the triad of The Zone of Potential, The Borderline and The Zone of Actuality. It is only in The Zone of Actuality that materialistic reductionism has a large measure of success but via intense states of consciousness even this apparent harmony can be 'interfered with' and in a sense 'penetrated' by mind. The essential unity of mind and matter in The Zone of Potential 'outcrops' transiently in The Zone of Actuality.

Given that mystical, pre-psychotic and psychotic states are all at the very edges of the phenomenology of person, I think we should at least seriously consider this 'flight of imagination' of mine as providing a qualitative framework for understanding 'the brink and the abyss' – where indeed it may be that the very deepest nature of mind and reality is revealed. At The Borderline there may be genuine discontinuity, despite the essential normality

Table 7.3 Symbolist and materialist views of reality

Symbolism	Materialism
The essence of reality is only captured by an integration of thought and feeling together with will	Thought and number capture the essence of reality
Reality is a co-dependence of the integration of matter and meaning	Reality is essentially matter
Persons and all beings are entities in their own right, Gestalts, beyond their constituents	In the last analysis there are only objects (particles)
Love is of the whole Self and hence brings the whole Self together. It is the purpose and meaning of life and work	Love is merely a means of facilitating sex and the bringing up of the young
Irrationality can be protective, life-enhancing, even life-saving. The ultimate, deepest level of reality is irrational	Rationality is always to be preferred, irrationality is the enemy within, childish and historically primitive.
In art, mysticism, microphysics and in the dynamic unconscious of psychoanalysis opposites are both true. Reality is based on 'both–and' logic	Opposites cannot both be true, matters are either one thing or the other. Reality is based on 'either–or' logic
The deepest levels of reality are to be understood by love, music and poetry	The deepest levels of reality are to be understood by mathematics
Some coincidences are genuinely meaningful	Coincidences are meaningless
Mind is imbricated into brain in gerund or participle mode ('minding') during life but transduces to noun mode and hence is separate on death	Mind is simply what brains do, just as 'balance' is what a dancer does, but there is no 'real stuff' that we can call 'balance'
Truth is a goal of science, art and spirituality	Truth is the preserve of science
Understanding comes from being, knowledge from passion	Understanding comes from thinking, knowledge from finding facts
Some explanations require stories and complex narratives rather than succinct equations or compact interpretations	Parsimonious explanations are the rule
Close involvement with one's subject matter is critical for veridical reporting and understanding	Close involvement with one's subject matter distorts observation; one should maintain some distance to keep an objective attitude
Reality is fundamentally relational and meaningful	Reality is 'atomistic' and purposeless
Since reality is contingent on mind and consciousness, all systems of understanding and life-enhancement are to a degree contingent and fuzzy and subject to different patternings of understanding both over time and at different levels of description	A system of IF–THEN rules and cause–effect or probabilistic laws accurately describes reality and can also structure and facilitate societal functioning
Reality is conditional on consciousness and mental state. Rational-aggressive attitudes close the door on a true vision of reality	Reality is harsh, red in tooth and claw, the strong will win

Consciousness may have existed since the inception of the cosmos and accompanies and interacts with matter, including brains where, in content terms, it is most differentiated	Consciousness emerges from brains and is a late addition to the cosmos
Quality can eventuate from agony and ecstasy, pain and pleasure. The way of love and coincidences is morally no better or worse than that of reason and experiment	Quality can only eventuate from self-denial and struggle. The way of reason and experiment is the morally superior way
God as an ultimate spiritual presence is in all and through all	God is an unnecessary illusion or delusion
Mystical insights are a profound understanding or apprehension of the true nature of things	Mystical insights are vacuous and regressive
Reality is to be understood as a system of signs. Even objects are instantiations of meaning	Reality is to be understood as different patternings of 'things' to no particular end

of the journey there (see Chapter 2) such that the phenomenology and biophysics of mind may radically change at a qualitatively different level.

Because the rappings, taps and clicks referred to above still happen to me, it may be possible to study them formally, perhaps with associated EEG recording. If they can be reproduced under self-doubt-inducing laboratory conditions (this could be brought about for example simply by me reading a compendium of ghost stories say) it would enable quantitative assessment of the phenomenon (see also Chadwick, 2005b on this). Mentally generated sound energy in coded form would confirm a model of reality in which, at a level beneath The Zone of Actuality, meaning and matter are essentially indivisible and co-dependent, as argued above. This is a line of reasoning constructed totally independently of but similar to Jung's constructs of 'the psychoid' and 'the continuum' (on the latter see Jung, 1969, pp. 318 and 412). The reliability of two people's independent lines of thinking on this matter of the psychophysical nature of reality is at least encouraging. Reliability in mentation does suggest the *possibility* of ontic status to that which is discovered, 'ontic' referring to entities and facts not only 'intrapsychic states'. It suggests at least that the findings are of THE mind not just his mind or my mind and may even, as we claim, capture the psychophysical not only the mental. We can, after all, at least try.

TRUTH/CLARITY UNCERTAINTY RELATIONS

The difficulty for the above model is that, although it is testable in various ways and does make predictions, it does not have mathematical precision. I have never been able to conceive of a form of algebra suitable to the task, as how does one imbricate emotion into calculus or put an equation to a crucifix or indeed a swastika? Meaning is a slippery entity. In the 1970s I did try to develop an algebra that would generate psychoanalytic propositions with certain terms standing for basic affects such as anger, sex and anxiety and operators of different kinds for processes such as repression, projection etc. At first the system was successful at creating valid psychoanalytic reasoning but with time I had to multiply the symbolism so much it was easier to simply write out the statement in English. The closed self-consistent (or largely self-consistent) system of mathematics had trouble with the open system of a meaning-based enterprise.

It may be that we are faced here with Bohr's 'Truth/Clarity Uncertainty Relations' (Bohr, 1958) in that the more truth we seek, the less clarity we can have and this may apply to such psychophysical investigations of 'The Edge'. The great clarity, certainty and definiteness positivists seek may merely guarantee only relatively superficial knowledge. The superficial knowledge of the 'safe valley' of life. This, like the uncanny, is also a possibility we must face.

Here I have articulated a theory as clearly as I can at least in the problematic medium of words. In the Deep Music of reality, meaning simply cannot be represented monochromatically. In a realm where ideally we need 'rainbow words', celestial music, poetry and 'rainbow equations' working together, formalisation is going to be difficult. My battle of old, however, with the algebra of psychoanalysis nonetheless left me feeling: 'Maybe'.

THE APPEARANCE OF THE SACRED

The mental state that I reached in the summer of 1979 to reach this 'phenomenology of The Edge' outlined above was one of transcendence of the Eriksonian concept of identity, the Kellyan concept of a construct system and the Freudian concept of an ego (see Chadwick, 1992 Chapter 4, for details and Appendix I in this volume). This state obviously has resonances with Buddhist thought but I have to say in closing this chapter, however unpopular this may be with scientists, that in interfacing with The Zone of Potential there was undoubtedly an experience of the Sacred, in both the Positive and the Negative – as if behind a thin membrane, but of awesome power. This I relived in September 1981 when reading the New Testament to destroy the psychokinetic rappings. It is clear that at The Positive Borderline, destructive rappings are just not the way things work, the manifestation is too showy and shallow.

It could be that if one were able to *hold* this transcendent state (see Appendix I), as spiritual masters such as Jesus, Mohammed and the Buddha seem to have been able to do, the results would be expected to be – as we have seen – of global significance. In their own ways they could be regarded as transducers of the Deep Music into the world, portals between The Zone of

Potential and The Zone of Actuality. This may throw some light on the conundrum of the relations between science and religion.

The idea of reality as symbolic as outlined here does have some attachments to previous thinking outside of physics. Wine, of course, is a symbol of the blood of Christ and Christians do believe that the meaning is 'there' *in* the wine not merely something we read into it. So this is an early conception of 'symbolic reality'.

The connection I make here between energy and symbol is not in itself bizarre. Every musician creates symbolic form out of sound energy when they play their musical instrument, as does every person when they use their larynx to speak. The seaman who sends Morse code via flashing lights turns light energy to symbolic use. The difference with what I am saying here is that the psychokinetic rappings, taps and clicks that I discussed earlier are really a sound-coding of a mind process not a mind-coding of sound energy, as in ordinary auditory perception. This is meaning eventuated *from* energy not meaning read in *to* energy. Similarly a vision seeable by others would be light-coded mind information rather than mind-coded light information as in the usual process of visual perception.

If, as in my own case, self-doubt can be symbolised by binary coded sound energy what *other* possibilities are there? And what energistically symbolises or could symbolise love? Does God appear symbolically and if so, how? And in what form? Was Jesus 'God in symbol'?

In this chapter I have spoken of meaning actually there *in* matter not of meaning created by the strokes of the paintbrush or the vibrating of strings by a human instrument player. It is about meaning as an intrinsic aspect of the world, not only as something we create ourselves by our own cerebrations.

A vision, shared by others, like the rappings in my case that were audible to others, involves processes of a projective kind that are the reverse of the usual processes of perception. It may be then that in some extreme mental states, the symbolic aspect of reality can indeed be catalysed and so reveal itself. This clearly puts a very different and more positive slant on reports usually dismissed scornfully as 'hallucinations'.

Chapter 8

Desmond

Comedian mystic

> You will never see the truth in anybody if all you look for is your own
> reflection.

INTRODUCTORY SKETCH

The so-called 'schizophrenic credit' (Claridge, 1985), in contrast to the oft-researched schizophrenic deficit, more commonly is to be found at the transitional zone between sanity and psychosis. Schizotypal individuals (Claridge, 1988, 1990, 1997; Stefanis *et al.*, 2004) may occasionally wander into psychotic styles of cognition but generally their psychoticism, to the advantage of their creativity, is suffused through their personality rather than manifesting itself in specific delusions and hallucinations, word-salad speech or serious disorganisation of their identity. This can give them considerable advantages particularly in spiritual sensitivity, sensitivity generally and originality of ideation. If they present themselves for treatment, however, it tends to be because of problems with anxiety and depression (APA, 1994).

Desmond Marshall, when I first met him, was an adult student of mine on an unconventional course I was running at the Working Men's College in North London in 1985. The course was unusual: it was called 'Supernormal Psychology' and was basically a positive psychology antidote, rather as this book is, to the emphasis on the abnormal in psychology (see also Maslow, 1968, 1971, 1973 on this). The first time I remember him speaking up in class was in a lecture I gave on some aspects of humour. Rather contrary to the spirit of the course I argued that, according to some views, comedians should be neurotic (and perhaps underneath it all, angry), both statements with which he heartily concurred. Perhaps it also was something about the way he spoke and the spontaneity of his agreement but he had a penetrating effect. I did not know at the time that he had been a professional comedian himself spotted in *The Melody Maker* at the same time as the Rolling Stones and Bob Dylan. But nonetheless I felt: 'This is a man who knows himself'.

Desmond became a lively contributor to class discussions but when eventually I moved the lecture topics deep into the areas of mysticism and the preternatural he left. But it was not because of lack of interest – it was obvious to me during a chat we had at one of the coffee breaks that I could teach him nothing in these areas.

Desmond is a small man, drawn in the face, only about 5′ 4″ tall and with a rather frail bird-like frame. Although physically he is a diminutive figure, there is a strange quality about him which makes him seem as if he is occupying more space than tangibly is the case. This in fact is slightly unnerving; indeed, irrational though it sounds,

Des Marshall.

there are times when Desmond seems to 'fill' the room he is in. I have 'seen' this at the Royal Festival Hall, where we used to meet regularly – and of course that is some space. It is not at all clear to me why this is so. He projects a curious blend of vitality and sadness. At times he has a rather portentous stillness about him (even when walking), yet his eyes may be darting everywhere. When seated he holds his head very slightly raised, so his (rather prominent) nose is ever so fractionally upturned. He also seems to have a quality of waiting or readiness about him – as if something involving him is surely soon to happen. This is also rather disturbing, as if a kind of 'field' emanates from him, into the future.

Des provides us with a running commentary on his thoughts in his book *Journal of an Urban Robinson Crusoe* (Marshall, 2002, pp. 13–14). The section below focuses on his stream of consciousness as he treks through the streets and alleyways.

> I went out into the street aware that my alienation would envelop me like a protective cloud. I felt numb inside. Each step was an effort, as my feet touched the sloping uneven ground of the paved stones. The streets were cold and grey. I looked at the faces of people. Some looked like they were in Hell with their haggard grief-stricken expressions and vacant eyes as they wandered the dirty litter filled streets.

The streets made me feel uneasy. People seemed to stare. I had to avoid staring back. The streets were filled with tension, and aggression wasn't far away. One man who happened to stare too long got a mouthful as he walked by – but he just went on walking without turning round.

The streets were important to me. I needed them to get rid of pent-up feelings inside. My long walks would relax me enough so that I could sleep at night. The nights were times of remembering but I'm not sure the memories belong to me, like times when I used to wait at the institution gate of the home I was in, waiting for my mother to visit me. Waiting, waiting, waiting, through the long drawn-out space of endless time. And now my life seems to be one long wait. For what? Somewhere I knew I had the answer, but dared not rake through too deeply the turbid depth of my knowing.

Here Desmond hopefully comes across. A sad and sensitive, at times tormented body and a harrowed soul thrown into the brutal wood of life. Periodically a refugee from reality yet noticing things that are usually only detected by the eyes of the deaf and the ears of the blind. He once told me something that John Lennon had said, namely: 'I am a violent man, that is why I talk about love'. This was a statement that resonated deeply in Des. As the reader will see, he too has had a life tinged with the violence of the Krays and the Richardsons – and perhaps that is partly why he too is a man of peace and of love. Yet, like me, Des also carries his past with him, some of it deeply buried, some of it more evident, and this past, as Kelly (1955) would expect, although not totally explaining him, is nonetheless what much of his present thinking has had to come to terms with.

Des is very 'fluent on self' to a degree that at times smacks of an obsessive self-preoccupation. This is a flaw. His background, as we will see, has cultivated his sense of humour, which he uses extravertedly to hold audiences, however small. This slightly dominating quality nonetheless is expressed in ways for which his friends do not chide him (although at times we should). Despite a rather lovelorn background, particularly when he was very young, he is a very endearing man.

He speaks quickly, with a London accent, often with eyes enlarged and pressure to his (rather poetic) words as if he must say what he is saying and one must hear it and fully understand. Desmond indeed takes badly to being misunderstood and can even be mildly insulting (at least to me) when this happens. Perhaps he has been misunderstood just too much in his life and can barely tolerate any further instances. But it could be deeper than this. Jean Cocteau (1891–1963) once wrote that the worst tragedy for a poet is to be esteemed through being misunderstood.

Desmond is a chameleon. He simply cannot provide reliable answers on personality questionnaires and on meeting him one never quite knows how the day has found him. What gives him his stability, at a level deeper than that of his changeable persona, is, amongst other things, his commitment to empathy and love and the basically mystical knowledge he has amassed over the last thirty or so years. Via all these things he lives a life at the borderline but without any anti-psychotic drugs. He is a testament to the use of an adaptive strategy that makes no recourse to biochemistry.

BRIEF BIOGRAPHY

Born on 31 March 1941, in Suffolk, during the Second World War, Des spent his childhood, from the age of about 2 months through to 11 years, away from his mother in convalescent homes in the wooded countryside because of disabling eczema and asthma. In a way he never really recovered from this awful separation. He also suffered from pneumonia, diphtheria and a mastoid in the early 1940s and very nearly died on two occasions. Really he was brought up by nurses and sisters. His father was Jewish, his mother Church of England. She later converted to Judaism but Desmond rejected it. Desmond's physical disabilities were in many ways his salvation from very destructive influences. His father knew both the Kray twins and the Richardsons, who opposed the Krays, and worked for the Richardsons in a cut-price store in Brixton, South London. When Desmond emerged from the convalescent home at 11, he was pitched throughout his teenage years into a world of anti-social people, street fighting and 'birds and booze'. He survived through his sense of humour. Though not at all identifying with them, he could make gang members laugh while playing the macho role well enough to get by. Fast reflexes (and a sharp tongue) settled many arguments one way or another.

Desmond's chronic eczema turned him into a revolving-door hospital patient but this at least reduced the amount of contact he had with criminals. The agony of eczema all over his body was also to make him eventually attempt to go *beyond* the body to the spiritual level of awareness. At first his method of dealing with it was to say 'I feel *nothing*'. But this was no use. Indeed, eczema (the Greek word literally means 'to boil') was to become not a leprous curse but Desmond's 'gift handicap'. He knew there was plenty of feeling there. As his younger brother said, without it he simply would not be the Desmond Marshall that we know. In fact, he could not be Desmond Marshall at all. He intuited, however, that he would have to change his life context radically if he was to throw off aggressive street-life values. But to do so too soon would make him unable to cope in the scenario in which he found himself (see also Bender, 1976, p. 60 on this).

He didn't like working for his look-alike father. His strange pedantic ways were irritating and they had occasional violent disagreements. Indeed, Desmond once dropped him to his knees with a punch – but ironically gained his respect by doing so.

His relations with his very moody and extraordinarily neurotic mother were little better. In late 1963, at just 22, in the middle of this quagmire, he attempted suicide by overdose and was hovering in a blissful state between life and death for many long hours – happy that he was dying. But this event was to produce not his own extinction but the first of the many strange coincidences that were later to pepper his adult years. Seemingly deep in coma, he suddenly awoke, sat bolt upright in bed with eyes staring and shouted out, 'Who's dead? Who's *dead*? Who's *dead*?' His startled mother quickly replied 'No one!' Then he immediately slumped back into stupor. He was subsequently to learn, without surprise, that President Kennedy had been assassinated while he had lain there at death's door. After this suicide attempt, his reflective capabilities, which he claims had been there since he was 5, started to accelerate. He desperately wanted to know why he existed. After all, why was Kennedy dead and he alive? Had he somehow para-normally sensed Kennedy's death? It sounds ludicrous but perhaps he had. It was this train of unsettling events and their immediate impact that awoke Desmond's spiritual consciousness. Returning from the borderline between life and death had kindled a flame in him that no amount of bodily or psychic torment was ever to extinguish.

The effect of this spiritual flame on Desmond's life was relentless but gradual; not superficially apparent to others at first. Always a man who felt that he looked odd – but who had nonetheless always made people laugh – he worked as a popular professional comedian at Butlin's holiday camps and in clubs between 1970 and 1974 (and later from 1988 to 1990), with the stage name 'Dizzy Desey', but dropped the stage career as a serious endeavour largely through ill-health but also when he felt it was becoming too much of an egoistic experience. After his days in show business he became anonymous and worked as a luggage handler at Britannia Airways – and took advantage of cut-price flights around the world. But during time off, he took to reading *An Autobiography of a Yogi* by Paramahansa Yogananda. This was to be a transforming experience. It firmly set him on the spiritual path.

Over the years that followed he read with passion: Gurdjieff, Ouspensky, Sartre, Camus, Stendahl, Meisster Eckhart, Colin Wilson, Hermann Hesse, the teachings of Sai Baba, the healer Edgar Cayce and those of St John of the Cross all being deeply influential.

But while such people have helped Desmond validate his spiritual self, he has also needed, as he puts it, to be 'grounded'. He has thankfully never lost touch with the down-to-earth and practical matters of life (something a mystic can very easily do), and this has been thanks to a completely unsung friend of his, a man called Fred Robinson, who sadly died in 1992. Fred was in the Black Watch regiment in the Second World War. He was an ardent Socialist and had a family of seven boys and two girls. He treated Des like one of his sons and always helped to return him to the here-and-now, the immediate, the present. Fred was a vital influence in Des's life in providing care, love, balance and a sense of belonging, a sense of rootedness. All of his family, Des included, somehow cannot believe he is no longer with them. Des himself is obviously still reeling from his loss as Fred in many ways gave him the family he never really had.

One of the cardinal features of Desmond is the way that he does indeed allow his feelings to buffet him; there is no room for stoicism and spartan denial of affect in his soul. So, unlike the vast majority of men, Desmond is one man who really can cry. He has cried for Fred as he has cried for everyone.

OF WHAT USE IS A MYSTIC?

Widely travelled and quite widely read, what has he to offer to life? Desmond, alas, though he is now 66, has been for many years one of our many millions of unemployed. He existed on invalidity benefit, his legs and arms still racked with the agony of eczema to the extent that some nights he sleeps not at all. Officially Desmond 'had no job'. His extreme sensitivities sometimes hamper him. For Des doing is not being. To quote him: 'If I do without being I am dead'. The paradox is that he operates in the world and loves people and humanity through the state and act of being – but 'has no job'. Are people of this ilk of any real use to society in these days when marketability counts for so much, indeed for some counts for all?

Perhaps it could be said that Desmond is vital to the world? He is in a way a kind of 'street mystic' – rather than one who lives remotely in the hills or in the temple. Rather in the spirit of a community psychologist (Bender, 1976; Orford, 1992) his is a seeking rather than a waiting mode. Des is present in the world, there on Regent Street, in Camden Town, on Oxford Street. A 'cafe cosmopolite', he roves the sandwich bars of Drury Lane, High Holborn, Finchley Road, Swiss Cottage, Belsize Park, Bloomsbury as if 'everywhere', talking, talking, talking. He breaks all the capitalist rules yet he brings people together, gives ministries at Quaker meetings, inspires, yet 'has no job'. Weaving tales across cafe tables he takes away the lofty, pious quality of mysticism, makes it relevant, and available to all. 'The only difference between Jesus and me and everybody else is that Jesus *knew* what he was.' He goes on: 'Other people do not. They don't see their own divinity! I am *consciously* aware of God. For most the presence of God is unconscious.'

But despite these portentous remarks, there is really no heavy quality to his talk. My wife even thinks of him as a 'comedian mystic', rather as was Oscar Wilde, using comedy to rip aside the pretence of forced erudition or fashionable ideas to plunge through to the raw truth (e.g. short of cash in a cafe one day: 'Jesus didn't pay for the Last Supper').

'By their fruits shall you know them' was one of the teachings of Jesus. Des really in his own way could be seen as a cementer of the world. A deeply empathic man who lives at a level deeper and higher than the action movies, computer games, fashion shows, fast cars and Mediterranean holidays. He is a man who inhabits a realm which is the *real* foundation of life. The world of love, of meaning and compassion, of the absolute essentials without which ritzy glitzy life could not obtain at all.

THE UNCANNY

The thinking of this man is clearly far removed, both in form and in content, from anything that most academic researchers in the human sciences are familiar with – unless they happen to meet people of this kind as patients. It is known that although 68 per cent of British adults do believe in God (Cox and Cowling, 1989), 67 per cent of psychiatrists do not (Neeleman and King, 1993), and hence it is very difficult for professionals such as these to establish 'joint reference' (Freeman *et al.*, 1982) with people like Desmond. It is doubtful that they could productively help him even were he to consult them and indeed it may be that such professionals in the field of psychopathology have counter-transference difficulties with those of Desmond's ilk and underestimate the health of religiously minded people (see Shams and Jackson, 1993; Neeleman and Persaud, 1995). The situation regarding beliefs in the paranormal and supernatural is, however, more positive in certain other cultures (Idemudia, 2003; Furnham and Igboaka, 2007).

Although volatile, Desmond's scores on one of the psychometric measures of schizotypal personality, the STA (Jackson and Claridge, 1991), oscillate over time (three testings over two years) in the upper half of the range reported in that validation study (his scores range from 20 to 24), given a mean for normal males of only 13.00, SD 7.43 (N = 97) (Jackson and Claridge, 1991, p. 316). His most noticeable 'symptoms', to speak medically, are occasional ideas of reference; excessive social anxiety; 'odd' beliefs and magical thinking; unusual perceptual experiences and speech (perhaps) that a standard-minded diagnostician might easily regard also as odd. He has also suffered from inordinate paranoid ideation concerning people's reactions to his appearance. However, it has to be said here in his defence that he certainly does not look like a prototypical Englishman (see Stefanis *et al.*, 2004, for the importance of the paranoia element in the overall picture of psychosis-proneness).

Believers in the paranormal, clairvoyance, 'sixth sense' and so on have many cognitive biases and defences which sustain these beliefs (French, 1992; Irwin, 2003). However, it is recognised by researchers that believers in the paranormal *really do* score more highly on tests of telepathy than non-believers (Schmeidler and McConnell, 1958; Palmer, 1971). Hence a cynical attitude to such belief is not warranted by the evidence – and indeed in this light it is arguable whether such convictions should be regarded as symptomatic of pathology at all. (In this and related contexts Russell (1994) argues that the authors of the 1994 DSM IV manual, which includes both 'spiritual disorder' and belief in the paranormal as part of the schizotypal personality diagnostic criteria, might be validly accused of having 'overtight associations'.)

Researchers also recognise that actual belief in the paranormal (which is also high in incidence in schizophrenic people (Irwin, 1993; Thalbourne, 1994)) is very often initiated by real events which were genuinely strange and even uncanny (see references in French, 1992, p. 295). It is worth dealing briefly with some of these events that have taken place in Desmond's life so that the reader can judge how *they* might adjust their ways of construing the world-inclusive-of-Self had these incidents happened to them. Three will suffice, I hope, to convey the flavour of what Desmond has had to deal with in order to come to the philosophy he has constructed and to the way of life he has chosen.

First: he was at a Quaker meeting at the Friends' Meeting House in Euston. A man by the name of Dougan was there, a pleasing man of child-like temperament. Des was not really very surprised when he looked across the room to see seven or eight children sitting around Dougan at his feet, looking up at him. But he was staggered when, in the blink of an eye, these children *disappeared.*

Being no angel, Desmond has always had a weakness for gambling. In his heart he took it lightly until he began to win, and win . . . and win. Over a period of several weeks, betting intensely but only in single pounds, Des literally won scores of pounds day after day, week after week by visualisation of winning on the race, visualisation of moving to the counter and collecting the money. The names of the winning horses would stand out from the board to him. There was no doubt of the outcome. Every gambler's dream? Yes and no. For Des it became a nightmare. The quality of relentlessness is a quality we associate with processes that move from present to future. To experience relentlessness transmitted from what seemed to Desmond to be *the future to the present* turned out to be positively terrifying. Rather than going eagerly to the betting shop, Des eventually became afraid of the strange active/passive state he was in that seemed, fragile though it was, to permit this kind of thing to happen. He had to stop gambling for a long time. It was as if his intuitions of the future, if that's what they were, became a burden of immense weight. He sensed that they would crush him if he did not stop.

Finally, he was attending a 'Self Transformation' weekend workshop in 1984 to explore and benefit from childhood experiences. There were about thirty people in the hall being used for the weekend arranged for this particular exercise, in six groups of five. Desmond took his turn to be in the centre of his group with other members standing round him. The task of the central person was to face some critical question by making an emotive statement and simultaneously hitting the floor with hands and feet. Desmond chose a time when he was distressed in the convalescent home as a child. He shouted out, 'I wanna go home!' whereupon the group members around him were instructed to answer back with 'You *can't* go home!' This dialogue continued back and forth:

> 'I wanna go home!'
> 'You *can't* go home!'
> 'I wanna go home!'
> 'You *can't* go home!'

until a hopefully cathartic crescendo of inner anguish was reached At that moment Desmond heard an ear-splitting *scream* from across the room, presumably from one of the other groups. It really shocked him, how that person must be suffering!

At the termination of his exercise Desmond was laid on his side next to someone else who had also been 'in the centre' in order to recuperate. As he lay there he asked the man, 'Who was that screaming over there? God it was terrible!' The man replied naturally . . . 'It was you'. Clearly these incidents do not demand belief in extra-sensory powers or in an extra-dimensional reality. The first, of course, could have been a visual hallucination; the second the result of a misconception of chance (Tversky and Kahneman, 1974) (such 'unlikely' sequences do occur by chance, as in random number generation); the third the result of a temporary displacement of the position of the self's viewpoint within the internal representation of the room Desmond was in, as has been suggested to account for ('bird's-eye view') out-of-the-body experiences (Blackmore, 1982, 1987; Irwin, 1986). The best we can say for them, and for the attribution (that he did make) that he may have paranormally sensed Kennedy's death (p. 76), is that his interpretations are permissible and suggestive rather than required.

The scientific model of reality and its logic of justification, however, are not without their own philosophical contradictions and vagaries (Weimer, 1979; Gergen, 1985), particularly in the collection and evaluation of evidence (Chadwick, 1975a, 1975b, 1976, 1977, 1982; Chadwick and Hughes, 1980). It could be argued that there are indeed many permissible ways to construe the world and the Self (Bannister and Fransella, 1971). To actually diagnose Desmond as 'personality disordered' and 'cognitively biased' in a direction approaching schizophrenic illness would in this instance be a misuse of power and the anti-psychiatrists' perspective would here be fair because he has orchestrated his experiences into a usable holistic view of reality and of life that for him is functional and does indeed allow him to cope. For him 'in life' his model of the world has an intrinsic validity and at least an existential truth that is more useful and indeed coherent in accounting for his experiences than is the available scientific model of conventional psychiatry and psychology – which would count many of his daily impressions and intuitions as mere myths and illusions. Such a way of thinking would surely have anyone reaching for pills – thus circularly confirming a biobehavioural 'industry' that offers both 'the explanation' and 'the remedy' in its own terms for those who can find no alternative. In the interests of diversity we must ask: what then is Desmond's alternative?

HOW A MYSTIC AVOIDS MADNESS

We have seen that Des is far from ethereal but is clearly not a standard-minded Englishman either (if such a person exists). He is a nervous man, distractible, wary of strangers, a man of highs and lows, prone to overreacting. Perhaps many of his temperament and personality have indeed gone insane, particularly those who, like me, have sought mystical enlightenment (Greenberg *et al.*, 1992). But Des has not. Desmond's stability not only hinges on his creation of a coherent philosophy but on the use of functional techniques when he is under various forms of stress. Hence he blends, rather as does this text, atmospherics with practicality in contrast to my own use of motivating and self-organising metaphors (see Chapter 6). One pair of methods he repeatedly uses is that of visualisation and affirmation of benign images and phrases and positive consequences. For example, if he finds himself in a busy and slightly threatening environment, he shuns taking, say, a Valium tablet and instead visualises rings of white light surrounding him, protecting him as if a field of love is about him. If he finds his thoughts being steeped in vengeance and recriminations, he doesn't go further in to this state but changes the polarity of his experiences by stopping this flow and saying to himself repeatedly: 'No! I choose *love*' over and over until the calming and uplifting quality of the words transforms his feelings and intentions. When he feels himself overwhelmed by stimulation, again there is no reaching for medication. Instead he describes himself as voluntarily 'closing down', relaxing, focusing on some mundane, concrete everyday entity so as to become 'grounded'. (This latter process, which is obviously a protection against overwhelm and distractability and, in a sense, is a kind of self-created cognitive remediation therapy (see Wykes and Reeder, 2005 on such therapies) has, however, taken him many years to cultivate.)

Des is also extremely wary of imagining cruel and horrific scenarios. He argues that such imaginings, if repeated, have a subtle way of structuring one's behaviour over long periods of time in such a way that they really do eventually come true! '*Beware* of what you imagine!' is one of his most urgent claims. Therapeutically, the beautiful solace and closeness to nature of Hampstead Heath and Regent's Park as well as St John's Wood Garden enable him to disengage from human horror and indwell in the unity of the natural world.

He is also exceedingly dismissive of comparing himself to others in an envious way. Such a process of 'upward comparison' we do know is damaging of self-esteem (Weber, 1992, p. 54). His emphasis, however, is placed not on the esteem-enhancing converse process of downward comparison but rather on a more level attitude of acceptance of others. One might argue that spiritually this is a healthier and more enlightened strategy.

Now these are actual specific mental procedures that Desmond does not merely talk about as theoretical abstractions but really does repeatedly and consciously instantiate. All of these strategies are wilfully and frequently entertained as ways of coping with stress and of creating a resilient attitude which is protective of mental health. It seems at the individual level that he finds these stabilising and restorative (Victor Frankl (1959, 1963, 1969) also suggests positive meaning-seeking approaches related to these).

Once a comedian, Des is now not only a mystic but also a prose-poet. Perhaps it is also in the 'internal sentences' and affirmations (see also Chadwick, 2001a) that he both generates in such work and reiterates to himself that he finds strength. Here are some of these lines and couplets that act not only as spiritual philosophy but as informal spiritual-cognitive therapy. He writes:

Past is guilt, future is fear
Freedom and love is *now*.

We weren't born to be manipulated through guilt.

Fear is the forgetting of love.
In respecting all living things, I respect myself.

We are here to find out what we are
And what we are not.

Out of the head
into the heart
to rest.

(When in turmoil) My word is law . . . I erase those thoughts.

Empathy and compassion for oneself
is the same as for others.

In peace I understand myself and the world.

It is evident that imbuing oneself with thinking of this kind, some of it more, some of it less original though it might be, is likely to be calming and clearing of the troubled psyche. It is for some people perhaps even biologic-ally preferable to ingesting anti-psychotic drugs with their long-term dangers and side effects – although such medication has been suggested as effective for schizotypals (Serban and Siegel, 1984; Goldberg *et al.*, 1986; Soloff *et al.*, 1986; Szigethy and Schulz, 1997). The only medication that Desmond actually uses is steroid cream for his eczema. Despite the tirade of impressions, impulses and affects that populate and pepper his day he avoids the attraction of a chemical soporific in order to strive to be what he organismically is. To be what he is, however, may make his self unmarketable, but perhaps he should in any case be unmarketable, as that is not his way and not congruent with his values and aims. Des is not of the marketplace and productivity, he is of the borderline and of being. Here is where the ground of being itself peeps to the surface as a rim around a basin of 'pleasure, pain, money and facts'. This rim is where Des belongs even though our crass society has little recognition and appreciation to offer him – and really no place to offer him within either its socialistic or capitalist structures. The success he has had in his own personal endeavour goes unrecognised as artists and poets are only recognised in the West if they are truly astounding. Des's solution then is to weave his life into the world not as an entity-in-place, making money and achieving fame, but as a catalytic personified thread or theme suffused through the body of what is reminding it of its terra firma and its fundamentals.

DISCIPLINE AND REGULATION

It would be wrong, however, to overemphasise the romantic here and to neglect the importance of discipline. Through his use of affirmations (see also S. Wilde, 1987) Desmond does make a conscious effort to control his own thoughts. This is known as the use of metacognitive strategies. He also writes his affirmations down on pieces of paper and puts them on his kitchen wall or cabinet to remind him of strong, disciplined, loving ideas. At a more prosaic level he tries to minimise stimulants such as caffeine and generally, if not always, avoids alcohol. He also avoids illicit drugs and periodically takes time away at retreats in the countryside. All of this clearly is therapeutic. Now 66, he returns psychologically and emotionally to his 1950s teenage years via the music of Johnnie Ray, Frankie Laine, Elvis and Buddy Holly. He describes this nostalgic feeling (with an 'Aaah' feeling) as 'pleasant melancholy' and finds it very de-stressing in these troubled times.

HUMOUR AND SPIRITUALITY

Another powerful component of Des's protective armour is comedy and laughter. Unlike myself in 1979 he has made sure that he mixes with people who share his sense of humour and who can share his desire to lighten his load by laughing at it. In conversation a joke is never very far away.

It may seem strange to say this but despite his sporadic feelings of torment, Des actually enjoys his own mind. He likes, when all is said and done, the way it works and, like a true artist, is frankly accepting of all experiences, both good and bad. Des also has a slight tendency, when his stress level is low, to actually become depressed. But when this happens he becomes more affectionate socially (see Chadwick, 2001a, p. 54 and correlations from mood inventories on p. 57). This pattern, which I found in him in 1999, also reared its head when he had computer-mediated cognitive behavioural therapy (cCBT) in 2007. There is therefore a certain no-win quality to his mental state which keeps him rather vigilant to the events of his private mental life. However, at times when his threshold of coping, by whatever method, is being transgressed, if he cannot find a friend to talk to he visits a church. He opens himself up to forces beyond himself. He prays. He talks to God, the greatest of all friends. Des's spirituality cannot be overestimated in its protective and uplifting effects on his life. This sensitivity to the spiritual is a compensatory aspect of the schizotypal person (see Jackson, 1997) and reflects an arena of life perhaps more available to such people than to the standard-minded.

THE SORCERY OF THOUGHT

One very common characteristic of schizotypal people is magical thinking. This again has rewards and costs but its costs can be severe. This is indeed a road to both mystical enlightenment and, if the polarity reverses, to psychosis. One thing that Desmond seems to have avoided is the active seeking of *signs* (sometimes called the 'meaning feeling' or 'semiotic arousal') and any tendency, not only to connect, but to overconnect things. For example, if one thinks that 'people are out to get me', it is easy to 'connect' this idea with events in everyday life (a man stares at me from a doorway across the road; a car driver honks his horn as he goes past; some schoolgirls giggle as they walk by). In a threatened state of mind all these events can seem 'meaningful' to the extent that even a headline on a newspaper blowing past in the wind or lying trapped on a sodden pavement can also seem 'magically significant'. Some people have even seen significance of a personal kind in wind direction. This clearly is a very dangerous state of mind but Desmond has avoided it, despite his belief in Jungian synchronicity (Jung, 1985/1955) by being a strongly *trusting* person. People whose lives have collapsed into psychosis, although they are not alone in this, have often had their trust seriously damaged by abuse – either as children or in their teenage years (the latter happened to me in 1952 and, as we saw, again in 1963–64) – but Des has not. The idea of a major persecutory network, basically an 'external locus of control', operating against him never gets a hold – he has done nothing to deserve it and . . . anyway . . . he knows he's a lovable man. Thoughts like that are like an iron fist against the threat of psychosis.

CLEAN ANGER

There is also something particularly preventative of the onset of insidious turmoil in Des and that is his 'clean anger'. Some people, when they get angry, just say it, whatever needs saying, straight out, direct. Others, to their cost, simmer and smoulder – generating what Dostoyevsky in *Notes from Underground* (1972/1864) used to call 'the resentment of the stinking bog'. Des is well clear of this territory of emotion and behaviour through excellent self-assertion skills. The fetid, sinister world of 'dirty anger' is therefore not for him.

MIXING WITH THE RIGHT PEOPLE

Des is an introvert and his friends, such as myself and Ivo (Chapter 9), are also centrally interested in the inner life. None of us have much time for people who sit around recounting stories and who talk about nothing but 'the world'. A rich inner life, however, requires openness to preconscious processes and an enjoyment of the workings of one's own mind. Des's intro-version, however, relates to the world of the mind, it does not mean he is socially shy and withdrawn. Des's then is *cognitive* introversion (Guilford, 1959) rather than the social introversion of Eysenck (1967). It is an interest in internal topics (like psychology) rather than a state of being socially quiet and subdued.

Clearly Western society, certainly in Britain, if less so in the USA, more greatly values both social and cognitive extraversion. To be a sensitive cognitive introvert and be bombarded with nothing but stories in conversa-tion – my experience in 1979 – is boring, invalidating and, of course, reduces one to silence and passivity. One loses any solid 'Self feeling' (Cooley, 1902). But Des has not been forced, as I was, into an alien subculture via his sexuality (Des is straight), he has sought the company of people more simi-lar to himself. People who could relate to and confirm his style and interests not discredit or ignore them. This clearly helps self-esteem and feelings of personal substantiality. Putting oneself in the way of people who clash with and disconfirm one's identity, although challenging – and very much in the spirit of Popperian refutationist philosophy (see Popper, 1959) – is, as I found, very damaging of mental health (see also Chadwick, 1992, pp. 47–8 on this).

THE HAPPY SCHIZOTYPE

Schizotypy is not necessarily a personality trait with destructive or malign consequences. It may have advantages to such a degree that some authors have spoken of the 'happy schizotype' (McCreery and Claridge, 1995) and of 'benign schizotypy' (Jackson, 1997). These beneficent aspects of schizotypy relate to the access such people may have to profound spiritual and paranormal experiences which can be strengthening and uplifting even when the events of the secular world or indeed their secular situation itself would lead one to expect the person to be downhearted. The same can also be true of some psychotic individuals (Roberts, 1991). As a mystic and prose-poet Desmond has opened a window also on this beneficent aspect of his everyday thoughts and feelings, some stanzas of which I feel are worth reproducing here:

24 July 1995
The sun's rays sparkling pour through the window pane.
Feeling good, feeling happy, peaceful.
Another day dawns, as morning breaks.
The sun shines, just another day.
My friend is having a nervous breakdown, I am happy.
Another is in hospital having heart surgery.
An old friend of my mother's is dying of cancer.
And I am happy.

November 1989
Another day dawns, the sun shines, the snow falls.
Hilary terminates her existence because she cannot bear to be in her
    body with her thoughts and feelings.
It's too painful to live.
And I am feeling happy, just another day.
A child dies somewhere in the world of malnutrition.
Swollen belly, eyes vacant.
She succumbs to death that lulls her to sleep.
Just another day and I am happy.

A terrorist plants a bomb that kills a soldier and his child.
And rejoices in the act of violence on other human beings.
Just another day and I am happy.
Remembrance Day in Flanders fields 1914–1918 War.
When humans slaughtered other humans.
Regardless of their beings.
And STILL the poppies grow in Flanders fields.
Just another day and WHY am I happy?

Des, as we have seen, has said that he is consciously aware of the presence of God – though for most people the presence of God is unconscious. This 'access' to the deep ground of the world, the Divine ground, is for people of spiritual orientation a bounteous source of energy and vitality that is protective against the pain induced by profane and worldly events. But is this protection dispositional or are there windows of despondency and melancholy even in 'happy schizotypes'? Desmond's accounts suggest that there are and that the experiential life of the schizotype is a complex mosaic when considered over time in which facets of both the benign and the malign are present, sometimes alternating by the second and certainly by the day. This of course makes the inner life of such people challenging and demanding for them to cope with but it also reflects the intrinsic interest and appeal of that inner life, its basic colour and dynamism, something a cognitive extravert – interested perhaps only in sport, politics and current affairs – would have difficulty appreciating. It will be interesting to see how this complex mosaic comes across in the play he has co-written based on his *Robinson Crusoe* book. Felicitously, at the time of writing, funding for this play has just come through.

REFLECTIONS

Des has a vacillating and mercurial inner life. In many ways he is a rather Hessean character. It shows also in conversation, in his journal, and to a lesser extent in his prose-poetry. All these sources of information tell us far more than would a diagnostic label or manual. This is a man whose mind can only be still via meditation, whose mind usually is a theatre of surprises and shocks, word bursts and jazzing images. In the flow of everyday behaviour he is like a small bush animal, on its hind legs, looking sharply to the left, then the right, then sniffing the air, then down, then up again, left, right, darting forward, sniff, sniff, right, left, then away at high speed, tail held high. This is Desmond, although he is distractible, when he concentrates he really concentrates as if sending out a laser into the vicinity. When he talks to you, he never seems to blink and when he looks, he really looks.

People are never simple, at least not at the individual level. A dominant feature of him is that he seems to be 'in high revs', nervy, quick, agitated, jumpy. His eyes jump, his thoughts jump. Usually Des is a moving target, as a streetfighter in days long gone by he was extremely fast and won 80 per cent of his fights. One can sense this vivacity and unpredictable staccato quality in his behaviour even now. This actually has a wonderfully refreshing effect on people who know him. Part of his beauty as a person is that he does not have polished emotions and his behaviour and thinking have a wonderfully unmonitored direct quality about them that endears him to everybody. He is neither secretive nor overwhelming, neither bombastic nor subservient, somehow his executive processes keep this bubbling dream factory of a mind on the road in a beautifully tuned way. One sometimes thinks 'Des could be a racing car driver', because in a way that is his life. But the car is his preconscious processes and his track is that he has to get this car through London traffic.

Needless to say, Des is faced with a tall order. He at times tires just of living; seems sad; despairs; feels anguished; like Beckett, 'I can't go on . . . I'll go on . . .' and so he does. Having already set up Self-Esteem groups at the Brighton Unemployed Centre and the Quaker Friends meeting house in Brighton (where he lived for two years), his latest venture, after he returned to London, was giving a course at the Swiss Cottage Community Centre with Geoff Garfield on the challenges facing men today; obviously a flavour-of-the-month topic and a challenge in itself that he and Geoff rose to with gusto.

Basically Des has a spring-water beauty to his personality. That sometimes the water runs still is no detraction, it never becomes stagnant. Even in sadness one senses the latent vitality there, even in laughter one senses the depth. Des always feels that whatever the agony there is a part of him that is 'basically OK' and this he sees as his spiritual Self. This then is a glass mind that one feels one can know and yet one that always surprises, that always confounds predictions. For many people Des is their 'favourite person' and it is this strange blend of personal effervescence and directness coupled with a despondency that has a collective quality about it – as if he is being sad for the world – that is a dominant opposition in his personality and a contrast that is particularly engaging.

Science tends to be one-sided and to seek simplicity and economy. It can even be dehumanising. But when we study the individual beauty of the personality we come up against contrasts and contradictions and we find that nothing is simple and that to capture economically is crass. But with Desmond it is perhaps in these oppositions that one finds the essential tension and life-giving conflict that energises this protean, versatile and volatile soul. He is enigmatic and uncommon but whatever the threats and the challenges, the disappointments and the losses, his tail is always held high.

Chapter 9

Ivo

Fugitive from crassness

> Never give credence to any system of thought that destroys the joy of being alive.

In pre-war Germany the Hitler regime, with its crass philistine ways, induced many spiritual people to leave the country as esoteric thinking was in no way congruent with tough Nazi 'philosophy'. Indeed one of the slogans of the Hitler regime was: 'The butter is finished, now it's time for iron' (Short, 1994). It took decades after the war for the spiritual tradition to reassert itself in any measure. Ivo Wiesner, a young spiritual healer, who was born in north Germany in August 1960, was thrown therefore into a barren culture where his sensitivities found little endorsement. Unable to feel really at home in his own land, he came to England in the summer of 1991 to practise healing. Although there was no organised culture of this kind in Germany and no facilities there to develop spiritual awareness to any serious degree, he knew that there was a long tradition of spiritual interest in this country – represented particularly by the Spiritualists' Association of Great Britain (the SAGB) and also by the Society for Psychical Research in Kensington (the SPR).

He is a professionally qualified healer himself but healing by the lay-person in Germany is actually illegal unless one is a 'qualified alternative practitioner' and it is punished by severe fines there. This says something of course about the strictness of the Germanic attitude to esoteric practices, an attitude indeed which induced Ivo to leave. If they are allowed to exist at all, they must be harshly monitored, hence the bizarre arrest in Germany of the internationally known, and even scientifically tested, healer Matthew Manning (see tests by Brand *et al.*, 1979).

Ivo tasted of the preternatural at an early age. In the mid-1960s his father died in a car accident. He was a gentle man, then still only in his thirties, and he died when Ivo was merely six. However, a few weeks after his death cognac glasses in their home were *cut in two* yet undisturbed, as if sliced by a fine laser. The upper halves of the glasses could be gently lifted from the lower and then put back in place. A glass vase was smashed or rather 'imploded' in the room it was in and photographs of his father even rapidly changed colour. Remarkably, both he and his mother, whose flat was opposite the graveyard where the father was buried, could both see balls of blue light hovering and dancing around over the grave at night A noted parapsychologist, Dr Bender, in Germany took a great interest in the Wiesner family phenomena and made a film which featured these details and a book was published shortly afterwards including and discussing the events. It transpired later, when the father is claimed to have 'come back' through mediums, that he was still angry about his death, which he saw as premature and unnecessary.

Ivo therefore was left as an only child in 1966 and, as we have seen, quickly confronted with the uncanny. He was rather materially spoilt but he says that he was nonetheless basically unhappy until recent years. School was unenjoyable and he was a mediocre student although fairly talented in English, music and gymnastics. He also involved himself with martial arts at that time but the training was not spiritually based.

When he was eight his own sensitivities started to become apparent – he started to hear a voice inside his own head. It was like a thought that would appear when he was in an empty state of mind, a clear line of words. The voice did not echo his thoughts or comment or argue about them with another voice, as is frequently the case in schizophrenic illness (e.g. APA, 1994, p. 275); it would talk as in ordinary conversation and actually tell him things that were not, as far as he knew, in his own mind. It was a man's voice and to Ivo's astonishment on occasion he uncannily and correctly predicted events. Ivo, very frightened, told no one about all this, not even his mother. Though he thought he was going mad, this small, thin, unhappy but extremely brave child saw no psychiatrists and had no treatment of any kind. He was never diagnosed as schizophrenic – although probably he would have been had he consulted medical authorities, as hallucinations for many clinicians are seen as a first-rank schizophrenic symptom (Schneider, 1959). Instead he carried this experience around with him, in silence, unknown to anyone, for years.

One might imagine that Ivo could have been the victim of a cold, domineering or an overprotective, critical mother, sufficient perhaps to induce states like this. But not really. His mother has been a little over-emotional and possessive (more so, however, only in later years) but he was always brought up to have an independent mentality and a positive attitude to himself. Both of these things have been a great source of strength.

When he was ten he and his mother moved to Trier near Luxembourg, a totally different environment both physically and psychologically from that of his earlier years. But he still had few friends and the only subject he could relate to in school was music. The others meant nothing to him. Eventually he decided to study it at the College of Music in Cologne and became a professional musician for a few years. Then he moved on to train in alternative medicine and therapy and finally specialised in healing. This kind of training was able to give Ivo a meaningful framework which helped him to understand and cope with the eerie experiences he frequently had. He had realised that they belonged more to the realm of the mysterious than to that of pathology through involuntary out-of-the-body experiences he had had as a child. On several occasions he had tried in his bedroom to switch on a light while floating out of the body (interestingly not in 'bird's-eye view' fashion) but his finger had passed *through* the switch. He had been so frightened by this that the surprise would immediately 'fling' him back into the flesh. Clearly, by the time he was 20 Ivo's experiential life was discrepant with those of his unempathic contemporaries. What was common to him was quite outrageous to them! This has been a theme which has since remained pretty well unchanged.

IVO THE MAN

To most outsiders Ivo Wiesner is a totally inscrutable man. Here is someone who regularly 'hears voices', floats out of the body, 'travels' to parallel worlds (or so he claims), senses auras and has seen ghosts and psychokinetic events, indeed here is a man who seems to live in a five-dimensional (rather than four-dimensional) world and yet betrays not a hint of it on casual acquaintance. Ivo has no need of LSD, or PCP (phencyclidine hydrochloride), he has no interest in virtual-reality experiences, and he has no such interest because he can sample all of these things drug-free in his own head.

But Ivo is difficult to know. Physically he is fair, of medium height, a good-looking fellow always popular with the ladies. Soft-spoken and very serene, he seems to float as he walks and there is melody in his voice. His facial expression tends to be very still and, perhaps not surprisingly, he has a quality about him in which he always seems to be 'visiting' wherever he is. Just as Desmond seems to be 'waiting' and 'about to talk', Ivo seems to be 'paying a call on the world', popping in, looking the world up, as if not really of this world but temporarily *in* it.

Ivo is a slim man, basically quiet and seems more delicate than he is really. He is an empathic person who feels his way and never pushes himself. In conversation, whereas Desmond leads, Ivo tends to be a counter-puncher, he orchestrates his flow in reaction. Though rarely getting angry, he is very fluent and, more than this, inspiring, when the opportunity arises and holds his beliefs strongly. He cannot be argued out of them as (he says) they are rooted in life and his own experience.

Although he is now married, Ivo is what we English would call 'a man's man'. Among men he is at peace, his thinking, esoteric though it might be, is precise in its own terms. Under fire from men he is never in trouble, not seriously, and his mind, despite the strangeness of its contents, is obviously crystal clear.

Ivo Wiesner.

Ivo's phantasmal qualities, however, are a fair reflection of the essence of the man. His spectral characteristics do indeed project the man as he really is. If one's whole life has been spent in a realm that standard-minded people only experience when they go to the cinema, somehow one has to come to terms with it in such a way as to retain one's dignity and sense of inner peace. It is hardly surprising that Ivo is slow to reveal himself. Positivistic science is no route to dignity for men like him; it is only likely to be so for people whose vision of reality has no need or experience of anything beyond the material. Ivo could never be of this ilk as materialism makes no sense to him and could never do so. The system is inadequate. How then has Ivo come to terms with a life that would send most people into either a manic frenzy or a state of utter anguish? This has been no easy task.

In the pages that follow I am going to adopt an open-minded stance, and take Ivo at his word. This will be an empathic attempt to both understand and convey him in his own terms. Many psychotherapists may see Ivo's ideas as merely projections of phenomena that are totally intrapsychic but then again this may not be so. At our present stage of understanding, a prudent person would have to admit doubt. But whether or not Ivo (and I myself here) are 'projecting' to a dimension that 'really' is only psychological there is no doubt, as both of us have found, that these procedures and ideas do work as protective devices against the 'dark side' of nature, mind and perhaps cosmos. Even the very cynical reader then could productively regard this as an empirical practical chapter at least, and relegate it as theory to either the past or the future.

TAKING ONE'S HEALTH INTO ONE'S OWN HANDS

From an early life that would undoubtedly have led him to be pronounced as psychotic by the medical profession, Ivo has emerged now in good shape. Really he has done this, like Desmond, by taking his health into his own hands and searching for a positive and charitable rather than a cynical interpretation of his experiences.

Interestingly, Ivo has a very practical and sensible attitude to spirituality and to 'spirits'. For him spirituality does not any more mean talking with and being guided by people on 'the afterlife plane' as he calls it. This he has sampled, but now it means instead having a calm, creative, positive attitude. Having awareness of the subtler and finer vibrations of spirit energies, as for example in audioclairvoyance, does not for him by any means make a person spiritual. In his view there are many spiritualists who are not, in their hearts, spiritual at all and there are as many illusions to be had in communicating with this purported afterlife plane as there are in everyday life. It offers no guarantees. For Ivo dead people are only distinguished from us by the fact that they are dead. He does not regard them as wiser nor does he blindly trust them as guides. To have a model of reality in which spirits are making one's life decisions for one (as some people have) is not Ivo's way; this kind of experience and practice he totally rejects. In this respect he is close to Desmond in taking personal responsibility for his own life.

Having realised, where many in the mediumistic subculture have not, that spirits, if they do exist, are no more capable of coming to correct conclusions than we are, Ivo has moved away from spiritualism and is rather critical of it. He has stepped out of that belief system. He interprets spirit activity instead as merely confirming one's own belief system! To his way of thinking 'they' merely amplify one's wish to be confirmed, they 'pick up' on people's thoughts and feed back to them what they secretly want. However, if a person is latently suicidal, some spirits will, alas, take them along that path too. This not surprisingly is the way he interprets my own experience of paranormal rappings when I was in Charing Cross Hospital (see Chapter 7).

The true spiritual path for Ivo is therefore not to spend one's life sitting around tables at seances but to become self-loving and loving towards every thought and being. This, along with discipline, in itself gives protection as, without the right attitude and without discipline, disaster, as I found, is bound to overcome a person with etheric sensitivities. Ivo is quick to point out that such sensitivities will not automatically enrich a person's life simply because they are there. One has to be trained to deal with them, train oneself to 'close down' psychically when necessary lest they become overwhelming and be strong and sure of oneself in belief and motive. In complete contrast to the aggressive cynic, it is Ivo's philosophy that to be loving and sensitive is really the only safe state: it is not a state to be afraid of. And, in contrast to the ascetic, for him spiritual awareness includes awareness of the body, not flight from it (for recognition of the bodily dimension in therapy see Anderson, 2007).

SPIRITUAL LAWS

Like Desmond and also Deanna (see Chapter 10), Ivo senses the presence of actual spiritual laws. The spiritual realm is ordered, has harmony and a kind of predictability if one knows its ways. These are laws, for him, beyond the laws of physics, laws more powerful than physical laws, that he sees as being able to pattern our lives but that may reduce to physical laws in certain circumstances – rather in the manner that Einstein's equations can reduce to Newton's as certain terms approach zero.

Ivo's great wish therefore is for an understanding of these laws by a blending of esoteric knowledge with scientific knowledge. For this he argues that science has to realise that mystics are not all insane and mystics have to realise that scientists are not all cynical. Concessions are needed on both sides as deep prejudices divide the two – as, of course, does arrogance. It is his belief that integration will need awareness, open-mindedness and a vision, something positive, not bitter in-fighting and destructive criticisms – but that humanity is becoming ready for this integration. At a practical level, however, he does recognise that we will have to find that something is the case and that it works, then we can try to find why it works. This is the case in the understanding of both the physical and the spiritual. Practical techniques and advantages precede theoretical explanation.

THE SPIRITUAL ATTITUDE AS COGNITIVE THERAPY

The introduction above I hope gives the reader a taste of the flavour of Ivo's life and experiences and of his manner of coming to terms with the stream of his day-to-day awareness. My own access to realms such as Ivo speaks of is obviously pretty limited; I cannot travel with him to meet 'spirits on the afterlife plane' or try and press light switches while 'out of the body' to see what happens. I do not have to fight off seemingly alien voices in my own head by 'closing down' nor do I, unlike him, sense auras or physical mediumship capacities (e.g. psychokinesis) and the like. (Intriguingly he claimed to sense the latter in me minutes after we first met.)

Ivo lives in a land where I am merely on the shoreline, confronted with a cliff that for me is unclimbable. There is no doubt, however, that in terms of behavioural criteria Ivo is perfectly sane. Unlike many hallucinating schizophrenic people, his conversation is not odd, meandering or vague, he does not show quick topic or theme changes, he does not make 'plays on words' or pick up on double or triple meanings to what one says. He is neither paranoid, schizoid nor avoidant; on the contrary, he is a warm, affable, quite confident man, a man of charm and good humour, careful and measured in speech, clear, rational in all everyday matters, sober, responsive and extremely caring. If the overall clinical picture shows that, whatever materialists and rationalists might say, Ivo is not schizophrenic, and not personality disordered, if he shows no 'cognitive slippage', 'word salad' speech or 'interpenetration of thoughts', then what on earth are we dealing with here? Is all this *real*? Do these juicy anecdotes of weird happenings and strange talents represent tangible real events and real energies? This is all most peculiar. Some would just walk away but that way one learns nothing. No, I prefer that we go forward and *into* the deep and even dangerous mystery with which Ivo confronts us.

Let us go back for a moment to the analogy of the beach and the cliffs: I am on the beach, remember, looking up and, in effect, Ivo is at the top of the cliff from where he can see directly a vast countryside of rolling hills and dales but with some threatening features. In our time as friends he has called down to me on the beach and told me about lots of things that he has seen and all about where he's been. But I cannot see or experience what he can. The cliff is for me unclimbable; indeed, as you have heard, I am pretty lucky to have even reached the shoreline itself here in one piece, let alone be on the top of the cliff. Since I can't climb the cliff, since I can't see what he sees, I do the only thing I can do, I take what he says to me and use it to make a map. If I can't have first-hand knowledge of anything beyond the beach I can at least make a map with the help of better climbers than myself.

What Ivo is telling me and what his life really is concerned with is that he has moved on from the search only for coping with the preternatural to the very understanding of reality via the discovery of spiritual laws, even if these at the moment are only empirical. Ivo is like a geologist or geographer of another dimension, searching for an understanding of alien, if wondrous, territory by experiencing and studying it so as to discover its regularities and its pattern. If he can do this, then he can actually sample and move around in this territory quite safely, and come back and forth to the beach any time he likes without injury. My job, since I've at least (just about) got on to this dry land through my own nomadic adventures, is to collate my experience with his so as to create as good a map as I can make in the circumstances. Then if anyone crash-lands on this island they can at least survive here, as long as they have it in their possession.

The map is really a form of cognitive self-help or self-therapy for dealing with alien territory of mental experience. Very few cognitive therapists, however, know much about this land. This is not the territory of depression or anxiety, this is the territory of dealing with experiences that at least seem to come from beyond space-time and from beyond the Self. This is something else.

Ivo tells me that there are more treacherous areas here than most people realise, and more than he first realised himself when he came here as a youngster. The territory can only be safely negotiated in certain ways. Here then we have to look at these ways and also discuss whether they have any general use as well. Maybe if one can get around in this territory one can get by under any circumstances.

HOW TO UNDERSTAND AND GET AROUND IN ANOTHER DIMENSION

What follows is essentially a collaborative effort between Ivo and me. I have been mapping the shoreline and the beach/cliff junction where outcrop begins, but Ivo is giving other directions about expanses further inland. From now on the analogy breaks down as we have to move from a visual to a largely verbal format but I hope nonetheless that the sense of exploration and uncertainty will remain.

We are really at the edge of where the geology and geography of sanity still applies. Here, as Castaneda warned, life can turn bad just as easily as good. It seems to depend on two things: one's degree of spiritual development and one's current attitude. A feeling of fear, or of doubt and profound self-doubt or even a purely rational-intellectual attitude will lead one sliding into quicksand very suddenly. One must not be afraid, and one's thoughts and feelings must be together in harmony, not characterised by the schizoid split so endemic among intellectuals.

There is much evil in this strange land that we are now within but it can evidently only exert itself or manifest itself with the traveller's cryptic permission. It will indeed use you as a channel to eventuate itself in your reality if it can: the only way to block and fight it, as Desmond also has said, is to choose *Love*. Love somehow appears to be fundamental, a characteristic or quality of the deep structure of the reality here. We know not why. It seems that, by generating it, one simultaneously 'tunes in' to it, as if it were a feature of some Hegelian World Soul, Global Consciousness or Cosmic Mind to which the personal mind has access. Turn to hate and you will 'attract' the 'energies' of hate – which in one way or another will eventually destroy you. This seems usually to be so. If you point a gun at someone, someday, sometime in the future, someone will point a gun at you. This is the probability, but who it will be we cannot know – and maybe we are forbidden to know.

From this angle it appears also that all people's behaviour and attitudes have interactive mutual effects and rebound effects. What Desmond used to call a 'network of colliding ripples moving through time' is to Ivo 'The Law of Mutual Vibrations'. We ourself make the world and all the people in it. It is we in interaction who subtly shaped Hitler, the James Bulger schoolboy killers, the Yorkshire Ripper, the Suffolk Strangler, because in the realm of behaviour it is rarely the case that a genetic endowment is totally and utterly inevitable in its effects. Life is the result of mutual orchestrated influences. And as we influence each other, rather in the manner of the butterfly effect in chaos theory (see Gleick, 1994, pp. 20–3), we all in turn shape the world around us every second, every millisecond. We do not merely adapt to it, we creatively or destructively change it and transform it ourselves in turn, as indeed do all organisms. This indeed was also Piaget's view (Piaget, 1959).

The emphasis in this 'territory of the mysterious' is not on proving things (though Ivo is certainly mindful that his techniques or procedure do work in a practical sense) but on the cultivation of a sincere wish to help others, to be of service. The relentless search for empirically proven facts is not a route to a more loving state of consciousness more in harmony with the cosmos. The aggressive urge to dominate, control and standardise is irrelevant and even dangerous. Here one must approach phenomena with the same caution and peacefulness that one uses to approach feeding birds, lest the process or gift vanish. Phenomena usually regarded as 'schizophrenic symptoms' – the contents of delusions and hallucinations – must not be dismissed as merely pathological symptoms but accorded some truth or reality status, if only in an existential Laingian sense. Some such phenomena are merely mental, but others are profitably regarded as not so and hence may reveal the operation of 'higher' orchestrating forces and indeed other (unseen) forces but not necessarily representing the good. The most important strategy with troubling voices then is not to listen to them. Similarly it is actually therapeutic to regard weakening and terrifying coincidences as tricks intended to destroy via a force which makes use of one's own cryptic wishes for self-destruction. In these circumstances it is vital to 'close down' the feeling of fear as this will only exaggerate problems and permit further coincidences to follow. In a state of great anxiety, doubt and fear, parlour games such as tarot cards, pendulums and ouija boards are most definitely to be avoided. They are exceedingly dangerous and will only produce results (and there will be results) that worsen a negative state of mind. Even the occasional 'positive' result will be a trick or a confuser, it will lead nowhere and certainly not in a productive direction. Continued use of such 'pastimes' by the fragile and frightened can easily lead to a form of psychic and spiritual overwhelm. Their 'messages' must be ignored in such circumstances as just worthless dross sent only to capitalise on every weakness and self-doubt for the purpose of causing as much misery as possible. Although one need not be completely immune inside a church, the calm positive spiritual presence in such places is generally repulsive to forces that work in malign ways, so such havens are valuable (indeed vital) and hence well worth seeking. Many people who have ventured to these threatening realms of human experience have spoken to me of their dread of 'a churchless world' as materialistic atheists gain ground in the public consciousness (see Chadwick, 1997b).

Truth and real clarity come from calmness. The dimension of the Positive can even be visualised symbolically as white light which one can imagine surrounding one and indeed one can project it from oneself at critical moments out to others to bring peace, love and harmony. The very visualisation of this for Ivo has brought about a growth in strength which has kept negative 'energies' at bay. Through such visualisation (with affirmations) he has gained control of his own psychic sensitivities; they do not, as in some psychotics, control him. In this way he neutralises threats and attempts to create an inner sense of the positive to which others cannot help but respond or, as he says, 'resonate' to.

It would be wrong to say that he causes the positive in others in this way. Really he acts as a vehicle to facilitate the appearance of the positive as if from beyond. Some people, alas, can have the same power of enhancing the appearance of the negative. In this manner there have even been murders, one in Tottenham in the 1990s comes to mind, where no one knew, even the murderer himself, why it was committed! It was not a caused effect; it was simply 'inevitable' because of the 'atmosphere' at a particular moment and place – as if the act was pulled out of the person by a kind of psychic field. In this sense Ivo sees cause and effect, at a deep level, to be simultaneous.

These 'psychic fields' Ivo well knows can also be created in the positive but they will not be so if people are continually opening 'cans of worms' in their own minds, as I used to do. This can only facilitate the apprehension of the negative. The focus on positive beliefs about oneself – affirmations – is a far more powerful strategy. Similarly, as Ivo has found as a healer, doubt and fear in a patient can repel the healing force and prevent its effectiveness. It does seem that people can unconsciously prevent themselves from ever experiencing the kind of realms we are dealing with here.

Away from this land of the uncanny, reason and experiment are of, at least, practical relevance – as most scientific readers probably accept. But here reason has to be put to a new use: here events reflect the power of love and synchronicities. Here in the world of the Borderline it is clear that one can slide one of two ways, to the Positive or Negative. These territories, as we first saw in Chapter 7, are very different.

THE NEGATIVE AND POSITIVE BORDERLINES

This is a brief exploration into the ultra-violet and infra-red of human experience. One realm, the negative, is typical of persecutory experiences in psychosis where the individual feels trapped at every turning by Fate. Many people confused and muddled by the Negative Borderline have sought solace in suicide, others have claimed to be victims of demons, of a hierarchy of gods or of super-powerful destructive forces. What people attribute such experiences to is variable. The Positive realm, however, is also seen as real by many spiritual and religious people. It operates over the same dimension as the Negative but at the opposite pole and in the opposite way. Mental scientists will no doubt reduce these domains to different states of mind, the Negative to a manically paranoid state, the Positive to a mature healthy state of more carefully articulated intent. To infer the operation of external forces here they will see as superfluous. We would claim differently but in any case the description below is centrally empirical.

The Positive Borderline realm seems to build over time, decades or much longer if need be; the Negative destroys, as it has to, as somehow it must do. In the Negative Borderline state one has the mentality of a threatened beast, life is terrifying, portentous, one is hypervigilant, things are happening *fast*, there is little time for reflection, events happen *too fast*. There is a sense of destiny in death as if what one has stumbled across is forbidden territory and one's presence there is 'unwanted'.

But with different intent there are no 'kaleidoscopic coincidences' all happening too fast to absorb. Whereas the events of the Negative domain feel like Satanic tricks, the events of the Positive feel sincere. Whereas the events of the Negative happen just too fast to keep up with, the events of the Positive happen in such a way that one has time to use them and learn from them. Whereas the events of the Negative are spectacular and showy, the events of the Positive are of humble solidity.

The Negative Borderline is a mystical domain of negative implication entwined, it seems, with the psychotic. It is pervaded by coincidence. For example, a person finds that his or her thoughts are racing, but then a couple walk by and one says to the other: 'She'll never keep it up at this pace.' She thinks: 'Where is all this leading?' Enmeshed in another conversation nearby a man says: 'Hell!' These are the genuinely uncanny coincidences, horrific, terrifying, bewildering. The worst such instance I personally ever suffered during the 1979–81 crisis which I think is worth mentioning here in this context was at a time when I was desperately searching myself specifically for the strength to forgive. As if, were I to forgive, my plight would be eased, and perhaps I would be forgiven. I was preoccupied with these thoughts and feelings one day when I happened to be simply browsing in a bookshop in Fulham – a humble enough setting. In exasperation, stupidly needing some 'sign' as if from beyond to guide me, I took down a small black German–English dictionary from a stand and opened it at random. Unseeingly I placed my finger on a word, again at random (I speak no German). The entry read, with the italicised words being *where my finger alighted:*

verzeihen: forgive, pardon, excuse, remit (sins), *nicht zu-*, inexcusable, unpardonable, forgiveness futile.

It must be pretty clear from an example like that that the realm of the Negative Borderline is nothing less than a potential killer that feeds on self-doubt and uncertainty like a hungry vulture. This psychophysical dovetailing(?) must have led many to destruction and self-destruction. It is difficult to believe that such events are 'mere coincidence'. We hear of the results only transiently, for example in announcements such as: 'Person under a train at Waterloo' and so on – or in the press as a small item. Ivo remembers the attitude that enhances and facilitates these effects from his days of military service in Germany. During that time he felt that the slightest provocation would have induced him to violence. His wise solution was to become a conscientious objector.

The way to manoeuvre in the land of the preternatural is centrally via love: love seems to have tangible physical power. To be able to manoeuvre needs experience, if one stumbles across the uncanny as I did, as if from the back door it can overwhelm one. But for Ivo experience (rather than experiment) is the only way to grow into a loving being. Rationalising and analysing alone cannot bring about real development. It is necessary not to allow oneself to be drawn into violent or negative experiences. If one is so drawn, then one must step out of them quickly, then conditions will change.

Nevertheless, readers will in the end really have to demonstrate it to themselves at a personal level. One can only test these ideas against one's own experience: eventually the only proof is what works for oneself. For some readers their vitality may lie in total rejection of the above, for others there may be a feeling of 'yes . . . but not yet'. This is understandable. In this realm the time, place and context might be right, and if it is, then all will be well.

ANGER AND FEAR

It is implicit in the above that Ivo has considerable mastery of the emotions of fear and anger thanks to the development within that his belief system has facilitated during his trade with the world. Indeed I have seen him move from exasperated fury to calm in seconds. The attachment of anger and fear to things, people or events, he sees as futile. Nothing can ever really be destroyed; the outcomes of these emotions for him are only illusions. This particular attitude to anger and fear, similar to that in Buddhist and Hindu thought, may well be the source of Ivo's great serenity and calming yet inspirational quality as a man. His practice of Kundalini Yoga, which is embedded in his philosophy, has also induced great tranquillity and self-worth in him, feelings antithetical to anger and fear.

After leaving England and spending a relatively brief sojourn in New Zealand, Ivo now lives with his wife in Thailand, in fact in Chiang Mai near the northern tip of the country, some 400 or so miles north of Bangkok. The country is 95 per cent Theravada Buddhist with Muslims, Hindus, Sikhs and

Christians together making up only 4 per cent of the population. There have been periods of military rule interspersed with democratic government for a long time there (Crystal, 2000, p. 340). Ivo finds it refreshing that, whatever power-mongers are doing, the people themselves, influenced by the Buddhist ambience of the country, are essentially peaceful and do not really see violent conflict as likely to in any way improve the human condition. The emphasis there is on self-reliance and self-responsibility. It does seem a general theme of the thinking of people like Ivo to recognise that all serious spiritual questers basically are speaking the same message. At a profound level there is no fundamental conflict between the teachings of Jesus, the Buddha and Mohammed, although different people may be resonant to the different forms in which they are expressed.

Ivo's general perspective on life is holistic not analytic. It focuses on peace and acceptance not domination and control. In a way the view of reality that we, all together, gradually negotiate on this planet is the cumulative product of the intersections of our attitudes and expectations which subtly structure how we behave and act. We reap what we sow and our inner expectations in nuanced ways can critically influence what our life becomes. This is so whether we believe in God or not; we cannot escape the consequences of our own attitudes and the general timbre of our mental life. The violent person will be beaten, the loving person will be loved, the acrid cynic will die alone.

The, perhaps rather teenage, framework of interpretation that materialists have for people like Ivo tends to regard them (as indeed a very young person would) as either deluded, ignorant or stupid. We can see from all the above that none of these things is the case. Rather than being stupid, Ivo has been prescient in his thinking. People simply are not as naïve and doltish as the juvenile mind, in all its energy, self-importance and eagerness to laugh, thinks them to be. It is a felicitous outcome that Ivo has settled in a Buddhist country given the sensibilities that he has. Hopeful of finding England a more spiritually sensitive venue than Germany, the sheer cynicism and crassness of life here, as it has become over the last fifteen years, has sent him further afield. As Oscar Wilde knew, the real *motif* for life is not rebellion, but peace.

IN PRAISE OF DIVERSITY

Most psychiatrists regard the prognosis in childhood schizophrenia – the diagnosis which Ivo would almost certainly have received – as worrying (Werry *et al.*, 1994), although his basically sound 'pre-morbid' personality would have helped. (See Cepeda (2006) for an overview of the field and an antidote to tendencies to panic.) He might, however, have been put on small doses of anti-psychotic medication in all probability from an early age with the possibility of long-term side effects always looming as he grew older. Psychotherapists might have probed his 'over-close' relationship with his mother and his attitude to his deceased father, feasibly causing him, in his innocence, even more anxiety and confusion than he already had. There is a possibility that he and/or his mother would have been told that he had an illness and the events surrounding his father's death probably would have been totally discounted. With all the will in the world, all the vital leads could well have been missed (and in 1968 almost certainly would have been). This chapter shows, in a way that my autobiographical chapters do not, that there *are* 'other ways' than traditional mental health approaches, radically different ways, that we in the academy have only begun to explore (see Clarke, 2001; Barker and Buchanan-Barker, 2003; Lines, 2006; Pargament, 2007). Ivo's approach also, in dovetailing so much with Buddhist thought, has resonance with mindfulness approaches in therapy (P.D.J. Chadwick, 2006; Mace, 2007). Clearly the perspective that Ivo has brought to the challenges he has found is a potentially fertile one. This brief biography also reveals a rather subtle feature of Ivo as a person which may well have saved his mind and maybe even his life. As we saw when he was a 'hallucinating' child, he has an uncanny capacity to know or sense when to keep quiet. But now he is talking, and contrary to atheistic materialists, it is perhaps time that we heard what he and those of his ilk have to say. Ivo is far from his ideal. But he is also slow to reveal himself, at times exasperatingly composed, and talks of spirituality on occasion with at least a hint of Germanic mechanical efficiency. Yet he is a man with an excellent sense of humour, an enthusiasm for knowledge and, when all is said and done, is also a man who has a deep capacity to enjoy life. This is a far cry from the escapism practised by so many so-called 'spiritual' people and from the critical thinking cynicism of so many positivists.

REFLECTIONS

Ivo's conception of reality and of the interdependence of matter and mind jars uncomfortably with that of mainstream knowledge – and indeed people such as him are a threat to the claims of legitimacy that centrally placed authorities make for that knowledge. Hence it will be imperative that Ivo's 'model of the world' be ignored so that such claims can appear to reign untroubled. This is still the approach of materialistic science. An alternative strategy is to collapse his claims into intrapsychic psychology and interpret them as illusions or as 'projections'. Hence, on this view, there are no 'spiritual forces' eventuating via the situation when a tarot card reading is being done for a troubled mind (to produce even more troubling results). The cards merely are laid out on the table on a chance basis and what is then read into them (in a fanciful way) is the source of the distress. Similarly my 'forgiveness futile' event was not access to the negative side of the symbolic essence of the world but merely an unfortunate coincidence – interpreted by me in a portentous way because of my fearful state at the time.

The 'slicing' of the cognac glasses was a fault in their construction perhaps and Ivo's successes as a healer a pure placebo effect (see, however, reviews by Benor, 1990, 1993 and Hodges and Scofield, 1995, confirming via controlled trials the effectiveness of healing as a therapy). Ivo's 'travels' when resting or near-to-sleep to other dimensions or 'parallel worlds' could, however, be seen as the products of hypnogogic or hypnopompic forms of imagery (Blackmore, 1987) and the balls of blue light hovering over his father's grave were (surely?) visual illusions or perhaps even a form of ball lightning. The effectiveness of love rather than fear in taking a person away from the Negative Borderline could be seen by mental scientists as due to its de-arousing properties, which therefore could reduce activation spread through semantic networks and thus reduce magical and 'wild' remote associative thinking. Anger and fear, in turn, could be seen via this scheme of things to have the effects they have only because of their activating properties producing difficulties in the modulation of thought and impairment in the capacity to dismiss 'irrelevant' cognitions.

Ivo presents us with nothing that demands our acquiescence to a symbolic and psychophysical world view. However, just as materialistic science is based on an act of faith that such an approach will produce valid generalisations about the world, Ivo's construction of events is also so founded. He begins from different assumptions, evolves strategies and particularly an attitude of mind and an holistic stance on the world that works for him and that he passes on to others, and strives for a conception of reality that makes sense out of his experiences and enables him to operate effectively in life. Really his mission is little different in procedure from that of mainstream science and conventional psychology (Kelly, 1955), with the exception that he considers there to be limits to definiteness or factual certainty. It may, however, be that for these techniques he uses to work a psychophysical conception of the world in the bearer, and a belief in spiritual forces, is required. Freud recognises that an external threat is easier for the mind to deal with than one which is internal – hence the use of the defence mechanism of projection (Freud, 1911). Also distracting oneself and deflecting attention from the negative, rather than embroiling oneself in it, are now known to be techniques that more success-fully make for human happiness (Sackheim, 1983; Argyle, 1993). Focusing on negative states, although brave, is likely to exacerbate depressive and suicidal tendencies (Nolen-Hoeksema, 1987).

Sufferers of spiritual crises do feel that they are being assaulted by forces that emanate from beyond themselves (indeed this was how Jung would describe the spiritual experience). If this 'externality' is accepted for what it seems to be, counselling of a spiritual nature, taking advantage of the person's belief system and working within it and with it, is arguably a flexible solution of merit (Bilu and Witztum, 1994; Leff, 1994; Pargament, 2007).

We are left with the puzzle of why an understanding that accords the spiritual some reality status is so helpful, life nourishing and comforting.

Unlike fact-finding empiricism it has helped Ivo move towards greater wholeness, integration and inner peace. There is always the troubling possibility of course that this may be because the approach has essential ontic validity. Since the living systems produced by materialistic intelligence and those produced by spiritual intelligence are both grounded in faith and will, eventually we will have to know them and assess them by their fruits in life.

Chapter 10

Denys

Adventures in meaning

Sensuality penetrates far deeper in one's being than does thought.

The abstract artist Kandinsky always saw the bourgeoisie as self-satisfied, immovable and narrow (Robinson, 2006, p. 376). For the safe and comfortable, transsexualism truly is a strange disturbance of the ambience. For the proletariat, the disturbance seems even greater. Nevertheless there are indeed men who firmly believe that really they are women and cerebrally they probably are. There are other men who think they are women when in actuality they're another man and there are yet others who want to be a woman on a part-time basis; if they try it full-time, it becomes exhausting for them. All kinds of gradations exist between these boundaries in the veiled world of transgender males.

In my three or so years of intense involvement in the sexual underground (1977–80) it was transsexuals whom I related to best, and in the years that followed some were close friends. One such transgressor of the common law was Denys Cole. Denys was 47 and a divorced father of two when I met him in 1986. He had been diagnosed as transsexual, by an eminent sexologist, in 1971 when he was in his early thirties. His 'femme name' was Deanna. He takes us, however, like Ivo, into the intriguing world of psychotic phenomena as opposed to psychotic symptoms. He enables us therefore to see a much more positive and productive side to mind-expanding and kaleidoscopic thought than crassly stamping a label on it and regarding it as 'disturbed' (which, of course, usually then leads on to the search for the 'deficits' the person harbours within).

THE EUPHORIA OF INIQUITY

I knew Denys for nearly eight years between 1986 and 1993 when my contact with the underground sadly was more peripheral. Both of us were fascinated by the strong links that exist between sexuality and spirituality, links totally misunderstood, and indeed, denied, by Western religions but not of course by Hindus or believers in Tantric thought. Christianity divorces sex from beauty and sees it, at least outside marriage, as dirty. It is only legitimatised by marriage and reproduction but has no intrinsic validity, or beauty, in itself. The Eastern view is that sex is transcendental. We were both also sympathetic to the concept of the four gender rather than two gender society, an idea central to the thinking of North American Indians, particularly the Crow Indians and the Mohave (Williams, 1986) and one sympathised with in the Polynesian islands (Sweetman, 1995).

Denys was a man, very much like myself when I was younger, who enjoyed living right on the very edges of sanity and society. While working, as a man, in a high profile security post in the northeast, a job he had gotten because of his many years in the police force, he simultaneously worked as a transsexual prostitute, floating forward in life on a wave of perfume, poetry and silk as a dominant mistress, in a sadomasochists' brothel in London's West End, a lifestyle that required a *lot* of travelling!

Work of this kind is not by any means uncommon for transsexuals, as stigma tends to prevent them obtaining more conventional employment. They are then of course scorned by the very 'moral' people who have stigmatised them in the first place. There also is a great fascination in men for a woman who has the supposed sexual urgency of a man, the archetypal and powerful 'phallic woman' of classical psychoanalysis. The trade in pornography, which presents beautiful pre-operative or non-operative transsexuals in just this light, is huge. Denys and his transsexual partner Deborah managed to capitalise on the delights and desires of this dark, and usually secret, room in the male psyche.

Denys was in many ways a sexual mystic, and that is how and why we met, but his orientation to transsexualism seemed to me to be very motivated by the cerebral excitement and glamour of 'dressing' and the misandric power, as a woman, it gave him over men. I was never 100 per cent confident that he would sustain the transsexual identity because if a man literally does want to be a woman, he is in for 'the long haul' and the excitement of over-the-fence behaviour will simply not sustain him. By 1993 his interest in that scene in life was fading and he seemed ready to move on – or at least move on within it in a different way. The double gender lifestyle also was proving incredibly energy draining (as I found myself in the late 1970s (see Chadwick, 2001a)) and Denys was finding the machinations to 'pass' as a woman very time-consuming and not successful enough to allow him to fully be at peace, and feel reliably rewarded, in the female role.

It also seemed to me that, as in transvestites, the female role for Denys was not a truly 'at home' peaceful place but a rather euphoric altered state of consciousness and, again, this is not a good basis for a permanent lifestyle. Although sporadic cross-dressing can give a man intermittent highs, and a kind of 'time out' experience, one cannot indwell in such euphoric behaviour all the time without exhaustion and burnout.

There was little doubt that in the years I knew him, Denys was on an erotic, emotional and spiritual trip. In 1993 essentially he came in to land, but during this somewhat otherworldly and spectral adventure he bravely unleashed forces within himself that most would have shrunk from expressing.

Whether Denys's rather occult and esoteric ideas (see later) were delusional is a matter of opinion. Psychiatrists he consulted in the context of his transsexualism reacted more with laughter to his general way of thinking rather than with clinical concern, but nonetheless those ideas were the cognitive content that orchestrated his life for several years. (In a similar vein Stuart Baker-Brown (2007) has time slip experiences dismissed by psychiatrists as delusional simply because he has a diagnosis of schizophrenia.)

Denys and I saw cross-gender activities as reflecting a double gender *capacity* rather than 'gender dysphoria'. We see people's scorn of the transvestite/transsexual culture merely as 'the un-normal through normals' eyes' rather than moral people viewing institutionalised pathological behaviour. Denys often spoke with venom of people's 'petty little middle class suburban value systems' and the bias of the ignorant to 'destroy that which they don't understand'.

SEX AND TIME

Hailing originally from that hotbed of machismo, the northwest, Denys was, like me, down in London out of *fatigue du nord*. He needed far more than the stifling norms for which north of England life gave licence. He needed least of all self-appointed macho moralists and most of all the discovery of his *own* virtue.

Is it psychotic, however, to believe that one is possessed by the spirit of a woman from another time? The spirit of a Borgia, known for their whiplash cruelty and cunning (Wright, 1985, p. 104), a powerful woman, using one's body and mind to eventuate herself into the world? A woman who longs to *be* and who will use her vehicle, her puppet to seize once again the gift of life? A woman, wielding not only the riding crop but the wicked swish of a taffeta dress, who must be obeyed, at whose feet men lay, in chains and handcuffs, reduced to slaves to be mere fodder for her pleasure? If one did believe this, how many would dare to act on the belief? Who would transform themselves so as to indeed give her life, instantiate her in the world, allow and permit her to *live again* through them?

Reincarnationist beliefs are, not surprisingly, far from uncommon among transvestites and transsexuals (Davies, 1995) and certainly taking individuals at their word and working within their belief system is productive for the sympathetic and empathic exploration of their experiential life – and what in that life they really see as meaningful. Treating them as a product of aberrant learning experiences or dysfunctional cognitions about women tends to make them emotionally freeze and retreat from mutually engaging dialogue. Relating to someone only with the blinkers of the theoretical box one inhabits is hardly likely to lead to any real understanding – only to transduction of the person's psychological situation into terms with which one is familiar. This may put the clinician at his or her ease but not necessarily the client.

It seemed that Denys's reincarnationist belief (tainted though it was for me by the usual bias to famous, rather than ordinary, people of the past) was nonetheless productive in his life. It impregnated his existence with meaning, gave goals to strive for, ignited his own fetishistic and sadomasochistic tendencies, all for the good, gave a strong sense of identity and purpose, put a system in his life and turned a relatively rule-bound monochromatic life into one of iridescent colour, magic moments, surges of eroticism and, of course, the delightful experience of surrender to the bewitching power of glamour.

THE SIN OF SILK AND SATIN

To those of spiritual orientation it is interesting that matter in certain forms commonly is taken to have magical properties; e.g. certain geometrical shapes: the circle, the mandala, the cross, the star; certain sounds: the mantra; certain materials: black satin; certain smells: incense; certain numbers: 3, 7; certain colours: deep purple. All of these often are thought to be gateways to the spirit. Denys, as a person, had a wonderful open-mindedness about these things which endeared him to clairvoyants, whom uncannily he always brought the best out of, and creatives alike. He saw his penis as 'of no use' to him and his male identity as 'a shell' and 'an act', hence his erotic pleasures were cerebral rather than literally phallic. Nonetheless important to Deanna's rituals was the presence and power of black and purple satin.

This indeed, as is usually the case in truly devoted and committed fetishists, was not a fetish he had, it was a fetish that *had him* – particularly when such materials presented themselves as ball gowns and 1950s wear. As writers on transvestism also have said, 'You don't wear satin, satin wears you!' and uses him or her to show itself to the world (Watson, 1987). In the silk and satin fetish underground it generally is agreed that one cannot use these most feminine materials known to Man as a tool, they are too powerful. The true devotee therefore is the vehicle to show them to the adoring eyes of all present. One sees here the passivity and sadomasochism inherent in dedicated fetishism – as well as the seeds of religiosity, as true satin lovers even claim to 'worship' the material and warn that devotion to it can 'strip you down to your very soul' (Watson, 1987, 1993).

Materialists of course will see nothing here but perhaps an unusual pattern of temporal lobe functioning or perhaps 'aberrant conditioning' but psychologically and spiritually what truly is being related to is not a 'thing' but a symbol, a symbol of the essence of femininity, which such materials often are taken to be. This clearly is a leap of abstraction and an indulgence in transcendent sex, not 'thing worship' at all. We are dealing with meaning here, not matter. Like Oscar Wilde's and Walter Pater's worship of youth, and indeed Keats's own preference for relating to 'femininity' rather than to a singular woman (Thorpe, 1964/1926), it is relating to *an idea*. This is not local brain area functioning, it is the involvement of the whole Self.

Clearly the sadomasochistic and fetishistic aspects of Deanna's life, as the female alter-ego of Denys, were activities deeply impregnated with significance and connotation. It was particularly these intense semantic associations that were central to Deanna and which were the real motive for her choice of lifestyle. The profound feelings of meaning and portentousness to her life were undoubtedly enormously productive and rewarding and although a hostile critic might see her behaviour as possessing elements perhaps of mania or hypomania, absolutely nothing at all is gained by such an assessment. One might retort that it merely turns wine into water.

PARANOIA

One area, however, of the psychic economy of Denys/Deanna that was of concern was Denys's increasing paranoia over the years he indwelt in the role of Deanna. This was coming to have a quality of clinical intensity because he was developing paranoid inferences, and vacuous inferences of betrayal, in relation to me whereas the reality was that Jill and I were devoted friends and he could have trusted his very life to me. Soon after he did break off contact, as he seems also to have done, in extremely angry disgust, with sex reassignment consultant psychiatrists. As far as they were concerned he was one of many 'losses to the system'.

To have a partly female brain in an indubitably male body and appearance is one of the greatest tragedies that can befall a human being. He felt monstrously uncomfortable in the very stereotypical male role he had to adopt for his conventional employment but did not have the looks, at nearly 50, satisfactorily to live full-time as a woman. Like me, his upbringing in the north-west had also filled his mind with abominable experiences surrounding the issue of the feminine in men which are incredibly difficult to live with. Betrayal of 'sissies' is standard practice there and it seems that Denys could never quite shake off, because of his upbringing, this paranoid hypersensitivity to what he was. Nonetheless his talents of open-mindedness, imagination, sensitivity to detail and empathy, his great love of beauty and his thirst for meaning and for 'that which is beyond' all do, I feel, have the potentiality to enrich his life in myriad ways.

THE VITALITY OF GLAMOUR

Was Denys/Deanna deluded? Was Denys an instance of possession? Was he indeed an exemplar of atypical hypomania or paranoid personality, even the beginnings of clinical paranoid symptomatic problems? The really worrying undercurrent in Denys's personality, to me, was however at a deeper level. It was his terrible *depression* in the male role at being caught in a no-win, no way-out situation. His paranoia may well have been a defence against this (Zigler and Glick, 1988) and the glamorous role he played in London as Deanna probably also kept depression at bay. Personality and mood tests I gave Denys in the male and female roles did seem to indicate this (Chadwick, 1997a, p. 98). The role of Deanna, however, was a capacity that reflected enormously powerful female inclinations. Attributing this to possession by a powerful woman from across time, a kind of 'warrior queen' archetypal image a Jungian might say, certainly did no harm – whatever its truth status – and was doubtless esteem enhancing and vitalising. Truth, after all, is not the solution to everything (see also Bernstein *et al.*, 1996; Siever *et al.*, 1996 on this co-occurrence of depression with paranoia).

It was not productive for Denys to talk to him in terms of 'the inadequate male'. A spoon is not 'inadequate' as a fork, it was obvious to him that really he was meant for other things. Having 'started late' he did not have the body and looks easily to indwell in the role he preferred – but was also unwilling to have his male personality reconstructed to fit with the demands of the standard minded. He saw that as utter hypocrisy and capitulation.

In circumstances such as this, it is likely that the attributions an individual makes for his or her feelings and sensations, if they are not troublesome but life galvanising and do no harm, can be taken as pointers to the directions they will have most vitality to explore. Admittedly sometimes attributions can be defensive, but then vitality may lie with defences. If a person sincerely does not wish to capitulate to established norms it would – whatever the organic basis for their way of being – be unethical to take any other approach.

ART AND THE UNCONVENTIONAL

What was most positive about Deanna's lifestyle, and that of her close friend Deborah, was its progressive, courageous stance as possessing what I call 'intrinsic validity'. Certainly, coming from the northwest, the 'internal objects' in Object Relations psychoanalytic terms, in Denys/Deanna's mind were sadistic and those earliest introjects were certainly projected out into the later 1980s and 1990s society (see Meissner, 1978 on this process). But still the fight for validity was sustained.

Deborah and Deanna themselves have written not of cross-gender activities as dysfunctional but of more refreshing ideas such as Surrealistic transvestism, abstract transvestism and of the indwelling in the feminine as facilitating growth (Watson and Beaumont, 1989). Looking at the (supposed) symptoms as possessing beauty is, of course, congruent with the attitudes of Warhol and of Laing.

The enhancement in the feeling of meaning that one sees in fetishism and sadomasochism also is, I admit, a characteristic of delusion (Chadwick, 1992, pp. 91–2). Some also regard seeing magic in clothing as a sign of mania (Zaehner, 1957). But while behaviour of this kind is merely a repetitive and distressing compulsion it may be that the mental health professional has some relevance (Halberstadt-Freud, 1991). But when the phenomenon is ego-syntonic and starts to 'move' away from the status of a private problematic enslavement to something that attracts creative life and life-enhancing properties, then psychological reductionism and the 'psychologisation' of distress lose their impact.

When, for example, fetishism becomes itself an art form, as in the work of Patrick Robinson, Marcelo Benfield and Mike Francis, and also in Mimi Parent's Surrealists' exhibition of 'The Fetishist's Room' (Alexandrian, 1991, p. 227) or when de Sade-inspired sadomasochistic creative imagery emerges (Short, 1994, pp. 160–5), we are progressing beyond symptomatology and pathology. Outré sexuality is now creating new meanings, becoming of social relevance, becoming a form of art in itself. Now the human scientist is not faced with an inert distressing personal problem but with a competing semantic system from people who have the same confidence in their rightness of being as have they. When the art form attracts some degree of popularity and aesthetic appeal, the human scientist, following culture at a safe distance behind, is not seen as refreshing and clarifying (see e.g. the positive reactions to chaos theory in Gleick, 1994) but, in total contrast, as boring, backward looking and degrading as well as arrogant and patronising.

This battle that Deanna and Deborah had to assert their right to be was truly a brave mission. Denys did indeed wish to continue the fight when I last had contact with him. Essentially he moved from experientialism, which he had with me, to politics. However, the protest against the standard minded in the service of being 'a female out of male' is certainly contested by the Church and fiercely so by evangelicals. The Bible (Deuteronomy, Chapter 22, verse 5) presents such people, in the eyes of God, as 'an abomination' so, on this occasion, is not helpful at all. One cannot separate the sin from the sinner here as transsexualism is not something a person does but something that they are. Hence Christians do not have the *will* to be loving towards such people.

Psychiatry and psychoanalysis, the values of the latter being of course closely parallel to those of Judaeo-Christian religion (Collins, 1988; Webster 1998), also conveniently see the way of being here as reflecting intrapsychic pathology (Stoller, 1969, 1975; Beatrice, 1985). Sadly the direction of causation problem is not given sufficient attention by investigators here.

Transgenderals in other 'pre-literate' societies in India, Oceania, Africa, Siberia and North America (Kinsey *et al.*, 1966/1953, p. 679) are often respected and thought to possess magical powers. In Tahitian society, their equivalent, the *mahu*, occupies a near sacred position (Sweetman, 1995, p. 275). The blend of male and female they represent is also generally valued far more in the deeper, more philosophical Orient than it is in the more empirical, practical West – where usually it is scorned. What is unambiguous, however, is that these people are as deserving of love and capable of love as anybody else. The devoutly moral and conservative may despise them as unworthy or dysfunctional but one characteristic I have noticed in almost all transsexuals I have known is their *wisdom*. This may well have been what has elevated them in psychologically less mechanistic and less spiritually simplistic societies. Rather than being 'unsuitable' as parents, they probably would be *very* suitable. Their wisdom may not entirely be a result of their terrible struggles in life, which can indeed precipitate paranoia problems and suicidal intent, but a genuine feature of the blend of Yin and Yang that is a reflection of the very fabric of who they are. Ironically, in the brutal evolutionary game of things this may in fact be why they exist at all and have, over the millennia, survived.

CONCLUSIONS

Psychology, psychiatry and psychoanalysis have no positive narratives at all on psychosis or transsexualism. Both are seen as deviance or dysfunction and hence regarded, overtly or implicitly, in pejorative ways. Yet both psychosis and transsexualism, as well as alternative sexuality, open the door to positive possibilities that tend to be ignored or undervalued by the agents of Western society – where centrally placed authorities tend to believe that nothing is real unless measured, 'all is number' (itself a rather distorted version of Pythagoras's teachings (Waterfield, 2000, p. 90)), knowledge is synonymous with fact and meaning is all and only a brain process. Indeed positivistic scientists have taken everything from Pythagoras and Aristotle to Russell and Wittgenstein and turned it from a feast into a hamburger. Denys was not only 'realising' what was within but, in some of his activities, actually *surrealising* his inner Self. He explored the fetishistic avenues of 'material magic' and profited, admittedly not without some suffering, from opening himself up to forces seen as eventuating from beyond himself. Shifting from Apollonian Man to Dionysian Woman he punctuated a monochrome life with one of iridescent sparkle and exuberance.

In a culture dominated, as the West has been, by war, empire building, technology, physical competition and heavy industry, it hardly is surprising that the male has been forced to indulge in 'the flight from woman' and from femininity in any guise. It is difficult to create finely nuanced lines of poetry while working on a building site and carrying bricks up a ladder or to think of dress designs while shooting bullets at people. Coal mining and factory work are not good environments to cultivate one's aesthetic sensitivities and few people realise their capacities for nurturance and grace on the rugby pitch. Man therefore has tended to become what he has invented and worked with – a machine. Even the relatively staid, bland style of dress of men is not a 'natural' thing but a mid-nineteenth-century 'industrial' invention (Hollander, 2002; Kuchta, 2002; McDowell, 2002). 'Peacock Man' is now buried in the mists of time. In England, retailers for transvestites not surprisingly say therefore that more, not fewer, of their customers come from areas of the country where masculinity standards are more cramped and severe, such as the north of England and Scotland.

In such a high 'muscle tension' male environment, some men choose literally to switch all muscle tension off by utilising hidden feminine capacities in cross-dressing. They seem also to have done this since Stone Age times (see Timothy Taylor's work in Dobson, 2007) so the latent capacity has always been there. Other men, more commonly, switch it off with alcohol, cannabis, ecstasy or heroin. Clearly both machismo and materialism are stressful – rather than 'the only way to be'.

The sensitivity to the spiritual such as is highly evidenced in schizotypal people (Jackson, 1997; Clarke, 2001) comes through here in Denys but more as schizotypal personality capacity than as disorder. Few people, other than obsessive-compulsive personalities, have 'ordered' personalities anyway.

My greatest remaining sadness concerning Denys had nothing to do therefore with his outré style of life. It was that, towards the end of our relationship, he was 'becoming like his enemy'. One sees this very often in people, including philosophers (see Appendix II). At a personal level I worry a great deal when I see this tendency emerging in people. In his virulent hatred for those of the middle ground (for him the 'out group') he developed the very same in group/out group thinking style that characterises the people who stigmatised him in the first place. In fact his speech was developing a verbal pugilism quite unlike and unbefitting of the person I had known.

My sadness at Denys Cole moving on therefore had numerous aspects but it was time. Perhaps it was indeed 'time for politics'? Denys also liked a rather less abstract and conceptual style of conversation than me and that put an ever-widening gulf between us over the years. Deborah's 'red light' domicile provided him with more spacious and comfortable surroundings for dressing than the flat Jill and I had to offer in the relatively cramped space of a West London terrace. The travelling – to other contacts as well – was, over the years, also taking a tremendous toll. Indeed it is a tribute to the enhanced vitality for life that cross-gender activities and alternative sexuality can evoke, that Denys was able to sustain this remarkable lifestyle for as long as he did.

The direction that Denys wanted to take over the years I knew him was into *thunder*. He didn't want 'facts and evidence', he wanted 'deep satin': Wagner,

Dorian Gray, Goya, Caravaggio. Earthquakes not 'nice decent, middle class, middle of the road research' or 'nice intellectual debate between cultured people' and 'nice psychology'. He wanted the battle between Heaven and Hell, lightning, thunder, earth tremors, all presided over by a high glamour, glossy-lipped, stiletto-heeled blonde goddess in a purple satin negligee. Like a character out of *Revelations* that basically was the music of his mind. (Of course even Christians would have to admit that music, thunder and honesty are all known in both Heaven and Hell.) No wonder he didn't want starch put in his personality by empirical truth and scorned safe, leafy suburb life. A talking cure cannot, after all, reach an ineffable joy (and neither can numbers).

Denys certainly lived and thrived on the irrational life, a life that psychoanalysts (Chrzanowski, 1977) admit is not always destructive but one that can stimulate creativity and self-actualisation.

Words, as I have used here, sadly are often the inferior libretto to the music of the emotions – and it is that music that really matters (Namier, 1953). It always, to be sure, helped me in resonating to the being that Denys was, to listen to the music of that great pilgrim to silk and satin: Richard Wagner – who was indeed his favourite composer (see Pettitt, 2007). If one hears Wagner one hears the essence of Denys/Deanna far better than any written words can convey. For Denys, Wagner was 'satin in music'. As I once did with Ivo (Chadwick, 2001a, pp. 66–9), to present him via a musical score – rather than via numbers in tables and graphs – would probably enhance deeper understanding. Sadly there is not the space that would be required. Listening to Wagner, however, certainly was a path to harmony for Denys comparable to that provided by the creation of Deanna.

The eventuation, in a male, of 'the woman within' is in many ways a work of art and her behaviour the creation of a piece of personal music. Malevich, the Russian abstractionist (1968, p. 17), always believed that such creations had to be done in the absence of reason and that it was essential to free oneself of the objective factual world. What Denys did was a product of 'inlook' and inner acuity not outlook and veridical perception. He lived for movement, fluidity, change and adventure, not the stoic virtues of stillness, firmness, arrest and endurance.

The emphasis on rationality and evidence in psychology can not only numb the affective faculty but numb deep understanding and produce crass interpretation. But despite Denys's torrid infractions of the rules of 'normal' behaviour, in an increasingly postmodern world (see Butler and Ford, 2003) the increased diversity that Denys needed (and our species needs) seems more likely to come about – hopefully freeing us from a world dominated by male metaphors and materialism. Denys essentially was talking to the future whilst feeling within himself, the past. The future, after all, is made at the margins of society.

As the decades go by, in the large metropolitan areas of the Western world, it is coming to be difficult to *find* 'normality'. The female side of the male may yet find still further expression. If so, then serious paranoia in cross-gender males may become a thing of the past. It might also be that female metaphors (rather than male metaphors) for knowledge-seeking, Man-as-flower metaphors, rather than Man-as-beast, and Man-as-music, rather than Man-as-machine metaphors may all yet reach sufficient acceptability to help those parts of the keyboard of male capacities previously electrified by fear to be playable (see Chadwick, 2007b and Appendix II in this volume on this). If this does come to pass, it will bring far more out of men.

To *do* as one really is, one should *be* as one really is. When one is not being true to oneself, nothing means anything. Not only 'measure and cognition' but art and spirituality are part of the human essence – and are far from superficial spin-offs from a basically rational generatrix. The fact that the mechanics of the brain can be understood by reason does not mean that all the brain does is reason. When one thinks of the dour, bland, po-faced world of fundamentalist masculinity one has to face the likelihood that anything that needs such ridicule, ostracism and violence to sustain it is not by any means entirely biological.

The Masculinity and Heterosexuality Thought Police (MASHTOP) (see Chadwick, 2006e), which one can find on the terraces at any football match, always scorn, even drive to suicide, people like Denys. Yet Denys Cole was a living instantiation that the scientific world of the possible, rational and factual ('scientific sanity') is not at all necessarily the best guide to how to live. For some, maybe most people, something more and different is required. People have capacities that go far beyond truth and truth-seeking that are indispensable to survival and to quality. Denys embodied something he (probably) wasn't, yet he made The Impossible live in the world.

Chapter 11

Reflections on the biographical sketches

Can you bring out the beauty in someone's personality or do you merely bring out their ugliness, as do cynical people?

THE NEGATIVE AND THE POSITIVE

Wicked, rebellious and heterodoxical people are curiously attractive. They fill the broadcasting schedules of television companies; they fill the pages of newspapers and magazines; they are everywhere on the internet and while atheists proclaim that God is dead and that Satan doesn't even exist, Satan's powers seem to have thereby crossed the oceans. What do we have here? We have Travis, wallowing in the transporting delights of the forbidden weed; Steve, paying a terrible price for the same sin. We have Desmond: gambler, ex-gangster, ex-street fighter, joker, egocentric, mercurial, wicked, lovable, now blending the passion of past sinning with the chromatic glow of the spiritual positive. We have Ivo, moving from martial arts to meaning, private hell to public healing; we have Denys, transmuting from married, mortgage-paying policeman with two children to whip-wielding, brothel-cohabiting, transsexual prostitute, now an agent of the four gender society inspired by Wagner, himself a blend of satin-inspired, musical genius and prescient Nazi. What have I, in turn, done with my life? I have eaten too much, drunk too much, smoked too much, trained too hard, studied too hard, worked too hard, travelled too much. I am utterly overeducated, over-qualified, I have luxuriated in the delights of the senses, from the fragrances of perfumes and the intoxications of wine bars to the iniquitous caress of chiffon, the lines of sin show on my countenance and the curve of my lips and my body aches with the pain of decades of physical delight – from running to sex, from weightlifting to dancing, from boxing to modelling. Like all maximalists I am almost ready for Oscar Wilde's 'Club for tired hedonists'. Like Denys, and like Wagner and Keats, I know the penetration depth of sensuality. Sensuality is in no way disjunctive or incompatible with spirituality. Via sensuality hidden reaches of the Self can be externalised by taking advantage of inner chromatic music to plunge deeper than reason.

Somehow, if sometimes narrowly, we have all avoided jail, if not always the divorce court, therapist's consulting room or psychiatric unit. But the purpose of life is to live and not, as Wilde's tutor Walter Pater would say, 'drag out some false shallow existence that the world in its hypocrisy demands'. These people have *lived*, if they often have paid the price, so be it, one goes forward, looks as ever for the opportunities in the difficulties and accepts that, in life, one has to welcome *all* experiences, both good and bad.

It is not surprising that some patients (e.g. Kaines, 2002) see schizophrenia-like illness as a product of the ways of God and Satan mysteriously working together as a 'Bipolar originating Consciousness'. That would mean nothing to materialists, of course, but in the kaleidoscopic tapestry that is life, one cannot help feeling within oneself this continual battle of the positive and negative. The resultant is hardly one or the other but something different and in a real sense more, which eventuates from them as ever-present polarities there at the microlevel of mental life. Though a brain cell can either be on or off and just as there always is good and bad, yet life and consciousness are more than this and beyond both these opposites. Life takes us eventually to realising, not in rebellion but in peace, the massive, beyond words complexity of the amalgam which has properties beyond either. The Positive beyond the positive and the negative.

It is very sad that in the lower classes, where it is well recognised that there are more mental health and antisocial problems, the negative is so relentlessly pervasive. Because of the deprivation, the crime, disrespect and disloyalty, violence, even the ugly surroundings (as well as such people's paranoia about the manipulativeness of managers, capitalists and governments, usually not in directions that are in their favour), people's negative and paranoid schemata are forever activated. Lower class people therefore come to *value* the negative more. The negative is very important to them, the focus of their conversation, what they have most vitality and interest talking about, what they think they have to look out for and also where they like to think the truth really is. In being like that they tell themselves how 'raw', 'close to nature', shrewd and honest they are. The brutality of the negative also convinces them how strong and wise they are to face it and deal with it and flatters their ideas of how perceptive they are, particularly about people's attempts to deceive them. This all makes cynicism seem 'real' and makes lower class people feel that they are 'nobody's fool' and hence makes them feel better about themselves.

But of course the negative is all 'the easy stuff'. Any fool can see the negative. It is always very obvious, to spot it needs little subtlety, depth or reach of mind and to think about it so much shows the relentless confirmation bias of the negative mindset and the lop-sidedness of one's thinking and personality.

It is dishonouring that a learned culture such as that which investigates the mind should so much and so often descend as a field, in its thinking, to low life styles of construing, in yet high literary language – even in its high valuation put on realism over fantasy, and logicism and practicality over poetry. The fact there there is an endeavour called 'positive psychology', which hence features 'positive' as an adjective, shows that psychology usually is synonymous with the negative and that its negativity can be taken for granted. It is a field that has tended to find something 'wrong' with *anything* that is out of the ordinary and the very mention of the word makes people feel they will be interpreted in a cynical (i.e. low life) way. In counteracting this one has to go to this microprocess Positive beyond the (obvious) positive and (obvious) negative.

THE EVERYDAY NATURE OF MADNESS

When Oscar Wilde said, as he did, that he could never quite rid himself of the grief he felt at the death of a fictional character (Balzac's Lucien de Rubempré in *Splendeurs et misère des courtisanes*) was he indwelling in an essentially psychotic process where fantasy is imbricated into reality? When the public is upset at the 'death' of a popular character in a soap, are they similarly utilising a psychotic propensity in the service of perpetuating a rather sorrowful romantic experience? Surely they are. When the young man is obsessed with feelings and with imagery of the young lady with whom he is infatuated and cannot, as he says, 'get her out of his mind', is he far from, or near to, madness? These everyday experiences show us that the actual basic fundamental processes and qualities underlying psychosis are there, usually to a lesser degree, in all of us. The blurring of the distinction between fantasy and reality, the preoccupation with and intense emotional investment in something or someone, the willingness, as in romantic love, to risk the whole Self, to gamble everything, is all not that far from the deluded psychotic, enchained by a delusion, who allows it to structure his or her life right down to the fine details. It hardly is surprising that the repertoire of processes discussed so far occasionally come together with catastrophic consequences for a person's sanity. All this also shows that psychosis is very much about simply being human.

As we saw in Chapter 5, I crossed from the world of sanity to that of insanity via *one* incorrect bridging inference (p. 47). Bridging inferences we use all the time meaningfully to connect one event with another. For example, our younger cat went out half an hour ago, the other, the elder cat, is abed asleep. As I write there is movement at the cat flap in the kitchen. It is probably (bridging inference) our younger cat returning. This elementary cognition 'connects' or 'bridges' the event of our cat going out with the sound at the cat flap. Obviously we could not live our lives without the continual use of bridging inferences, most of which are correct. When my wife and I returned from a shopping trip once, I felt concerned, as one does, that we quickly put any perishable items in the fridge. When she said, 'Can you put the whoosit in the thingymibob?' it was 'clear' to me (bridging inference) that she must mean 'fish' (the only perishable item we had bought) in 'the fridge' (a computer or android would probably have had difficulty with this one). Alas in the summer of 1979 I made one rather too dramatic a bridging inference and we saw what happened.

This drift of reasoning certainly reminds us, for example, if we gave up our job on which our livelihood depends, how close most of us are, really, to the abyss. In states of extremely high stress, one wrong inference can ruin a marriage, or a career, or even our hold on sanity itself. It is not reassuring or comforting to talk in this way, but madness is not really that remote a state. Lower animals do not suffer it perhaps because they just don't have the imaginativeness of a human being or the complexity of social relationships and enormous knowledge about them (and how they can go wrong) that we have achieved. The very language capacities that we have may well be the price we pay for the presence of schizophrenia in our world – see Tim Crow's research which uses a different approach to the multiple gene, vulnerability-stress model adopted here but similarly argues for the singular 'humanness' of schizophrenia (Crow, 1993, 1995, 2004, 2006).

Sadly, in life, 'going mad' is one of those 'Once is too often' things (see Chadwick, 2004b); many people will never let you forget it and the radius of behaviours that you can run off before they think you're 'going funny again', is very small. While people like Madonna and Robbie Williams can pretty well 'do anything', because they're performing artists, once you've been psychotic one can 'do nothing'. You really have to behave yourself to prevent the diagnoses and more general insults flying from some people's lips. No wonder the stigma of the schizophrenia label is more pernicious for many people than the illness itself.

THE COGNITIVE AND THE SOCIAL

Cognitive approaches are exclusively Self to World, there is little World to Self dimension to cognitive thinking. For example, Dryden (1999), in discussing self-help therapy to enable people to accept themselves, focuses exclusively on modifying the intrapsychic processes of self-depreciation. The text totally ignores the social dimension of seeking and finding people 'out there' who accept oneself so as to help one change 'outside-in'. Self-acceptance, on the cognitive view, is 'all in the head' and social relationships (Dryden, 1999, p. 8) are addressed only one way in terms of how self-depreciation can affect one's relationships Self to World, leaving the World to Self dimension somehow to 'look after itself'.

This one-way orientation also is a reflection of the reductive theoretical bias in cognition which sees social processes as the bottom-up resultant of individual cognitive processes. This contrast between Self to World and World to Self dimensions (Peters, 2001) was brought home to me starkly when I was a professor of community psychology in the 1990s. The people in a nearby estate were suffering dreadfully from the dilapidated condition of their flats and immediate surroundings. As I had contact with some of the people who lived there, via a neighbour, I wrote a *cri de coeur* demand to the council to upgrade their estate which was backed by a massive number of signatures from the people themselves. To their credit the council acted immediately on receipt of this petition and the estate was cleaned and renovated. This, as far as I am concerned, was infinitely preferable to sending in an army of cognitive therapists to help the residents at the individual level cope intrapsychically with the depression-inducing state of their surroundings. Instances like this highlight the contrast between community psychology (Bender, 1976; Orford, 1992) and the encapsulated world of cognitive psychology. Clearly the attractiveness of the latter is only going to be high for people who cannot relate their difficulties primarily and critically to their environment and so are willing to say, 'the fault lies in me'. Life being what it is, in all its multidimensional richness, this is rarely, if ever, entirely the case (see also the critical discussion on this in their paper, 'Beck never lived in Birmingham' (Moloney and Kelly, 2003)).

There is no doubt that cognitive interventions are effective (Morrison *et al.*, 2004, p. 25), and in Chapter 13 I discuss circumstances where I am supportive of them, but when, like a good entertainer, they centrally distract the miserable from their misery, they thereby distract our attention not only from socio-economic and political issues but from the dense microprocess two-way interactions at the Self/World interface. The way tragedy in theatre can encourage conformity with a 'look what happens when you don't behave yourself' implicit communication (Boal, 1979) is a related example of how individually targeted forms of life can mask the multitude of microprocesses involved in our everyday trade with the social world in reticular, feedforward and feedback fashion. See McHoul and Rapley (2000) and Sacks (1995/1992) on how behaviour so reflects the cultural order. Like the fish, it is so easy to be blind, at least in such an individualistic subject like psychology, to the all-pervading water in which one swims and the enormous (often 'too tiny to notice or mention') interchanges with it. It is psychology's enormous task in the future to face these too-tiny-to-mention aspects of life and mind. (For video study of microsequences see Jenkins and Barrett (2004) and for microstudy of the patterning of behaviour in relationships, including therapy, see Miell and Dallos (1996).)

PERSPECTIVITY AND 'CONCEPTUAL SHOPPING'

Don Bannister (Bannister and Fransella, 1971) always used to show how differently any issue can look from different perspectives. Given the multiple alternatives that pervade this postmodern world it is necessary, to some degree, and as I did myself, for sufferers of mental health problems to go – and to have to go – 'conceptual shopping' for approaches that fit their situation, within and without, most appropriately. In Chapters 3 and 4 we see reported experiences that take us into totally different worlds on the issue of cannabis smoking and in Chapter 9 Ivo Wiesner shows how a completely alternative frame of reference to the bio-cognitive can be constructed on hallucinations and on, what human science professionals would call, 'magical thinking'. We see the same in Chapter 10 where Deanna and Deborah reap the rewards of a more positive artistic and of course also more rebellious stance on transsexualism than the dysfunction-emphasising narratives of some professionals in the human sciences.

There is little doubt that the constructors of diagnostic manuals overvalue the bland as the model of normality as normality is defined linguistically as the absence of abnormality (Rosenhan and Seligman, 1995/1984). But normality also should be accorded to those who make productive use, as did Churchill, of processes otherwise seen as underlying pathology and hence live with such processes without incapacitating distress.

Psychiatrist Peter McKenna (2003), on a positive note, has argued that in daily practice, psychiatry has *no interest* in people who are not suffering incapacitating distress to the point of seeking services. He would be against the contemporary drive of many media personnel and journalists to 'psychiatrise' everyday life (see Chapter 13 also on this). In the middle part of the century it was the case, as I found, that once labelled 'a patient', the full weight of tendencies to pathologise and diagnose was directed at one (e.g. Rosenhan, 1973). In a repeat of the Rosenhan study (Slater, 2004) it seems, however, that this tendency, to the credit of psychiatry, might be decreasing.

STAFF, PATIENTS AND 'STATUS-LEVELLING'

In the field of psychopathology, staff are not patients and patients are not staff (Hinshelwood, 2004). Because of this, being in my position as a 'peer-professional' who actually works in the field is highly unusual. Although I have done formal counselling work and a very considerable amount of educational counselling, which often turns out to involve addressing many intimate and challenging emotional, family, life and career-planning issues, the vast bulk of helping experience I have had in psychopathology itself has been with people as equals. My students I also have always regarded as friends, my only advantage being that I started the subject sooner and when, at the height of the Thatcher business ethic revolution, I was informed by the Head Office of one of my employers, 'Remember you should regard your students as your customers' I replied by saying that the day I regard university students as customers is the day I will give up university education forever.

The 50-minute hour is not a good opportunity for what I call 'status-levelling experiences' as spending the session, say, talking with a male client about the local football team (which can indeed, if rarely, happen) could only occur as a one-off or he would likely see interactions like that as 'not really what I came here for', even though, through the levelling experience, it could well have been therapeutic. Actually getting things *wrong* can also be status-levelling and not at all automatically counter-therapeutic (Marsh and Leroux, 2002).

In the history of the therapy movement, Ferenczi, Adler and Stack-Sullivan were all prone to behaving at times in a status-level way. Ferenczi even made the first (albeit rather *too* informal) attempts at a kind of co-psychoanalytic therapy. Adler and Jung, though not Freud, would also have their patients seated so as to be physically level with them. Treating the patient or client as if there is nothing wrong with them may be therapeutic via communicating implicitly this very message (see also Chapter 12 on this). Being spoken to always as 'the sick one' can itself make one *feel* ill. One of the advantages indeed of living in a psychiatric aftercare hostel, with staff, is that so much of one's interaction with them is peppered with status-level talk and events. To some extent this is true also of Day Centre experience. It is interesting that some professionals are so dedicated always to being 'up there' in their inter-actions with patients or clients that they are temperamentally *incapable* of talking to them in a status-level way and will put them down even in the occasional chatter of an everyday nature, for example about their computer or the bus route home and such like. One has to wonder whether profes-sionals of this kind are *using* sufferers to preserve their own psychological equanimity in singularly sinister ways.

A FINAL NOTE ON SELF-EXPRESSION

Richard Gregory, who was one of the professors at Bristol when I was an undergraduate there, said many years ago, in a short article on perception for medical students, that in science there is a way in which one's research somehow externalises that which is within us. Indeed the emphasis on self-expression and the facilitation of possibility in person-oriented forms of psychology is itself a theme of Expressionist artists (Britt, 1999). It is there-fore good to see scientists thinking in ways that put bridges across from science to art.

I have never personally believed in the blank-slate view of the infant and as the centuries ahead of us unfold, I feel sure we will discover realms within of which so far we have rarely, if ever, dreamt. There is something, for example, about being on a beach that somehow models the human condition. As we face the ocean and gaze out over it, it seems, subliminally, to remind us of the ocean within and without. As we discover more 'out there' it does indeed seem to enlarge our understanding of what we are and opens up canyons within which nourish our perception of humanity itself outside-in.

Sometimes, as in the actual practices of education and therapy, one feels that one puts knowledge from the outside in, only to light up what, though dormant, is already there. This uncanny ambience to the growth process I feel holds many mysteries for us. What are these canyons within? And how did they get there? When, as with people such as Newton, Einstein, Shakespeare, Milton, Nietzsche, Wagner . . . we feel that we are indeed seeing 'the other side of the carpet', whether they be scientists, artists or philosophers is secondary to their ability to fully realise some given power to the mind and instantiate publicly what intangibly is somehow there in some degree in all of us. Like all outstanding creatives, they seem to mirror the power, character and possibilities of the cosmos-inclusive-of-mind while reflecting ourselves back at ourselves.

All the biographical and autobiographical sketches here deal with people who have been sent many challenges, though Travis alone is, for the most part, quiet on this aspect of himself. What I call 'clear-run personalities' always seem to have the most simplistic identities and views of life; for a Self that is multifaceted and that has richness in outer and inner perception, there are benefits to be had from hiking on the harsher path. What I have tried to convey in this first part to the book is the knowledge to be gained from diversity rather than from the standardisation of consciousness. Schizophrenia and related ways of being, whether one talks of them as characterised by psychotic phenomena or by psychotic symptoms, open up a variegated, and often terrible, riot of menacing colour within. The task the person has is to mutate and transfigure this, not in the service of capitulating to blandness, but in the service of growth and proliferation of all that one can be. The outer reaches of human experience give us glimpses; our task, as Keats knew, is to see what bearing they have on each other. If we continue to do this, and to dare, we will share the quest of Einstein and Hawking, eventually to know the Mind of God.

Chapter 12

On the acceptance and emotional understanding of psychotic thought

When you're not being true to yourself, nothing really means anything.

UNDERSTANDING RATHER THAN DIAGNOSIS

An extremely important conference on 'Phenomenology in Psychiatry for the 21st Century' at the Institute of Psychiatry in London in September 2005 symbolised a renewed vitality and openness to the experiences of sufferers of serious mental health problems and paved the way for a rapprochement between psychology, psychiatry, psychotherapy and psychoanalysis, a possibility which I felt should be grasped with enthusiasm. At the conference Nancy Andreasen suggested that a 'reverse Marshall Plan' was now needed and possible where the United States could benefit from the more qualitative approaches to understanding that have long flourished in Europe (e.g. Jaspers, 1963). Many contributions at the conference made reference to the works and ideas of artists, philosophers and spiritual questers (see *Schizophrenia Bulletin*, 2007, volume 33, number 1 for several of the papers presented) and it was clear that semantic understanding was at last being respected as opposed merely to mechanistic reductionism, categorisation and prescription.

In the same spirit many psychologists do now work with methods that 'resist the diagnostic gaze' (May, 2006) and use non-judgemental, accepting frames of reference, in this case for psychosis sufferers. The formulation-based approach (e.g. Morrison *et al.*, 2004) in clinical psychology is itself an 'understanding'-based alternative to diagnosis. Rufus May (2006) opens the conceptual door for his clients to benefit from such traditions as yoga, mindfulness, meditation, Daoism, acupuncture and so on. Beliefs are not judged or categorised but respected and listened to compassionately in the service of the relief of distress and in helping people to deal with their beliefs in the context of the wider social world. Indeed periodicals that give voice to service user perspectives and experiences, such as *Open Mind*, *Your Voice* and *Mental Health Today*, although I will not labour this point, are replete with tales of discontent at the past judgementalism of the human science professions and their incapacity to respect the dignity, individuality and the subjective perspectives of the sufferers themselves (e.g. Taussig, 2002; Knight, 2004; Cobb and Roberts, 2007). However, see Strauss (1989, 1994) for a strong compassionate voice from the professionals.

My own recovery from psychosis (see Chapter 6) focused a great deal on the use of perspectives from psychiatry, psychoanalysis and cognitive, humanistic and social psychology. But clearly in a postmodern, multicultural world, different people will find different forms of knowledge and understanding meaningful. In order for clinicians to maintain 'joint reference' (Freeman *et al.*, 1982) with clients, perspectives other than the rational-empirical and deterministic style of much scientific humanism have to be available and respected. Because of this it may often be necessary to move outside of conventional professional boundaries, diffuse boundaries between conceptual boxes and indwell in the world views of the clients to see the frames of understanding and the directions for which they have most vitality. This, sadly, requires a flexibility of mind and a tolerance of paradox and ambiguity for which traditional Western education gives little preparation. In my case my own total absence of any substantially meaningful spiritual education proved, in 1979, a serious source of vulnerability. Had the territory of experience I moved into had any notable familiarity to me I might not have been so deranged and destabilised by it.

EXPERTS BY EXPERIENCE

Professionals do welcome service user contributions and self-disclosures but, as yet, make little move to recognise them in the works they cite and, at the end of the day, frankly admit to 'holding the trump cards' (Hallam, 2004). Service users themselves therefore need to continue to self-organise as in the *Hearing Voices* and *Paranoia* networks and the *Mad Pride* movement so as to utilise the advantages of insider knowledge and of peer support (Marshall, 2003; Lawn *et al.*, 2007).

Sometimes this can take refreshingly new and therapeutic directions such as the involvement of previously very withdrawn sufferers in patients' football leagues (Carter-Morris, 2001). The therapeutic value of football for bonding is also stressed by Pringle (2004). All manner of activities not usually seriously considered within the conceptual walls of state-approved academicism, such as photography (Glover, 2001), golf (Carless and Douglas, 2004), dance (Stanton-Jones, 1992), music (Turner, 2006), poetry (Tolton, 2004), writing generally (Bolton, 1999) and drawing (Ah-mane and Holloway, 2002), have all received considerable service-user support (see also Carless and Sparkes (2007) on sport for sufferers of serious mental illness). On the arts therapies in perspective, particularly see Thomson (1989), Waller and Gilroy (1992) and Kaye and Blee (1997). The idea of from-the-inside narratives in which 'a day in the life' is portrayed also turns out to be a remarkably revealing way of giving outsiders a 'taste of the soup' of the insiders' private and usually secret worlds (Chadwick, 2001b, 2003b; Butler, 2004) on a moment-by-moment basis. A day-by-day fictionalised account of a psychotic crisis, based on actual cases, from pre-psychotic state to the inception of psychosis through to hospitalisation, is given in Chadwick (1995b, Chapter 3).

Clearly as service users themselves become, as indeed they have become, more active in protest, peer support and in demand of alternative approaches to the individualistic and rational-empirical, the hierarchical structure of the mental health culture is slowly in the process of a change to a participatory heterarchical structure utilising many service users themselves as mental health workers (Grant, 2007). Those people, in any individual case, who have the most relevant skills and resources, then become the focus. If this happens to be a faith community, of course anathema to some scientists (see the Autumn 2007 issue of *Open Mind* on this), or a small self-created service user group (e.g. a 'delusions group') who accept the individual, then so be it.

THE CENTRALITY OF ISSUES

All of this, of course, does not pre-empt the relevance of biomedical approaches which, as Chapter 6 shows, have certainly been of tremendous help to myself. But the fact remains that a substantial percentage of psychosis sufferers recover without anti-psychotic medication (Harrow and Jobe, 2007) and this has always been the case (Mayer-Gross, 1932; Bleuler, 1978). Others, such as myself, do need a small dose but do perfectly well on it for life while others, it is true, do deteriorate (see Hafner and an der Heiden, 2003 for an overview). The picture is complex and each person has to be considered in terms of the *issues* central to them (Alanen, 1997a, 1997b). It is quite wrong and dangerous to adopt blanket argument, extreme positions which try to 'wipe out' certain approaches and perspectives via angry, political pressure. In the sinister multi-faceted diamond that is schizophrenic psychosis, one simply does *not* know, in the foresight situation, whatever meta-analyses and randomised controlled trials may state, which avenues a particular person will find productive. Research is now producing positive and replicated findings of a genetic mediation to schizophrenia (Kalidindi and Murray, 2004) so it is likely (though not inevitable) that biochemical support will benefit a sizeable percentage of sufferers, particularly those who are more seriously ill. There are others, however, who, perhaps not quite as ill but also through their own efforts and through congruent environmental factors, will be able to recover drug-free (Harrow and Jobe, 2007). For example, it has been known for some time that those returning from hospital to families who are *not* highly critical, overinvolved and overprotective and who are warm and also perhaps not overtalkative and guilt inducing are liable to progress more favourably (Bebbington and McGuffin, 1988; Martindale *et al.*, 2003). Those people who find subcultures, whatever they are, that are more tolerant of outré and unconventional thinking, may also feel less stressed and more accepted and through such involvement they may find a path to a more consensually shareable style of being. The importance for recovery of subcultures of this kind whether they be UFO groups, anarchist groups, eco-warrior groups or whatever has been recognised for some time (see Heller, 1988, Chapter 15; Chadwick, 1995b, p. 62). Evidently there are circumstances, at the individual level, where accepting psychotic thought, rather than increasing distress, actually decreases it. From a commonsense point of view one might well argue that the best way to keep a person 'mad' is to stamp a madness label on them, make them feel in subtle ways different from the rest of humanity and regard and treat them as if they *are* mad. In contrast to this it hardly is surprising that so many people recover from psychosis by mixing with tolerant, accepting, warm people who treat them pretty well as 'one of their own' and as if there is nothing seriously wrong with them. I know personally that this would not work for everyone, I do not believe my own psychotic state in Charing Cross could ever have been alleviated without medication, but it does seem that we need a spectrum of approaches and a considerable degree of open-mindedness about how a psychotic person can be eased out of their predicament and distress. When psychosis has led to such violent and dangerous behaviour as it did in my own case obviously one has to adopt a more conservative position because the risks involved are extremely high. However, individual people vary tremendously in this respect and in the issues that they face so what is appropriate in one case is not by any means appropriate for all. That I believe applies generally. I believe service users would strengthen the overall impact of service user contributions in the mental health field if they did not generalise so broadly and often so vituperatively from their own singular experience.

SPECIFIC EXAMPLES OF 'PSYCHOTIC' THOUGHT

The acceptance of psychotic thought can, in specific instances, be calming and reassuring and indeed can prevent problems from escalating. What, for example, would the average clinician's reaction be to a woman who suddenly uttered the words, 'Is this letter a telephone?!' This was a question a woman with a diagnosis of schizoaffective psychosis asked me after she had received a letter that day from a former lover who had gone to live in America. She really felt that her estranged lover could hear her thoughts via the letter and that it put them in real-time contact.

Now of course a traditional bioscientist might say 'She needs more medication'; a cognitive behavioural therapist that her irrationality needs to be turned into a rational attitude. But another approach is to turn the thought around and embed it in a positive context: 'There's a poem there'.

Over the next half hour, while I was there, we did create a quaint poem out of the supposedly 'thought disordered' cognition:

> Is this letter a telephone?
> I read your words
> Sent from so far away.
> Can you hear my thoughts
> Now as I read them?
> Are we really apart?
> Do the miles really matter?
> Reduced to nothing by paper.

Obviously this blank verse effort is hardly Keats, but soon after this little creation the 'delusional glow' of her idea subsided and her specific kind of thought-broadcasting worry disappeared, never to return. Perhaps a sense of closure is achieved by making something constructive out of psychotic/poetic sparks. This really is what Salvador Dali also was trying to do.

'Letter–Telephone' is, of course, a very wispy association: both words refer to communication. So, since one can hear 'down a telephone', can one hear 'down a letter'? The woman's preconscious reasoning might indeed be best captured by the poem but, at semantic network level, it can be seen as an example of a creative 'knight's move' (Freud) associative style. Since all nouns have an array of properties, this is an example of accessing a particular concept ('communication device') and then associating from one exemplar of the category (letter) to a property or subset of that category ('real-time communication'), producing the notion 'He can hear me thinking' and then inevitably on to 'telephone'. One might say that her great need for contact produced the emotional drive or activation spread through the semantic network to evoke a wider range of associating than usual. Emotional needs involved in romantic love obviously override any inhibition necessary for reason or reasonableness even at (perhaps especially at) microprocess level. Under romantic love, scientific impossibility becomes possible.

'I'M A RADIO!'

Our flat in London in the 1980s and early 1990s was a kind of 'three-quarter way house' for sufferers to drop in for company and a chat. One afternoon in the late 1980s a woman diagnosed as 'paranoid schizophrenic' by psychiatrists noticed in our kitchen that as she moved around she changed, because of her positioning, the volume of music and talk on our kitchen radio. On first picking this up she exclaimed, with eyes burning like gems, 'I'm a radio!' She was not mindful of the act of deflecting radio waves, this was to her 'paranormal'.

At the time this woman also believed that she was having telepathic 'hypnotherapy at a distance' from her consultant at the local hospital. So, this latter belief would be made more likely and realistic, and hence would be confirmed, if she were herself a living radio, sensitive to 'signals' through space.

This and the previous example of the 'telephonic letter' at the time emerged like 'psychotic pop-ups' seemingly from nowhere. But both at source were emotionally based and drew on emotionally tagged stored information ('emogens' rather than 'logogens', in the sense of Dixon, 1981). The human radio lady desperately wanted a real close connection with her (beloved) consultant, while the telephonic letter woman wanted the same with her (beloved) former partner now in America. The cognitive irrationalities made sense in the context of the strong needs associated with romantic love. Put this in minds with an additional hunger for the spectacular and magical poetic sparks connecting physics and psychology result. Human radios and telephonic letters seem to become reality (and, of course, perhaps one day they will).

JUNG ON JOYCE

When James Joyce's *Ulysses* emerged in 1922 Carl Jung, having battled with and been bewildered by the text, described it in 1930 essentially as a 'schizophrenic' book (Jung, 1971/1930, pp. 112–14) and then seemed to see everything in it through the lens of the diagnosis. In all credit to Jung, he did ponder the (slight) possibility that there was some limitation in his own psyche that prevented him from appreciating and understanding the work (Shloss, 2003, p. 278). He eventually put it down to his irritation at Joyce's apparent disregard for the reader, but it could be that Joyce was able to dare more unfettered, fluid thought than Jung, yet still maintain executive control and retain organisation of thought. This may well have been a lamentable case of the weaker, more limited ego feeling a loss of control and slapping a psychiatric diagnosis on the stronger ego simply because he didn't really understand irrationality as anything other than pathology and may even have felt psychically threatened by the book (see Shloss, 2003, pp. 274–81, for details on this).

By way of contrast, the Dadaist artists John Heartfield and Wieland Herzfelde (Elger, 2006), on meeting the self-proclaimed 'Christ' and 'President of the Universe' Johannes Baader in Berlin in 1918, warmed to him and declared him 'The Supreme Dada'. They treated him with respect and affection and encouraged his art. Raoul Hausman, within the Dada group, always stood by him and accepted his eccentricities. There was never any question of banning him for 'madness', he merely was 'controversial' (Elger, 2006, p. 56).

Pathologisation of the subjectively odd is very much part of the dark and murky authoritarian past of the human sciences as a whole. One could, of course, reverse the process and, as we saw in Chapter 2, smack the labels on the bland. Sadly, categories in themselves don't explain anything and mud-slinging both ways shows the futility of categories where nature has not been 'cleaved at the joints'. Alas, this is the usual state of affairs with the blurry, often organically meaningless categories in psychopathology.

A POSITIVE VIEW

In the 'Theatre of the Impossible' that is the psychotic mind there is always a danger of crippling service users' liberty and stultifying their imagination by the overuse of rationalism. Determinism has also always been seen by artists such as Louis Aragon as an enemy of freedom and morality. The acrobatics of psychotic mentation can be frightening, it is tempting to 'put starch in' (as Joyce himself would say) to tighten up associations. Are we really any different, ever, from Jung with Joyce?

Because of their focus on mechanism within a monistic framework, materialistic scientists may well not fully respect the spiritual and artistic values of the psychotic experience. Such realms of phenomenology certainly deserve much more research (Clarke, 2001; Barker & Buchanan-Barker, 2003; Kliewer and Saulty, 2005).

If we move outside scientific humanism and adopt a more flexible, accepting mentality in the context of psychosis, we could talk of sufferers' object classifying as 'unconfined' or 'floating' (a credit approach) rather than 'over-inclusive' (a deficit approach); of their associations as 'varied' or 'supple' rather than 'loose'; of the mercurial spirit as 'multiple identity capacity' rather than 'identity disorder'. Sometimes a person is in temporary, but necessary, 'identity suspension' rather than 'identity crisis' and is 'productively well organised' rather than 'obsessive-compulsive'. Indeed, sometimes delusions can be 'imaginative passion' rather than 'thought disorder'.

It may be of value to indeed use far more art, music and video in understanding and recovery ('Draw your "illness"') and perhaps materialists can come to recognise that imposing a more prosaic way of life on people naturally more Dionysian can itself have long-term disadvantages (see the poet Ted Hughes on this in Cornwell, 1999).

SURREALISM AND PSYCHOSIS

Materialistic science and atheism compel and challenge investigators to explore that in people which is most animal and machine-like. Art, however, compels and challenges us to seek that which is most human (Rothko,

2004, p. xxxi) and – as the novelist Philip Roth said (Kettle, 2006) via celebrat-ing rather than ignoring the nuance – takes us to the very secrets of our hearts at the individual level (Collingwood in Lines, 2005, p. 18). This is why I believe true knowledge seeking (*scientia*) that is a blend of empirical science with art and spirituality will take us further in the understanding and the healing of minds than materialism and positivism.

The human psyche naturally spawns both prose and poetry, is both logical and lyrical. It is possible, as Dali did, to creatively misread the world and, as the eugenicists were, to be deceived by reason. Pre-emptive scientific imperial-ism and cognitive correctness may make our endeavour more 'physics-like', but could totally fail to fruitfully engage with passion and the splendour of 'knight's moves' in ways that will help people eventually to be truly who they are in generative ways.

Salvador Dali was, and is, a much maligned figure, but he showed via his 'paranoiac-critical method' (Short, 1994; Waldberg, 1997) that one could take psychotic thought and, with critical discipline (and, in his case, strong academic technique), turn it around into something fascinating and beautiful rather than simply eliminate it. Perhaps students in psychology and psychiatry need somewhat less training in cognitive neuropsychology and CBT and rather more training in how to think in, and empathise with, more fluid, lateral thinking ways?

Psychotic delusions and speech can often involve the juxtaposition of the incongruous and the seeming arrangement of sense into nonsense. But the poetic spark (Max Ernst in Elger, 2006) can, like psychotic perceptions, bring alien worlds together in ways that can delight, shock or disturb. The Surrealists (see Chadwick, 2006c), were interested in the way that changing a singular letter can bring worlds together (FAST/FEAST), put them in direct oppos-ition to one another (MUSTARD/CUSTARD) or, for visual artists, charac-terise their very endeavour (PAINT/PAIN). At low (and, during crisis, falling) thresholds of consciousness, what Pierre Janet used to call *abaissement du niveau mental* and that do indeed obtain in schizotypy and psychosis (Evans, 1997), subtle and tiny, otherwise unthinkable connections between things become available.

Connections such as the word plays above and previously unthought of anagrammatic connections (e.g. ELVIS – EVILS; SINATRA – ART A SIN) or sound associations (EIGHT – HATE, SIX – SEX) start also to occur to people. 'Mad thoughts' that were the very currency of bohemian artists (Franck, 2002), among them the Dadaists, Fauvists and Surrealists (see Sass, 1992; Short, 1994), such as an apple that fills a whole room or a rainfall of bowler-hatted men (see Calvocoressi, 1984 and Meuris, 1992 on Magritte) become one's own very currency. One starts to think the never-before-thought, the unthinkable, and to become fascinated with the unknowable.

It was the contributions of the Bleulers, Jung and Laing that have helped us to recognise that madness does have narrative sense and some measure of communally shareable meaning. Psychosis sufferers, in what they say, are trying to communicate and to regard what they say as 'empty' is to turn them away to the path of despair.

ACCEPTING THE MYSTICAL

The underpinning ideology of academic and clinical psychology does tend to be that of scientific humanism. Although this orientation can be helpful for clinicians to deal with unusual beliefs that do not clash with secularism, it can be disastrous when dealing with service users with spiritual or religious beliefs that conflict with the professional's worldview.

Psychologists are generally scornful of mystical intuitions, preferring to ground the subject in empirical findings rather than revelatory intuitive insights. But another tradition argues, with the ancient Greek thinker Parmenides, that truth is indeed rooted in the mystical experience (Firth, 2004, p. 29) and in a sense if our reason is grounded in something deeper than itself, our reason may be better. Even theoretical and quantum physicists such as Schrödinger (1955) and Pauli (Laurikainen, 1988) have subscribed to this.

Sufferers with mystical beliefs that contain life-enhancing aspects may be better dealt with by acceptance of the beliefs or discussion of them within a spiritual framework than by challenging them and proving them wrong (Knight, 2004). As one woman, reported by Knight, profoundly damaged by CBT said, 'I thought I was a shaman, now after CBT I feel terrible, all I am is a mental patient'.

The fact is that secular humanism is not a system or ideology that can contain or validly assess mystical intuitions (Deikmann, 1977). One doesn't drink soup with a fork. In my view the treatment of that woman was a gross misuse of rational-empirical psychology and was felt to be so by the sufferer.

So far this text has focused on the understanding and acceptance of more flamboyant psychotic thought and behaviour, the so-called 'positive symptoms' or excesses rather than lacks and deficiencies. In Western society these latter 'negative symptoms' are states with which we have some difficulty but I certainly remember myself the help that Gestalt gave me at times of ennui, listlessness and passive bewilderment. It is inevitable in life that there will be times when we feel lost and devoid of motivation. It is sometimes helpful to see such times simply as necessary transitional periods rather than punishing oneself with regard to them because one is not 'dynamic enough'. Often a great deal can be going on within but outside of awareness such that 'being with the calm' and 'acceptance of stasis' can be highly productive.

In other cases, however, the onset of a seeming void within can be far more dangerous. At these times one has to think more in terms of tertiary prevention in the sense that such states have to be managed to avoid chronicity and terminal decline.

GRIEF AND MOURNING AFTER PSYCHOSIS

Patients can be well aware of their increasing deficiencies, not all totally lack insight. The onset of negative symptoms such as apathy, lethargy and anhedonia can be perceived as an experience of loss and so a certain element of mourning and grieving can be involved which clinicians may not recognise.

Service users can still use their memories to compare how they are to how they used to be and of course comparisons like this are not favourable for them. What I have experienced over the years with a number of people is that the really dangerous time for sufferers is when symptoms that have been troubling them for a long time actually become boring, relentless and seen as never ending except in death. This kind of grief is deadly. While one can keep a spirit of challenge and interest alive and the person can be helped to see their problems as still worth tackling and battling there is a good chance of keeping them alive. It's not so much where there's life there's hope as where there's hope there's life.

CHAT

The air of apathy that negative symptom sufferers can radiate can be incredibly demoralising for everybody. Nonetheless, hearing themselves described by staff chatting as 'cardboard cut-outs' and 'burnt-out schizophrenics' is degrading for them. People are not deaf, they don't lack feelings in every sense and they are not fireworks that have gone out.

It is worth pointing out, however, that even extremely withdrawn people value being treated not as 'mental patients'. As the neo-Freudian psychoanalyst Harry Stack-Sullivan realised, they need to be spoken to at times not as patients but as persons. It is therefore useful to talk to them about ordinary things like local football or fashion news, things in the paper generally and matters other than medication, medication effects, cognitive and psychodynamic distortions and their general mental state. They enjoy ordinary everyday chatter; it is a change from the 'illness talk' that often surrounds them. That in itself only keeps reminding them over and over again of their position. They can do without it because first and foremost they are people-in-the-world and only secondarily patients or residents-in-care.

REFLECTIONS

We worry about psychotic patients showing signs of negativity especially when they say they are not depressed. In driven Western society such people are 'not motivated enough', 'not interested', 'not lively enough', are 'an energy drain', 'lack drive', 'lack earning capacity'. The whole area of the negative and the passive in an increasingly market-oriented planet seems to be problematic for us. It is not an aspect of being, and a potentially productive one at that, it is 'a symptom'. We should be wary of scorning stillness and silence.

Perhaps it is necessary to recognise that some people are naturally far removed, but sometimes productively so, from the bland model of normality as sanctioned by science in psychiatry and psychology. If we were to allow ourselves to see the intrinsic goodness in the unusual and focus more on the constructive enhancement of uniqueness than on orienting the person towards a more middle-of-the-road way of being, patients and clients would likely feel a great deal more peaceful within themselves and would eventually come to recognise their own intrinsic validity.

It is part of the essence of psychotic thought and feeling that to a greater or lesser extent it sends a person out of control. Yet in many artists, and one sees this particularly with Magritte, Dali and Joyce but also in the work of Kandinsky, Jackson Pollock and Sylvia Plath, there is a tremendous blending of the capacity for abandon and 'wildness' with that for discipline and structure. In more recent times one sees this also in a gentler way in the contribution of Veronica Etro, the designer for Etro Fashions, who always stresses how her work blends the sensual and the rigorous, the structural and the romantic, and the designer for La Perla Fashions, Anna Masotti, who combines the soft, feminine and dangerously romantic with the tough and metallic. Turning the relative wantonness of free imagination and psychosis with its remote associations, daring and iridescence around into something both self-transcending and productive requires practice, education and a willingness to find creative space away from the Self. This is not, however, automatically the same as reforming a person's mentality into a style of sanity more acceptable to positivistic science.

Chapter 13

Issues in diagnosis, therapy and understanding

People don't want to be changed, they want to be loved.

MANIA DIAGNOSIA

For forty-four years I have been studying texts and articles in psychiatry, psychology, psychotherapy and psychoanalysis, first as an amateur, then as a professional. I also have taught psychology and various forms of therapy at university level for 30 years. Needless to say, in that period of time one has a lot of discussions with both professionals and trainees particularly, in this context, in psychiatry and psychoanalysis. I had relatively brief psychoanalytic psychotherapy myself for about 8 months in 1967–68 and of course, as we have seen, I was treated, using various methods and techniques, for psychosis and Tourette's syndrome in 1979–81. Over these four decades or so I have, sadly, had a large number of labels attached to me. I will outline some of these here that have popped up in both formal and informal interaction.

I initially entered this arena of thought and quickly 'discovered', for example, that I had an 'Oedipus complex'. On realising not only my love for my mother (which I can assure the reader is there) but my intense hatred for her and her abusive behaviour, it was suggested that I had a 'negative Oedipus complex'. On hearing how precisely and accurately I was able to recall the *dates* of everything that had happened in my life, a houseman in psychiatry diagnosed me also with 'obsessive-compulsive personality disorder'. Unlike most psychologists I believe in God, the paranormal and the supernatural, and this was, to some people, 'magical thinking' and 'schizotypal personality disorder'. I am actually quite a cheerful person at the worst of times ('hypomania') and am, as one needs to be in the research business, a confident man who, like Kierkegaard, likes to use his own life and personal struggles to enrich his work and writing ('narcissism' or even 'narcissistic omnipotence'). I am also very good at giving up smoking, to date I've done it 37 times, but never truly quit ('addictive personality') but like most smokers I do fear the damaging effects that smoking has on personal freshness. At the height of my teaching years, when I was giving eleven classes a week I used, for the students' sake, to have four or five *baths* a week ('delusional olfactory reference syndrome'). I also have an uncanny tendency to think things which at least my wife and close friends then say ('thought broadcasting delusion') and I have the admittedly rather unusual quality of having a mind that, no matter how much reading, studying generally, thinking or writing I do during the day, seems to have large supplies of energy and so doesn't seem to tire ('atypical hypomania'). In my younger days when I was into transvestism, I was obviously conflicted about it because it clashed so much with my macho upbringing ('ego dystonic paraphilia') and, having some religious sensibilities, it caused me a lot of trouble in my relationship with God ('spiritual disorder'). As we saw in Chapter 5, I did develop delusional ideas ('schizophrenia'/'schizoaffective psychosis') and memories of my suicide attempt for a time would disturb me at night when I was trying to get to sleep ('flashbacks'/'post-traumatic stress disorder'). On a different tack I have always favoured girlfriends with beautifully shaped breasts ('partialism') and who went against the grain in their style of life ('latent anti-social tendencies'). When I was younger I certainly was a rebel who detested what we'd now call 'doing normal' all the time ('sociopathy') and in my affairs with men, a lot of the excitement was due to how *forbidden* the behaviour had been in my formative years ('manifest anti-social tendencies'). In 1979 I did indeed develop a mild coprolalic tic ('complex vocal tic disorder') and for many years I was very bitter about the abuse I suffered as a child ('ruminative worrying'). At times this would very seriously lower my mood ('clinical depression'). At times I have taken the whole psychological profession to task in the things I have written ('grandiosity'). My wife also has at times been drawn into this whirlpool as we are a very close couple ('co-dependency'/'symbiotic relationship'). Like most transvestites, when I was younger my heterosexual drive was more intense than that of straight men, something researchers have noticed in male transvestites (Kinsey *et al.*, 1966/1953, p. 680; Ruse, 1990, p. 3). I was perennially 'girl crazy' ('hypersexuality') and, as we do, found them so attractive I actually wanted to *be* them, if only on a part-time basis ('boundary problems'/'narcissistic object attachment'). I have always thought exceedingly well of women ('idealisation'/'unresolved Oedipal fixation') but, given my life experiences, am wary of children ('specific social phobia'). I do enjoy public speaking ('exhibitionism') but sometimes I find myself wanting to give everything up, just 'crash', and just sleep and sleep ('demoralisation syndrome').

This list could be extended; in forty-four years one comes across a lot of categories in to-and-fro dialogue of a psychological or psychiatric nature but sadly, apart from the terms 'psychosis' and 'tic disorder', I cannot say that *any* of these labels have furthered my understanding of either myself or anybody else one single iota. Indeed the houseman who diagnosed me with obsessive-compulsive personality disorder on the basis of my vivid recall of dates didn't even bother to enquire more deeply into this. In fact my father had a Derren Brown style photographic memory for numbers and when I was a teenager I too had this capacity (making history and the memorising of societal statistics obviously very easy for me). The capacity faded in my thirties and forties but my number recall is still very good. The houseman saw none of this and made no such enquiries, to him it didn't reflect a capacity but a *disorder*. One wearies of seeing this happen so often in one's dealings with human scientists and indeed one's exasperation leads to the worrying possibility that some of these professionals deliberately use their nomenclature – for reasons best known to themselves – to socially down-rank people. (Ironically psychotics seem to have been socially down-ranked quite enough as it is and this is itself an issue in their illness (Birchwood *et al.*, 2000, 2002).) In this respect the so-called 'formulation' style of therapy used in clinical psychology, which takes the whole case history into account to formulate an approach and which avoids stigmatising categories and labels, is far less humiliating, and infinitely more informative and helpful. I personally believe that psychiatry would benefit from adopting this approach (see Morrison *et al.*, 2004; Johnstone and Dallos, 2006; Tarrier, 2006).

The use of diagnostic categories and conceptual process labels in psychiatry and psychoanalysis seems such, at least in the journeyman practitioner, to have an almost magical, magnetic pull for these professionals. They only have to 'get a whiff' in the content of one's speech of a category and *immediately* you are IN it! So strong is this tendency that one cannot help thinking that they are giving the representation actual physical reality status – a psychotic process (Segal, 2007, p. 111) – and simultaneously jumping to conclusions and showing exaggerated confirmation bias – again both psychotic tendencies (Freeman and Garety, 2004a, 2004b). Are psychiatrists and psychoanalysts taking on some of the characteristics of their patients?

Refreshingly it is the case that the leading professionals in psychiatry I have had dealings with simply see me as having had 'a relatively brief psychotic episode' and, apart from the tic problem, see all the rest as 'just life'; this also is the case with colleagues in clinical psychology and those on the frontiers of psychotherapy. So any students reading this can be comforted with the thought that 'at the top' in actual daily practice, whatever the diagnostic manuals would lead one superficially to believe, it does in my experience seem to be that there *is* common sense in that the people who really are at the top of their game see the *person* not the category.

NEGATIVITY AND STIGMA

The social down-ranking of people with mental health problems is a phenomenon that pervades the human sciences, the general public, the world of business and the media (Singer, 2001; Pinfold *et al.*, 2003, 2005; Corrigan,

2004; Thornicroft, 2006; Fung *et al.*, 2007). However, at the level of interactions between individual people, the stigma associated with serious mental
illnesses such as schizophrenia is, in form, basically an (often ill-informed)
inference and a *prediction* that one will, say, be unable to do the job properly,
or be unstable or frightening or whatever.

When I got back into work in early 1982 I decided not to tell my employers
about my psychiatric history. When I *did* tell them, some eight to ten years
later, nobody even batted an eyelid, as we say in England, because they had
seen for themselves that I could do the job perfectly well and hence the
'implicit prediction' was refuted. I suffered no effects of stigma at all from
any of my employers.

The stigma problem in the human sciences themselves is probably greater,
however, in a general sense (not less) than elsewhere because we are studying
the mind and professionals are likely concerned that serious mental health
problems in the past in one of their own personnel will affect one's source
credibility and the clarity, reliability and trustworthiness of one's thinking. In
the arts there tends to be an implicit belief that the rebel, the person on the
edges of society, or even, like Caravaggio, outside it, has somehow the best
vantage point from which to view mind, person and the human condition.
Because of this, people who are, say, homosexual or manic-depressive or
whatever are often greatly valued in artistic circles. In science, however, and
this certainly is so in psychology, the general implicit belief seems to be that it
is the very stable, middle of the road personality, even bland person, with no
sharp edges to their being, that has the best view of mind-in-life and that the
exotic personality might be rather cavalier or too off-centre in their thinking
and feeling to have a very clear view of person and human nature. There are
exceptions to this of course, such as Stuart Sutherland, who was manic-
depressive, but exceptions are rare. Obviously, as a psychologist pitched right
into the middle of this dilemma I have experienced the pushes and pulls of
these attitudes to some degree, but they have been rather more detrimental to
my research career, as professionals generally adopt an aloof 'Us and Them'
mentality (even towards patients who are themselves professionals) than to
my teaching work, where my insider experience has always been an advantage. The situation seems similar in psychiatry and indeed Robin Murray
(2006), professor of psychiatry at the Institute of Psychiatry, advises colleagues (psychiatrists) who have suffered schizophrenia NOT to reveal this to
the profession. This is a very sad state of affairs in professions where one
might expect people to be *more*, not less, understanding but it is the state of
play in these endeavours. Like myself, Rufus May, who is a clinical psychologist, has been open about his own psychotic episode, and the head of his
training course at East London University, Mary Boyle, proved understanding and supportive. The inside knowledge that Rufus and myself have of the
psychotic state has, however, been of some advantage to our work and writings and I think, looking at this in the round, that our self-outing generally

has been beneficial to us and to the profession of psychology. I would *not* go so far as to say, however, that self-outing on these matters, in psychology and psychiatry, is to be recommended.

Though this text is not centrally concerned with these matters I should mention briefly that in science, inclusive of psychology, the self-outing of my transvestite past has, however, proved not less but *more* stigmatising than the self-outing of my schizophrenia – though again this was much less a problem for students than for professionals who have far more restrictive (indeed 'soul-battering') pressures on their lives and on their thinking (Schmidtt, 2000). Psychology selection committees that I admitted this to in days long gone by would cringe with embarrassment, look at their feet, stare at me saucer-eyed as if I was from Mars and so on. Once a whole audience of a hundred or more clinical psychologists immediately, and in unison, looked down at their feet in embarrassment once the words, 'I used to be a transvestite' came out of my mouth. There also is a noticeable streak of homophobia in the British Psychological Society with transvestism, it seems, so out-of-the-window as to be unmentionable. Since I also give a lot of lectures to artists and art therapists on the topic of artistic approaches to recovery (e.g. Chadwick, 2004c), it is refreshing to see the audiences, if anything, look up and smile faintly when I make an admission about my transvestic past to them. In conversation afterwards it transpires that they see my exotic history as adding colour to my personality and as being (as indeed I saw it myself) 'a symbol of rebellion'. It is to them a capacity and a good thing not a deficit and a disorder.

Service users themselves have done a great deal via protest and their own self-outing to counter such negativity and stigma. The March 2002 issue of *Mental Health Today* carries many stories by service users writing openly in their own names deliberately to reduce prejudice. Having patients or clients forever shrouded in pseudonyms, even first name pseudonyms, and impersonal initials, simply and sadly maintains the shame. The Autumn 2002 issue of *Open Mind* also specially features service user research. In my own case I am a hybrid of scientist, artist and spiritual quester (in my religion I am a Pantheist) so it is perhaps natural for me to come out and state flatly what I am. Given the present state of society there is a necessity, different in different areas of life, for a delicate balance between concealing and revealing. Despite the brave and vocal self-outing in the *Mad Pride* movement there is still, in my view, excessive and shame-maintaining self-concealment nonetheless about mental health problems, a shame really that, in modern times, dates from the days of the asylums and the public's fear of them. The project by *Rethink* and *Norwich Mind* to decrease such stigma via their controversial statue of Winston Churchill, who seems to have had considerable volatility of mood, in a straitjacket, was an excellent eye-grabbing symbolic gesture to the effect that even the very greatest people can have mental health problems. (Thanks to the somewhat manic side of his personality, Churchill was 72 years of age before he ever found himself feeling too tired to do things.) Fortunately, investigation into prejudice and discrimination against people with serious mental illness (SMI) is now an extremely active area of research internationally (see Pinfold *et al.*, 2005; Song *et al.*, 2005; Dietrich *et al.*, 2006; Chiu and Chan, 2007).

As the reader can doubtless tell from this text, I have been fighting stigma all my life. I have also been, as many people are, a victim of 'the spiral of abuse' (Chadwick, 2005d). I was abused for being my father's son and for my bisexuality and femininity of temperament; this abuse made me ill with paranoia – so some people then abused me for being an ex-mental patient; I developed Tourette's syndrome at the time of the psychotic illness, itself a socially humiliating condition so I smoke for its powerful anti-Tourette properties and am then stigmatised for smoking! If one complains too much about these things one risks politically minded people abusing one for talking 'victimspeak'. It never ends. Like most of my close friends I see myself now as being perfectly sane and quite stable. An old friend of mine, Ron Clarke, who was a life-battled footsoldier like myself and who first met me when he was 60, found me, encouragingly (and doubtless to some readers surprisingly) to be 'the sanest and most stable person he had ever met'. He was astonished at what I went through in 1979 and said that there 'must have been damn good reason for it' if it had happened to me. Remarks like that, particularly from very shrewd people as Ron was, are a lot more beneficial than categories of deviance.

More seriously, however, it doesn't seem to me that these four main human science endeavours can regulate themselves when it comes to the issue of mental health problems and/or off-centre sexuality in their own personnel. Some external monitoring of these professions on these issues is obviously required. The central problem they have is that they are victims of their own negative narratives. These professions have very few substantial *positive* academic narratives (though the present works and Kay Jamison's text on manic depression (Jamison, 1993) are examples) on any form of psychosis or any form of sexual orientation other than heterosexuality. As a rule they, like Christianity, almost glorify straight sex, particularly in classical psychoanalytic narratives, and choose neutral or negative, rather than positive, anecdotes to exemplify or demonstrate all their trains of thought in the fields of mental health and alternative sexuality. It seems it is almost implicitly forbidden in the human sciences to say anything actually unambiguously positive about behaviours that are not sanctioned by the general cultural order of the state.

One can see the effects of these 'vocabularies of denigration' (Laing, 1990/1960) in the wary attitude of the general public to psychology and indeed to all the forms of life that the human sciences instantiate. In addition, in the sexual underground, the style of self-presentation expected is always defensively superficial. The gay sensibility (Landesman, 2003), though this tends to apply to the transvestite sensibility as well, is dominated by artifice, theatricality and a focus on surfaces – because the people DARE not go under the surface as they know only too well from the culture in which they live that there are NO positive narratives to guide them. Once under the surface it is all 'character assassination' as that, one way or another, is all the human sciences have to offer them. All of this really is *abuse* of everyone but the bland, itself almost a teenage, secondary school mentality, and it really should not go on. Admittedly psychology as a field is, in recent years, trying to 'turn its oil tanker around' somewhat in the development of positive psychology. This is a field that does have roots in the far less 'assassinatory' narratives of thinkers such as Ferenczi, Jung, Horney, Rogers and Maslow, as well as the ego psychoanalysts Hartmann, Loewenstein and Kris, all of whom saw human nature, generally speaking, in a much more favourable light (as did Fechner, Winnicott and the Gestalt psychologists Köhler, Koffka and Wertheimer). There is a glimmer at the end of the tunnel ... but the darkness is still oppressive. It is sad to enter an endeavour which shares the social representations of the very people who put one in hospital in the first place. This, of course, is what is known as 'sleeping with the enemy'.

THERAPY: EXISTENTIAL ISSUES

Although it is true that no therapy works for everybody and any therapy will work for at least somebody, the present state of our knowledge in the field of psychosis research is that usually a combination of medication and cognitive behavioural therapy (CBT) is probably the optimum treatment that professionals can offer for people with these problems. Rather than focusing on diagnoses and deficits, practitioners target actual symptoms and biases, such as the Jumping to Conclusion (JTC) bias (Garety and Freeman, 1999), as well as, in cognitive remediation therapy (Wykes and Reeder, 2005), more general cognitive problems of what one might call a 'cognitive hardware' nature. Difficulties in social, relationship and self-care behaviours may well reflect these, often neglected, cognitive difficulties (Green *et al.*, 2000) so merely removing or reducing a person's delusions and/or hallucinations and/ or the distress associated with them is no longer regarded as being enough to consider an individual a treatment success. Problems in previously neglected processes such as attentional capacity (Chadwick, 1992), contextual processing (Hemsley, 2005 and references therein) and a whole host of issues relevant to readjustment to work and everyday life (social skills; assertiveness training; time management; non-verbal behaviour; self-organisational skills etc. (see Craig *et al.*, 2003; Martindale *et al.*, 2003)) are now also targeted to enhance quality of life.

A number of texts already exist on CBT for psychosis (e.g. Kingdon and Turkington, 1994; Fowler *et al.*, 1995; P.D.J. Chadwick *et al.*, 1996; Tarrier *et al.*, 1994; Morrison, 2002; Morrison *et al.*, 2004; P.D.J. Chadwick, 2006; Freeman *et al.*, 2006); it is not my purpose here to repeat material already available in those works but to focus, in the next two sections, on issues, not as yet made very explicit in the literature, which I believe could nonetheless be incorporated into the CBT approach.

It is common for both behavioural scientists and psychoanalysts (though not cognitivists) to regard conscious experience as the basic (if important) roughage for interpretation but to focus on tacit, implicit or unconscious processes where 'the real action' supposedly is taking place (e.g. Hinshelwood, 2004). However, alternative theoretical models such as those of attribution theory (Heider, 1958; Hewstone, 1983), Gestalt therapy (Perls, 1969) and the broad approach of phenomenological psychiatry (see the January 2007 Special Issue of *Schizophrenia Bulletin* on this) argue that the style and contents of consciousness have an important part to play in the understanding, prediction and indeed explanation of a person's actions in life.

Working within such an ideological and epistemological framework, I think it is worthwhile re-evaluating previous phenomenological contributions (e.g. Laing, 1990/1960; Jaspers, 1963) to see what they now have to offer in the task of empathically indwelling in the worlds of sufferers whose behaviours and actions are proving not entirely reducible to such tacit or unconscious processes.

The purpose of this section is to re-examine in a contemporary context Laing's (1990/1960) concept of 'ontological insecurity', which I will deal with here under the broader and more neutral term 'existence status' so as to address certain experiences which sometimes (if not always) arise in psychosis and in pre- and post-psychotic states. These are experiences of fragility to the very ground of one's being that are not usually discussed in the context of cognitive-behavioural therapy but which, I think, could be formulated in such a way that CBT as well as narrative therapy practitioners might well be able to deal with them. In presenting this material I will draw on some of my own pre-psychotic experiences but also make use of reports from and experiences with people in co-counselling and in group work over the years.

PSYCHOLOGY AND EXISTENTIAL PHILOSOPHY

Existential writing (e.g. Heidegger, 1962/1927; Sartre 1956/1943) can be very obscure and opaque and is not easily attached to the concerns of people such as cognitive neuroscientists, cognitive and narrative therapists and social psychiatrists. It is my aim here to discuss these issues, in the context of psychosis, in ordinary language, so as to relate the phenomena involved to the interests of the mainstream in psychopathology research and therapy (see also Webb, 2005 on this). This is not, as previously was the case (Laing, 1990/1967, Chapter 5), to overthrow the mainstream with a totally radical (and in my view, dangerous) approach but to enrich it by relating the concepts to extant procedures and ideas, particularly in cognition.

I am speaking here more of the actual experience of 'existence status' as a generic term within the endeavour of experiential psychology rather than working within the philosophy of existentialism. The emphasis of existential philosophers, since Kierkegaard, on free will and on the personal responsibility of the individual in taking charge of their lives (see Magee, 2001) has not endeared them to reductive scientists who focus on determinism and the supposed impotence, causally, of conscious experiences. The existentialists' denial of the existence of any 'Real Self' also has made communication complex with adherents of some humanistic schools such as those of Rogers (1961) and Maslow (1973). The 'authenticity' of Heidegger (1962/1927, p. 68) and Sartre (see Thody and Read, 2005, pp. 56–61 for a summary) is not the 'Real Self' of Rogers although, of course, the concepts are related. Here I am disengaging the discussion from the free will/determinism debate to focus on the ontological issue of how solid, substantial and sound psychosis sufferers' very *being* in this world really is. Some people may have achieved existence status but be battling to preserve it but others may feel that they have never fully achieved it in the first instance (Laing, 1990/1960). One also has to address the concern, of people in stigmatised minority groups – who are of course particularly vulnerable to paranoia (Bentall, 2003a) – and people whose parents have brought them up to feel valueless and 'no good' in themselves, about the *right* to exist. What happens to your mental life in general, and even the microfeatures of your cognitive processes, if you're not even sure that you have the right to exist at all? Clearly, as Kierkegaard would understand, this also has spiritual consequences since, if one feels one has no 'right to life', one may feel that one cannot have a positive relationship with the Divine.

Whilst admitting, at the outset, the spiritual benefits for less disturbed people of (as in Buddhism) the 'loss of Self', in an age of evidence-based practice, primary difficulties of an existential kind may seem rather hazy and 'atmospheric', not easily assessed by standardised methods or addressed at all by behavioural science. But it may be that such sufferers, of brittle foundation to their very being, can benefit from a blend of approaches more usually found in cognitive, narrative and psychodynamic therapy and pastoral approaches as dovetailed with aspects of the existential approach. Laing's concept of the 'schizophrenic voyage' (Laing, 1990/1967) deep *into* the crisis (with no guarantees) and then (maybe) out to a better level of functioning has not proved a solution popular with most professionals treating individuals with such difficulties. Alternative ways are needed without I believe, at the same time, denigrating Laing's insights.

THE RIGHT TO EXISTENCE

Although it is now a truism that existence precedes essence (Heidegger 1962/ 1927, pp. 67–8), many people, as I was, are 'born into hatred' and they do not feel that their existence can in any sense be taken for granted as safe, wanted, good or acceptable. Lesbians and gays in Uganda and Nigeria, Jews in anti-semitic communities, transvestites in the north of England or Scotland and of course black children in racist white communities, all may suffer in this way. One may also be born to a mother, in a single parent situation, who bitterly resents having been left to bring one up. A child may take, in his or her 'ways', after a hated grandparent or be 'a disgrace' to the family in their way of being or in their sexuality. Clearly there are innumerable scenarios where a child can grow up feeling 'people wish I wasn't here at all' even if they never voice such a feeling in words.

The various forms of capricious existence, namely: 'I'm not really here'/'I shouldn't be here'/'I must justify my right to exist'/'I am being abused simply because I exist in the first place' involve or can involve existential guilt and shame – as if the person should be ashamed of, or apologise for, taking up space in this world at all for what they are. Whatever is the case logically, essence or 'Whatness' can have feedback or feeddown effects psychologically on the integrity of existence or 'Thatness'.

It is not usual for CBT therapists, themselves outside of the existential or Laingian domain, to probe deeply for, or deal with, such fundamental flaws or vulnerabilities in the very bedrock of the Self. Issues *of* existence that are discussed philosophically with clients of less psychiatric morbidity in existential therapy, issues such as the point and purpose of life, meaning and of course hope are predicated on the actual, reasonably firm, experience of existing. But if the latter is compromised a priori the mental dynamics take on quite a different complexion (van Deurzen-Smith, 1993, p. 155). This is more than the usual reference of the psychiatric concept of 'existential distress' (Kissane, 2001) and becomes a genuine uncertainty about being at all. At this level of disturbance, as Laing himself realised, a philosophical orientation to therapy is not appropriate.

MOTTOS AND NARRATIVES

Being helped to verbalise these uncertainties in the very ground of one's being at least brings the issues into conscious focus where they can be fully felt, admitted and discussed. It may be that they relate, if not exactly, to the 'mottos' of Karen Horney (1937), the 'internal sentences' of Albert Ellis (1962) or the 'automatic thoughts' of Aaron Beck (1976) irrespective of the usual philosophical baggage that comes with formal existential therapy. The more usual mode of existential guilt, being in debt to life (van Deurzen-Smith,

1993, p. 163), may manifest itself consciously and verbally to a person as the motto or sentence: 'I am alive, I must *do* something in repayment for this gift of life' or 'I must *do* so as to be *worth* something'. But fears for one's own personal reality may issue forth in the motto: 'I must *fight* the world to prevent it imploding me' or 'I must be *needed* so I have a reason to exist at all!' or (a frequent Laingian anecdote) 'I must win this argument with you, not to make the point, but for my very existence!' or 'If I am not in a romantic relationship I don't exist!' or 'If I don't have children, my whole life and existence on this planet has been wasted!' In an emotional sense these have implications of a profound spiritual nature additional to those usually involved in the concept of 'automatic thoughts' – but at least dovetailing such problems with extant cognitive concepts does give us leverage upon them. As Webb (2005) has argued, we need to face the subjective and acknowledge 'First person data' and 'First person methods' in the human sciences (see also Guishard-Pine (2006) on the neglect of existential therapies and the discussion of existential difficulties in Chadwick (2002c)).

If upbringing at both home and school is among people who do not value or respect one's basic capacities, presence or identity, the narrative or 'thumbnail sketch' one can receive of oneself by the age of, say, 18 can be horrifically negative. People who feel that they're 'a waste of space', 'a nothing', 'a hole in space' might more easily tolerate abuse as 'just what I'd expect' or 'nothing less than what a no-good, nothing like me deserves' etc. People in a state like that are obviously vulnerable to the loss of their sanity. Eventuating the network of mottos and threads of storylines that make up a totally invalidated or never-validated identity could at least manifest them so that they can be reframed and attacked. In my own case some of the critical 'counter-sentences' and, of course their emotional associations, that have helped me have been: 'Why should *you* suffer for the disloyalty of your father?'; 'Why should you devalue qualities that crass men are too insensitive even to notice?'; 'A male person can still be a man even if they're not suited to the army or the building site' and (borrowing a line from Jean Cocteau (1889–1963)) 'What the public criticises in me I shall cultivate, it is me'.

One sees existential issues of the kind discussed here in the poet Sylvia Plath, categorised as schizoaffective by Claridge *et al.* (1990, p. 211) who lived not so much by a motto as by a cryptic narrative of the seasonal nature of growth and decay. For her, repeated suicide attempts, in a sense shedding of her autumn leaves, would be used to revitalise her being and enable her, rising phoenix-like from the ashes, to move into a kind of spring and summertime productivity. Never, it seems, unthinkingly secure about her very existence, independently of her parents, Plath needed this periodic resurgence to feel alive at all, as a singular person, and of course by identifying herself so much with the cyclicity of nature, paid the ultimate price. It is clear that she was living via a very, very dangerous storyline and it is a tragedy that in therapy this cryptically hazardous narrative was not deconstructed and replaced by one more unambiguously life-affirming (for detail on Plath in this context see Alvarez, 1971; Stevenson, 1998).

EXISTENCE STATUS AND COGNITION

Talking of the ground of one's existence is usually difficult as such language is a rather exotic mode of narrative in Western (or indeed any) society (Heidegger, 1962/1927, p. 63). Nonetheless even though such intuitions might be seen, on casual inspection, as ineffable, they are not really totally beneath the reach of self-examination in the sense that they are not necessarily held down by a repressing force or truly beyond formulation in words. We can at least try. It is certainly feasible that usually unverbalised existential issues feed into and structure cognitions and behaviour at a more superficial level and hence there is ground where existential and cognitive investigators could meet.

To give examples of how this could operate: given that sufferers of paranoia tend to have parents who have little or no respect for them (see Chadwick, 1997a, p. 33), an idea also mentioned by Richard Bentall (Bentall, 2003b) – and disrespect feeds disloyalty – it is feasible that lacking basic feelings of worth, substance and safety would exacerbate threat sensitivity and expectations of 'implosion', 'invasion' and betrayal. These would create a rich source soil for suspiciousness and self-assertion difficulties. With a compromised feeling of actual presence in the world or of Self as a causal agent, the very coordination of cognitive processes themselves may also suffer. If the sense of Self is diaphanous, retrieval of self-referenced memories may be affected and decision making difficult. One cannot in an existential sense be 'authentic' if one does not feel 'there' *pari passu* to make a decision in any case.

In such a fragile, 'skinless' situation, as Virginia Woolf's father, the critic, biographer and philosopher Leslie Stephen (1832–1904), would put it, threat sensitivity will likely also accelerate consequence ('look ahead') processing, expectations of betrayal, speed of thought and cognitive impulsiveness. Also since our sense of Self very much depends on our perception of our own history, disruption of or lack of formation of a coherent and substantial sense of existence and personal reality is likely to compromise storage and recall processes. Indeed a range of processes, such as retrieval, arousal modulation, jumping to conclusions, sensory integration and Gestalten formation and pronoun comprehension, are often seen as 'fundamental' and hence perhaps mediated by basic genetic, biochemical and physiological factors. But top-down interference with them could still, in part, be a product of social and family stresses on existence status (see also Chadwick, 2006a on this). Laing (1990/1960, p. 196) presents an interesting example of how the divisions within, of a schizophrenia sufferer, into 'partial systems' or 'inner objects' affected her discourse planning to produce word-salad speech. Each 'assembly' within independently produced perhaps a word or a phrase so that put together linearly, the melange of resultant speech seemed (but only seemed) to make no sense.

EXISTENCE STATUS AND THE SELF

The philosophical underpinnings of existential therapy dispense with concepts of the Inner Self or the Real Self (van Deurzen-Smith, 1993, p. 152; Magee, 2001, p. 210) but doing so may be to 'logicise' the issue too much. Looking at the more rational, functional side of the Self: one tends to need a strong ego to immerse oneself in the rather nebulous 'all-is-movement'/'nothing is firm' theories of existentialism (and also those of social constructionism and of idealistic models of perception) while, in those fields, simultaneously (and amusingly) disclaiming the existence of ego in the first instance. This paradox I have always felt to be the height of irony when teaching these approaches to students. At the neurological level it may well be possible, I admit, to see the Self, and its defensive operations in the ego, as only confabulations to maintain personal integrity and central coherence but it does seem that to understand such things as organisation of cognitive processes, allocation and deployment of resources, effortful and control processes of all kinds, production system run-off, capacities to discount and reject stimuli and general withstanding of cognitive strain, we have to recognise that the Self is a genuine and active psychological mentalistic reality of complementary status, both noun and process, however much it can be deconstructed philosophically, logically or biologically. If one is brought up in a scenario where the implicit communication from a parent is 'I am, you are not', it is hardly likely that a full capacity to develop 'Thatness' to Self and hence move on and apprehend or intuit one's Real Self will be at all easily achieved – and this could have serious cognitive consequences. These very 'cognitive consequences' could also lead specifically to the emergence of psychotic phenomena (Green, 1996; Green et al., 2000; Marland, 2000). Hence existence status and the differentiation out of a sense of one's Real Self are potentially intimately related constructs. It may indeed not be possible for all psychosis sufferers to make optimal use of the usual forms of cognitive or narrative therapies unless they are supplemented with more fundamental work on their sense of existence status. Indeed barriers to the very emergence of the Real Self may involve self-damaging internal sentences and automatic thoughts such that there is a case for blending CBT with person-centred approaches.

'MIRRORING'

Psychosis sufferers often find other patients, who really do know far more how it feels to be them, helpful in their recovery but do not generally find this of psychiatrists (Rogers *et al.*, 1993). Doctors and patients, because of their totally different frames of reference and forms of life, often engage in 'dualogues' rather than dialogue – or, to put it more brutally (Chadwick, 1997b, p. 169): 'onanism for two'.

The sensitivity and perceptiveness of psychosis-prone people are often too fine-grained and fine-tuned and their feelings too chromatic for them to find easy and frequent mirroring of how they are from the people around them. Though Thatness precedes Whatness there is no doubt that finding 'correlation' of positive (and even negative) aspects of one's Whatness in valued and liked others outside oneself is a potent procedure for enhancing one's sense of 'the rightness to be'.

Often it is playwrights, poets and novelists who can provide, by what and the way they write, those precious moments of mirroring, namely: 'Yes, I've felt that too!' or 'Ah! At last somebody else has noticed that!' whereas, at worst among crass and boorish people, sensitives are left to dwell only in their own world (Aron, 1999).

I cannot see how nourishing mirroring work can be done by therapists with such people unless therapists themselves are free to reveal a considerable amount of their own thoughts, feelings and experiences. Adopting a remote impersonal, scientific attitude with the clients' experiences as a source of to-be-tested hypotheses is simply not appropriate in dyadic work of this kind. It may even be that the usual large sample nomothetic research often done by therapist-researchers in psychology and psychiatry will not actually help them experientially in such finely differentiated phenomenological explorations. Large sample research, like politics, axiomatically ignores the nuance and the N = 1 situation does not count, for many such people, as 'evidence'. Bringing Whatness-into-being with psychotic clients, however, is very much about the nuance. Bringing this up in a group once, a man concurring with my reservations about the mass population research attitude, and the way it can numb sensitivity to subtlety, said, 'Yes, they don't look *at* you, they look right past you!'

The issue of therapist mirroring is more accented in more intimate, emotive therapies such as Gestalt, drama therapy, Eriksonian therapy and psychoanalysis but, life being what it is, this is more capricious and unpredictable a phenomenon that any texts tend to reveal. A very over-intellectualised man who in our group said back in 1993, 'I'm not born yet!' (something I rather felt myself back in 1977) lost this feeling and 'came into the world' as personally real after a long-longed for intense romantic and sexual relationship. The change in the 'music' of his personality was very noticeable and has not changed since despite the relationship becoming more distant in recent times. Clearly solutions like that are for the theatre of life, not the crucible of the consulting room. The therapist is a messenger of social life as he or she has known it but cannot be the flux of life itself.

This section has tried to deal with perhaps *the* fundamental experiential question. Do you feel that you have the right to be, to live, to exist, to move around, eat, drink and breathe *just for being you*? Not for what you can do, achieve, earn, own or how good you look but have you the right to be in this world at all and partake in any way whatsoever in what it has to offer, just for the intimate, private quality that is you as a being? It may be difficult to imagine that, for some people, it is virtually unthinkable to react to such a challenge in the affirmative. The therapeutic demand here is not the usual range of issues of existential therapy or CBT but the establishment of the person's very sense of being. It may be, in some cases if not all, that only if we can do this will we protect a person from falling victim to psychotic episodes in the very long term. My purpose here has been to address this problem in a functional and experiential rather than philosophical way and to argue that Laing's insights on this are not defunct in the modern age and access a level of understanding relatively neglected in contemporary academic treatises on psychosis.

THERAPY: PSYCHODYNAMICS AND SPIRITUAL ISSUES

In the voluminous literature on schizophrenia it is very difficult to find positive conceptualisations about sufferers, although generally the latter's proactive attempts to manage and cope with their experiences are recognised (Strauss, 1989, 1994). But as in the psychological study of memory and language in the elderly (Coupland and Coupland, 1990; Cohen, 1992) the laboratory paradigms, often operative, focus on deficits and departures from criterion and, of course, find them – to the extent that they under-rate, as the above authors state, the performances of participants in real life situations. In schizophrenia research, research on latent inhibition (e.g. Williams, 1996), which means inhibition of attention to an irrelevant stimulus, is found to be 'poor' or 'weak' in schizotypy and schizophrenia. However, such a tendency is liable to lead to a previously irrelevant stimulus being more available to consciousness on a future occasion when it becomes 'relevant' (Claridge, 1988). This clearly could have advantages for learning and for the richness of ideation and creativity (see Eysenck, 1995 on this).

Many psychodynamic practitioners for example, as sufferers in my own cohort attest, tend to see schizophrenia as a flight from reality whereas it often can be an occasion for actually confronting head-on one's deepest inner fears. In another sense, as both Freud (1911) and Bleuler realised (1955/1911), delusion is a way of creating an organised pattern of thought that prevents deeper emptiness and further derangement. Some patients themselves realise this (Roberts, 1991).

Psychotherapy and psychodynamic organisation (though not the mental health culture in general) disadvantage themselves from the outset by refusing even to consider for training people who have had serious mental health problems such as schizophrenia. This invariably leads to these fields being populated by personnel, in the domain of psychosis, who are talking of things of which they have no experience. Nonetheless, inasmuch as a capacity, at least to some degree, for psychosis is there in all of us, it does seem that practitioners do take advantage to utilise (and I would say bravely on their part) their own latent insanity genuinely to empathise with the psychic forces operative in schizophrenia sufferers (e.g. Federn, 1934; 1977; Bion, 1954, 1955, 1956, 1957, 1967; Winnicott, 1965; Searles, 1963, 1965, 1979; Segal, 1973; Kernberg, 1986).

In the 1980s and 1990s, however, the situation for psychotherapeutic and psychoanalytic approaches to schizophrenia was dire (Lehman and Steinwachs, 1998). It was said informally that such 'uncovering' and 'ventilationist' strategies were like sending a tsunami into a coastal town previously devastated by a hurricane. Mueser and Berenbaum (1990) after reflecting on the outcome evidence, argued that psychodynamic approaches to schizophrenia should at least temporarily be *banned* because of their harmful effects (see also Klerman, 1984).

Now in the latter half of the 2000s the predicaments of sufferers is being eased by practitioners realising that medication does have a part to play in psychological therapy (Busch and Sandberg, 2007) and also by advances in general knowledge in the broad schizophrenia field (Hirsch and Weinberger, 2003). An important advance, following insights by Freud (1940) and Bion (1957), was made by Molden (1964) who realised that the Jungian conception of schizophrenia as a distortion of the whole personality was questionable and that some areas of the psyche of the psychotic client are healthy and can be worked with to make inroads on the central problems. This was an approach also utilised by CBT practitioners (Kingdon and Turkington, 1994; P.D.J. Chadwick *et al.*, 1996). Recent meta-analytic research (Gottdiener, 2004) also reveals that the evaluations of the 1980s and 1990s may have been unduly pessimistic. In an analysis of 37 outcome studies it was found that psychodynamic psychotherapy was as effective as CBT and, surprisingly, that psychotherapy with medication was no more and no less effective than without medication. Apparent therapeutic success in the psychoanalytic treatment of psychosis also has been reported by Rosenfeld (1965) and Robbins (1993). It would seem that cynicism about this approach is not a fair or justified attitude, although it may be patients who are less ill and have more insight who are considered more suitable for such depth approaches.

The general openness of psychodynamic therapies (see Milton *et al.*, 2004) to many fields of knowledge, particularly biology and evolutionary psychology, philosophy and linguistics and in recent years to spirituality and to the findings of developmental psychologists, cognitive neuroscientists and empirical methodology is, I feel, encouraging (see particularly the integrative work of Schore, 1994; Solms, 1995 and Kaplan-Solms and Solms, 2000). There also is a burgeoning integrative psychotherapy movement (e.g. Alford and Beck, 1997; Anderson, 2007) and the present era does not, therefore, seem to be a time for therapeutic parochialism. Psychodynamics has also (see Milton *et al.*, 2004) been permeable to endeavours such as system theory, cybernetics and social constructionism while CBT also has incorporated imagery-based ideas from Gestalt therapy (Edwards, 1989, 1990) and adopted the unconditional positive regard therapeutic stance characteristic of person-centred therapy (see approaches in Morrison, 2002). Work applying empirical methods from experimental psychology to psychoanalysis has been ongoing for some time (e.g. Dixon, 1981; Kline, 1981). This encouragement of diversity in psychodynamics and also in CBT augurs well for their future – and the future of their hybrid, cognitive-analytic therapy (CAT) (Ryle, 1990). The formulation approach in clinical psychology also welcomes and encourages multiple perspectives to be drawn on case study material (Johnstone and Dallos, 2006).

The utilisation of the therapists' multidimensional subjectivities in therapy, a development in so-called relational psychoanalysis (Mitchell *et al.*, 2007), is an extremely promising advance which clients who have suffered psychosis are likely to welcome. The approach, as its practitioners admit, requires considerable courage in the therapist in an endeavour where therapist subjectivity at least in the early days of the endeavour had to fight for recognition of its vital importance. The insights of Searles (1963, 1965, 1974) to the effect that schizophrenia sufferers' critical problem is a failure in identity formation open a door between psychoanalytic and existential approaches to psychosis (see Silver *et al.*, 2004 for an overview of psychodynamic approaches to psychosis).

Spiritual issues and mystical insights, which have been dealt with in a positive light in the course of this text, are, of course, domains of experience which relate more to the concepts and approaches of Jungian analytical psychology than to those of the main schools of psychoanalysis. Before the 1980s, psychoanalytic psychiatry was unjustifiably scornful of such experiences (see the critical review of such work by Deikmann, 1977) as merely manifestations of regression to infantile states. Detailed reports on mystical states (e.g. Deikmann, 1966; Chadwick 1992 (Chapter 4) and Appendix I in this volume) show, however, that these involve profound and complex, mature experiences that need explaining rather than explaining away. The well-recognised high reliability of introspective reports of mystical states also shows that they are quintessentially human experiences of importance and not to be reduced to individual escapist pathology (see also Chapter 7). The artist William Blake always saw such experiences as not a 'cloudy vapour' but organised and minutely articulated, as he used to put it, 'beyond anything that the perishing nature can produce' (see also Chadwick, 1996, 2000, 2004d on this).

Much neglected but, in fact, pioneering work on the relations between the spiritual and the psychotic was done by Boisen (1947, 1952) and this perspective on therapy and mental health problems is now a vibrant research area

(West, 2000; Clarke, 2001; Barker and Buchanan-Barker, 2003; Kliewer and Saulty, 2005; Lines, 2006; Pargament, 2007; Cobb and Roberts, 2007). People's perspectives at the individual level on spirituality itself are, of course, highly variable. In the context of the present text, Desmond Marshall (see Chapter 8) always refuses to pin down spirituality with a concise verbal definition but instead sees it basically as facilitating his life *interpersonally* by catalysing a loving attitude in himself to life, the world and other people. He does not want to relate to a doctrine but simply leaves it as that which makes him more compassionate, forgiving and open to the world. This generally also was Ivo Wiesner's approach. This importance of spirituality in enhancing a loving and caring attitude interpersonally, and hence the transcending of the Self, is a critical dimension. Many artists, such as Edward Hopper and Frida Kahlo (Kettenmann, 2002; Herrera, 2003), have adopted a similar attitude (see Chadwick, 2004b, 2008).

The emphases, Self to World, on transcendence of the Self and, World to Self, on being open to forces from beyond oneself, however one construes this, are emphases at the heart, I would claim, of what most people mean by the spiritual attitude. It is a two-way process although interpretive perspectives on what actually is meant by 'the beyond' are, of course, variable. The nature mystic who feels resonant to all that is, has a regard quite different to the spiritualist trying to reach his or her 'spirit guide' while the more individually minded psychologist trying to engage with their 'Higher Self' is different again. In my own case my attempts to have a meaningful, positive and fulfilling relationship with God have been at the very heart of my efforts to get well again as was my dreadful casual but negative relationship with Him, when I was young, at the heart of my psychotic illness. After I survived my fourth suicide attempt (see Chapters 5 and 6) it seemed to me, as it did to most of the people who knew me at that time, that 'it wasn't my time to die'. God must, so I thought, have kept me alive for a reason and indeed I have always felt that my life, as Freud would put it, of 'love and work' since that time has indeed been fulfilling God's purpose. In a sense, once I felt that God did *love* me and did care about me, and that my life had some value, point, purpose and meaning, my cognitive processes at least to some degree somehow 'clicked into place'. This also, as Kierkegaard would expect, has strengthened me in an existential sense as I no longer feel that I have to apologise to the world for existing at all or feel (as I did before) that I have some kind of negative effect on existence itself. This has all changed the kind of 'internal sentences' and indeed the whole cognitive architecture that I have within about myself and the general patterning of my daily cognitive life. Clearly those interested in the spiritual, the existential and the cognitive do have ground where they can meet and talk meaningfully to each other. It would be wrong, however, for any of them to feel that they have 'the whole answer' to mental health problems.

The very experiential ambience of the feeling of being open to forces from beyond myself was, however, critical to those cognitive and existential changes. The effects were, as we say, 'top-down' so if my relationship with God had been examined in CBT, which is perfectly possible in this form of therapy, it could not have been examined only as a constellation of cognitions had this 'openness to the beyond' not been accepted and validated by the therapist. Again one has to ask, 'What is a human mind that it can have spiritual experiences?' and why, over the tens of millennia, have these been so vital and important to us?

Psychoanalytic thinking on these issues, far from being irrelevant, is I think important, particularly for getting rid of neurotic distortions in one's relationship with God, for example unconsciously (and childishly) blending Him with 'daddy' or with one's internal representation of one's school headmaster, or judging His powers of love, forgiveness, understanding and compassion by merely human standards or forgetting that God sees things not from 'outside eyes' (like a neighbourhood gossip) but through *your* eyes. This is not to undervalue work that one can do intrapsychically on oneself, for example in self-forgiveness (see Gallant, 2005; Worthington, 2005) and alternative narrative construction (Hinshelwood, 2004), as such changes mentalistically, in my view, allow genuine spiritual forces to work through one and on one in a more powerful and positive way (see also Chapter 9 on Ivo Wiesner on this). Strengthening and nourishing psychodynamic work focusing on relatedness, integration, transcendence as well as the self-acceptance of one's negative side can have enormous spiritual consequences. In this conceptualisation the physical, mental and spiritual are an interactive, permeable three-level system (Chadwick, 2005b) and all three levels have existence status. (Materialists might argue about the existence status of the mental and spiritual but then what would they say of the existence status of the past or the future or, indeed, of mathematics? See Sider, 2005; Chadwick, 2004a.) On this three-level view, even medication, in changing the configuration of one's brain processes and mental processes, can have spiritual consequences. The same could be true of CBT. Hence on this perspective, though I admit that this idea will be monstrous to materialists and to totally intrapsychic thinkers, very powerful, illicit drugs such as cocaine and heroin, in catastrophically influencing brain processes, do very feasibly facilitate the 'permeability' of the person to negative, and highly deceiving, spiritual forces (to say nothing of what they likely do to cognitive and psychodynamic factors).

The blending of the cognitive, the psychodynamic, the existential and the spiritual is an approach I have found of immense therapeutic yield. The relative compartmentalisation of these domains of study in the academy is very regrettable. However, the burgeoning integrative psychotherapy movement is one of great promise and theoretically there are no totally insurmountable barriers to it. This short chapter tries to present some 'bridges of hope' between these endeavours.

Chapter 14

Conclusions and overview

The context, as for the eventuation of a body's inertia, is infinite. In interpretation use all that you are and resonate to all that is, maybe not only across space but across time. This is how analysis is truly guided.

We are all so much more than that which we think we are. In the 1980s when Jill and I were living in West London, there was a terraced house near to Baron's Court tube station that had no curtains on the ground floor front window. The walls inside were all covered with floor-to-ceiling stacked bookcases. But once I had a dream that we were walking past, I glanced in and in the dream they were all, instead, covered with beautiful abstract paintings. When I awoke I realised that really I had *created* those paintings myself in my dreamwork, via my own unconscious self-organising processes. Yet no way could I create them in my usual conscious waking state. For that one would need a Malevich (Néret, 2002) or a Kandinsky (Robinson, 2006). This is our problem as human beings, realising what is within us, reaching this – what I call – Lower Level or the Deep Music. Reaching down and accessing 'The Ocean' within. There is *so much* there, but usually we just cannot reach it.

On a sadder note: there is an old saying (in fact known as Zymurgy's law) that once you open a can of worms, and one certainly does this in a schizophrenic episode, you can only recan them using a larger can (Bloch, 1979, p. 25). This is the challenge that faces a person trying truly to get better again after schizophrenia. It is not only a matter of taking a pill or getting one's thinking more rational, it is the task of nourishing the Self and becoming more and more what one is.

Education, of one kind or another, is vital in this. Lecturers who say to students, 'There must be nothing of *you* in the essay, stick to the facts' are only 'instructors' or 'trainers', they are not educators. Education is about bringing out from within, it is about self-realisation and self-fulfilment.

In recovery, patients do generally want to know about the causes of their illness, not only 'how to get out of it', although the latter tends to be the focus of professionals. In 'getting one's mind around' the crisis one has to learn more about oneself, and indeed life, and realise capacities (and limitations) one was blind to before. All of this in a real sense is still 'education'.

In this book I have talked a great deal about causes (particularly in the form of vulnerabilities acted upon by stress), about coping and about recovery. But there are certain meta-themes which do dominate. Firstly I have tried to blend atmospherics with practicality, to show some measure of vision whilst simultaneously being grounded enough to cope with 'life in the body'. In doing this I also have tried to show that mystical ideas are illuminating and nourishing to our understanding of reality and of other domains of experience such as the psychotic. They are not, as often they are regarded as being, 'theoretically useless'.

Secondly the ambience of the book has been integrative. I have tried to show the connections between schizophrenic experience and normal experience, indeed the very normality of madness; between the mystical and the psychotic; between the social and the cognitive; between the spiritual, existential, psychoanalytic and the cognitive and how all factors from the biological to the socio-economic are relevant to understanding and to recovery. I have, however, seen schizophrenia as a genuine *illness* in which a concatenation of essentially normal processes, in some exaggerated measure, come together in a toxic way.

Thirdly, and related to the above, I have avoided, or tried to avoid, writing from any one conceptual 'box'. Sadly the logistics of both the academy and the publishing industry tends to work against the integration of knowledge. One tends to have to be 'in a single category' and be a representative of 'a certain perspective'. So, for example, if one's agent sends around a proposal to publishers for a book entitled *Oscar Wilde – Psychologist* or *Psychology as an Art*, all such efforts, as I have found, fall between two stools as the publishers lack a singular box for them. Publishing psychological research in the journals of another subject also produces few, if any, Cubs badges or Brownie points for the research careers of academics. As this text reveals, I always have had, for better or for worse, this integrative, cross-disciplinary spirit but, fortunately, most of my efforts of this kind have eventually reached the printed page (e.g. Chadwick, 1976, 2001a, 2005a). Box thinking seems to be centrally about power and hence is a political stance. It is not in the spirit of *scientia*, true knowledge seeking, and has an unsettling pre-emptive quality about it in the hands of some.

Fourthly I have tried to maintain a positive, constructive and optimistic outlook throughout, without trying to make things look more positive than they are and without being blind to the difficulties and suffering involved in schizophrenic illness. Certainly schizophrenia can kill people; generally one in four sufferers attempts suicide and one in eight succeeds. Sufferers are far more a threat to themselves than to anybody else. But I remember from my days as a field geologist doing the mapping for my first PhD in Glencoe and Ballachulish, in the mountains of the southwest Highlands of Scotland, that thinking of *mountains* in that threat-sensitive way in no respect encouraged resolve or determination. Mountains do kill climbers but one has to keep going and harping on about the negative and the dangers, in the context of either mountain climbing or this illness, is demoralising. Indeed it is demoralising not only for patients but for staff.

As part of this positive perspective I have argued, like Laing, for the 'understandability' and narrative sense in psychosis (see e.g. Chadwick (2007d) on the supposedly 'ununderstandable' sign of psychosis of laughing at a funeral, usually taken to be an instance of organically based incongruity of affect). In this text we see also how seemingly 'psychotic' ways of being are acceptable in certain contexts (e.g. p. 129) and also the positive yield, particularly for creativity and spiritual sensitivity, of the schizophrenic pre-disposition. Delusion can indeed be the release of a fiction-making capacity (Chadwick 2005c).

Kandinsky (1982/1922) always saw the spiritual as a matter of tuning in to ever more subtle feelings and emotions. For Hindus of course (Burke, 2004) this is simultaneously tuning in to 'the presence of God within'. It may be that psychotics' cognitions of a spiritual nature and about reality are not always as deranged as psychiatrists habitually take them to be. Indeed, even in an everyday sense, there have been a number of reported cases where paranoid delusions have proved true or partly true (Lemert, 1962; Sagan, 1977, p. 181; Mayerhoff *et al.*, 1991; Chadwick, 1995b, pp. 15–16). Where delusions overlap with mystical and preternatural cognitions, it may be that the very 'open filter', as Aldous Huxley would describe it, of the psychotic mind in those states can apprehend things that the relatively narrow aware-ness of everyday consciousness simply is unable to grasp. This 'open filter' state, I admit, does carry many dangers, both emotionally and practically, as people in such a mode of awareness may have terrible difficulty relating to the trivia of everyday affairs. The chapters on Desmond and Ivo are critical here as they show how both have learned to modulate and regulate this state so as still to be able to go about mundane daily routines.

As in creative work, which often involves many different forms of mental attunement, the ability voluntarily to move from one mode to another is essential and indeed a developed skill (Martindale, 1975; Martindale and Armstrong, 1974). Being able to 'open the filter out' to achieve cosmic con-sciousness is good, but one still needs to be able to close it down, to varying degrees, as well.

Fifthly this text has definitely *not* been anti-psychiatry in spirit although I have had my tongue-in-cheek moans about 'mania diagnosia' (p. 135) and 'mania psychoanalytica' (p. 13) (see Galvin, 1989 also on the latter). I know that it is only by being mindful of the biomedical, psychological, psycho-social and spiritual perspectives that I have been able to have a productive life at all and hence I have tried to show respect for all the approaches whilst at the same time recognising the limitations of any one 'box'. A large number of writers and researchers of anti-psychiatry orientation never seem to stop to think for a moment what effects their comments have on psychiatrists and psychiatric nurses – who themselves receive very little gratitude from psychotic patients for what they do (see Hinshelwood, 2004, Chapter 1 on this). Vitriolic anti-psychiatry thinkers seem to feel that personnel in the biomedical domain are 'made of iron' (or of stone) and can 'take anything'. I know from psychiatric nurses I have taught that seeing a patient readmitted is a demoralising, sad and disappointing experience for them in a job where thanks from patients are few and far between. In addition, successful cases, because they are not readmitted, they often never hear of again. This easily biases their perception of schizophrenia further to the negative. Labouring usually under very limited budgets and resources, they still go into work every day and face as best they can the difficulties presented by patients on the wards. These people can not 'take anything' and they are not 'made of iron'. In this context I would like therefore, in print, to express my gratitude here to the professionals in London who set me on the path to complete recovery from schizophrenia: Steven Hirsch, Geetha Oomen, Peter Storey and Malcolm Weller (psychiatrists) and Frank Burke, Karen Leason, Dave Salisbury and Ruth Shippey (residential social workers). Given that my research also was immensely educative and therapeutic, I would also express my gratitude to Gordon Claridge, the late Hans Eysenck and Brian Foss and also my PhD supervisor John Wilding (for an excellent blending of human science and spirituality see Wilding and Boaden, 2005).

Sixthly I have done my best to show the profit of research and thinking by someone who is both a professional and a former patient and hence also of interactions I have had with people in 'status-level' situations. This 'peer-professional' or 'service user-academic' identity I am hoping will validate itself via having a perspective on mental health problems which blends the objective and the subjective while being less formal and impersonal than the more usual, rather dry, purely professional narratives. Sometimes things can only be discovered by people who have 'been there'. Also there is obviously going to be a realness and immediacy that an insider's narrative on schizophrenia can provide that one could not expect of that of an outsider. This, of course, can help to make for easier and clearer understanding in the reader.

I have written this book as a Pantheist not a materialist and I thereby see God and consciousness as in all and through all. Seeing psyche as both mind and spirit I regard reality, as did Wolfgang Pauli, as psychophysical and symbolic not just 'a domain of things'. This triad of the physical, the mental and the spiritual I take to be imbricated into all that is, objects, flora and fauna, both everywhere and everywhen. It has been a corollary of this book that this triadic, symbolic, psycho-physical view of reality is available to people at the outer reaches, if not in the safe valley, of human thought and experience.

Atheistic materialism has been powerfully attacked in recent years

(McGrath and McGrath, 2007; Watts and Dutton, 2006). The present book I believe breaks new ground and takes us beyond atheistic fundamentalism to the apprehension of a tangibly meaningful universe. In no sense, however, as cynics and sceptics might expect, is it written in a dramatic, or 'hot', psychological state. I can assure cynics that every chapter here has been written in essential tranquillity, as they should be. Vitality must co-exist with discipline and calm reflection. This was, in essence, 'a project'; I now move on to other projects such as the relations specifically between meanings and causes (see Chadwick, 2007a) and on arousal modulation in psychotics, in the latter case revisiting an old paradigm (see Claridge, 1967; Lapidus and Schmolling, 1975 on such matters).

Many people reading this book will be students of either psychiatry, psychology, psychotherapy, psychoanalysis or psychiatric social work. The broad integrative discourse that threads its way through the whole text, and that I hope you have been and will be nourished by, is this blending of science with insights and approaches from art and spirituality. Life is underdetermined by theory, it is bigger than reason and psychology is bigger than science. Mind is forever more than a representation of what we take to be reality. That is how our thinking moves forward beyond any contemporary view of what is. Many people think that science is coming to a close, once the problems (now) of quantum gravity and consciousness are solved, science will have 'cracked it'. We will have the essential understanding of mind and cosmos. There was a similar bullishness at the end of the nineteenth century that evaporated in the heat of contributions by Einstein (himself, I'm pleased to say, also a Pantheist) and the quantum physicists such as Bohr, Schrödinger and Pauli. I call this bullishness 'The Triumphant Generation Illusion', i.e. 'These problems have been there in the past but WE, *our* generation, will solve them and bring closure to knowledge'. I don't believe it for a moment as every solution or partial solution to a problem opens up ever more new questions. The funnel of the knowledge game is forever directed outwards, not to an apex. Students of today can march forward, not to an ending, but to an infinite sequence of new beginnings.

As closing thoughts for student readers: do not be frightened by this book and its talk of extreme states to think what you take to be The Impossible, it is one of humanity's greatest assets. Don't work either simply under the pressure of ambition, be true to your *talents*, not your ambitions. Always be guided by vitality and passion, including the vitality that precedes knowledge, and – whatever chaos is around you – always march to your own distant drummer.

Appendix I

Borderline thinking: mysticism as 'supersanity'

The man who is nobody . . . is everybody

This first appendix gives the best rendering I have managed to create of the 1979 'Borderline' experience which immediately predated my own psychotic episode in the summer of that year. It gives the ideation in full that led to the concepts of The Zone of Potential and The Zone of Actuality and that led to the insight replication of Jung's concepts of 'the psychoid' and 'the continuum'. I am sorry to disappoint seekers after facts but I have to say that it deals more with the 'thatness' of movement than the 'whatness' of things. It may be, though controversial, that this zone of experience does more reliably permit paranormal and supernatural events, particularly through the total dissolving of the boundary between within and without. Such states alas also make a person far more vulnerable to the delusional and hallucinatory symptoms of psychosis when, as eventually happened here, psychic organisation breaks down – particularly under the pressure of self-doubt (Chadwick, 2001c).

The appendix shows how the seeds of the Borderline concept grew out of my 1970s research on cognitive biases, which was part of my work on human factors in science. It led to the view that analytical rationality may be, in a profound sense, itself illusory, if psychically 'safe' for the integrity of identity.

When I went to London in October 1978 ('spirit freed') my psychological research had been, until then, entirely mechanistic and analytical. I had read neither Pauli nor Progoff and had only smatterings of Heidegger and Husserl. My knowledge of Jung was largely restricted to realising that he had introduced the terms 'extravert' and 'introvert' into the psychological literature, had done some interesting reaction-time experiments and had noticed that psychasthenic neurotics (what we now call 'dysthymics') tended to be introverted, hysterics more extraverted. All else, so I thought, was 'Jungian mumbo jumbo'. Being still a philistine I had also read nothing of mysticism, not even William James's important views on it (James, 1936; Knight, 1954, pp. 206–14), and if anyone had asked me what the *I Ching* was I probably would have guessed that it was a Chinese restaurant off the Earls Court Road.

I was determined, however, to use my counselling work – and my own, always ongoing, self-analysis – as an arena in which to develop and use my ideas about biases in human thought itself. My intellectual adventure was in part in search of a way to bootstrap myself past my own thinking biases. I felt that to 'see' mind I had, without drugs, to somehow get outside myself and 'look back'. By jolting myself out of my habitual ways of living into a quite different style of life, I thought I might see the chains that previously had bound my thinking and limited my vision.

By May or June 1979, insights about biases in thought began to coalesce. I started, in a staccato fashion at first, to write and think myself into what to me was a 'new attitude of mind'. Central to this attitude was a notion about what a truly liberated person would be. I called this person-of-the-future a 'Borderline Normal' for want of any better phrase. The most easily communicable feature of Borderliners was ambiguity. They were both good and bad, masculine and feminine, strong and weak, active and passive, etc. In a sense they lived between the opposites and transcended them. They had no one specific personality (or in artificial intelligence (AI) terms, 'subroutine'); their identity lay at the level of process (in AI terms at the level of the 'computational system'). The Borderliner had dispensed with ego, was not oriented towards the world in a focused, competitive or analytical way or in terms of a role or an identity. The Borderliner just 'was'. The Borderline state was a floating state of being with all that is. Having dispensed with ego, content jettisoned, *process* all important, the Borderliner was 'personified process'.

While regarding the Borderliner as an ideal, I tried to identify with it, reach to it, realise it in action. Always the emphasis was on process and ambiguity and the transcendence of it. Quoting from now on from my journal of the day, the latter emphasis was reflected in statements such as:

> The Borderliner both happens to be and chooses to be . . . is subject and object . . . is a coherent pattern of eventuated opposites . . . is the basic generalised person.

The emphasis on process was reflected in my belief that the Borderliner could only be evaluated in terms of the 'how' or 'in what manner' they did (and in particular *loved*), not in terms of 'what'.

> The Borderliner is process integrated or process useful, process practised. The integration is *that* the machinery is working well and ticking over. The integration is the tuning of the parts to do the job, the Borderliner's personality is well tuned, the integration is not *in* the job that the

parts do, it is not in the whatness of the parts . . . Hence the integration of the Borderline person is analogous to the process play of science in action over time.

The Normal sees the world through adjective and noun coloured spectacles, summing people up with nouns as integers, adjectives as fractions and conjunctions as addition signs . . . The Borderliner is probably most accurately perceived with infinitives and gerunds, hence the Normal's bewilderment – his apparatus just cannot handle the job.

In my view the structure of language had strangled our thinking. (I wrote that 'The Borderliner does not belong, not even to language'.) Rational man thought in terms of Subject (Self or *res cogitans*) operating on the world (Object or *res extensa*) with all reality characterised as atomised into dimensions with positive and negative poles such as More–Less, Good–Bad, Strong–Weak, and so on. The basic code of the mind was:

$$+$$
$$S \quad O$$
$$-$$

In this psychic condition I felt as if I was hovering conceptually away from the usual modes of mental life. If it was, as it is, functional to think in terms of Subject and Object both characterised in terms of the positive and the negative, then this basic 'mind code' was actually retreating from me. I saw it not as 'the true way' to think and be but as a shared bias. Where *I* was lay back of this, in an, at times, terrifying, undifferentiated realm. I was conceptually and experientially drifting away from life, away from the mode in which even space and time themselves are meaningful. I was moving experientially into 'the elsewhere'.

The Borderliner, however, lived, as I have said, in the middle ground between opposites and yet transcended them:

> The Borderline thinker sees the reality which the contrasts we usually deal with are merely differentiates of. Hence the Borderliner is the fluid reality between the concrete dogmatic reality of appearances.

In my own abstruse way I was viewing the Borderliner as in touch with the ground, the ground or 'All' which lay behind the naively accepted reality of everyday life. This is, although I did not realise it at the time, similar to the Buddhist concept of the Tao, if not exactly that.

The Borderliner was not just a mediator or a reflector, however, he was very much in action in the world, living as I put it at 'the point of potential to kinetic conversion', accessing the ground but effective and efficient in everyday life.

The Borderliner's resting state is at the potential to kinetic conversion – the sparking point, the contact point, between the inertia of the ground and the blinkered unreflective state of figure.

In this context the Eriksonian concept of an identity (Erikson, 1950) obviously was a naïve capitulation. Identity was a restriction, a narrowing down from the truly rich array of infinite potentialities available to person. Ego, content, identity and language were all snares; the human person in all his or her perfection was behind all these:

> The Borderliner attempts to be himself. The Normal role plays a pattern which weaves together all the positive poles of word-opposites that language has crystallised out for us and which trap us. The Normal then re-presents a 'good' image of himself to himself – he shuttles the bad away, inside or out into others. The Borderliner holds back from falling victim to language, he lives tersely in the opposites, accepting himself as himself.

My 'point of potential to kinetic conversion' is clearly identical with Jung's 'psychoid state' where psychological events are incompletely differentiated out from what he called 'the continuum' – there the psychic and the physical are no longer differentiated from one another. For Jung, 'psychoid' is 'touching the undifferentiated state of nature' (Progoff, 1973, p. 157). This was my 'All' or 'Ground'.

Thinking and feeling in this way I experienced the whole of rational thought as an illusion. The division of subject 'directed' to finding out about Objects or other Subjects usually construed in bipolar dimensions was a mistake. The Truth that I felt I had discovered was that these were the structuring rules of rational mind, it was how rational mind *had* to think in order to have any purchase on the world in the first instance. And yet this was a bias, the true 'reality' behind all this was undifferentiated.

There was also the sense, not only of 'not belonging to language' and hence to categories, but of not even belonging to any one place or time:

> The Borderliner is both behind the lens and in the scene he is taking.

> Too early, too late mean nothing too. The Borderliner is both out of date and premature, out of time and in it. Seen *as* failing/succeeding, 'chequered in career'.

> Triumph and Disaster – do not characterise the Borderliner's life from the inside. The Borderliner has nowhere to fall and nowhere to go 'up in the world' to. There is no room beneath a Borderliner, and the room above is empty.

The state of mind I experienced when reaching to these insights for the first time was one of vulnerability, yet of power. A feeling of passivity yet of activity. The insights had a quality of certainty, of absolute validity, which was beyond all question. My mind felt perfectly clear, as if psychically I could see to infinity. Rather than insanity, it was a superlative form of sanity. Unknowingly I had, of course, accessed a transcendent mystical state. Analysis and mechanics had been replaced by atmospherics and insight.

In this state there was a great sense of the unity of all things, time had no meaning; in the ground all opposites disappeared, all contrasts faded away, all difference and particularity was a consequence of being or actuality.

As the full force of these insights impressed itself upon me, words became increasingly difficult to find to describe the experience. Indeed, in the act of verbalising the state would be transiently lost. I wrote of 'throwing thoughts sling-like into the domain' but never being able to sit in it. As the Chinese philosopher Lao-tzu said: 'He who knows does not speak; he who speaks does not know'.

As my thinking became less verbal, journal entries decreased. Having used words as ladders into the Borderline domain I essentially and eventually merged amoeba-like with it. It is interesting that when attempting to write or verbally think myself into the state where the essence of Borderlining would be captured, I experienced a strange alternation between feelings of great clarity of my body boundary and an irrational fear that if I ever did fully capture the essence in language, indeed any language, I would, the moment I moved beyond the last word or equation, actually *disappear* (!). I therefore gave up language. I moved without explicitly knowing how or why I was moving.

In this psychic zone 'at the point of potential to kinetic conversion' I was in touch, so I felt, with an all-embracing, awe-inspiring force. The keyboard of my mind was immense and stretched out before me. I knew that if I could play it I could do or be anything (the Borderliner 'severalises the Self'). Great 'energy' surged through me. I oscillated between a state of exaltation to the greatest heights and a state of condemnation to awesome depths. A great truth had been revealed to me. I felt 'not of this world'. There was a sense of unearthly joy. I would walk miles in exhilaration, head-on driving rain did not deter me. When I tried as best I could to explain how I was feeling to a friend, he said, 'You're like a cylinder open at both ends'. Indeed this was so, feelings of saintliness and union with the cosmos alternated with feelings of possession by demonic forces and of being a *channel*, for both good and evil to come into the world. With the loss of ego and identity my feeling was that of being a vehicle. There was, to me, no doubt that what was happening was in some sense real and important.

It was also not surprising that at this fount I eventually came to feel in touch with 'a presence', an awe-inspiring force, which existed, now, as if behind a thin membrane. Any sense of ego or identity was gone, my existence was 'vehicular'. Psychosis this was not, at least not yet. For example, there was no Messiah delusion: 'A Christ could be said to *accompany* the world, but not a Borderliner', I penned. But there was nonetheless a sense of unearthly knowledge and of joy that pervaded me at this time – objectivity and ecstasy were now fused. My religiosity, such as it was, was magnified a thousandfold. The Lord's Prayer resonated and thundered through my mind. I felt I had been given a spiritual mission of the utmost importance. I could 'see to infinity'. I had reached a zone where 'the life system' was strangely making contact, through me, with 'the not-of-this-life system' – as indeed maybe it was.

I felt most at peace and 'together' when lying on my back in the park at night gazing up at a star-spangled sky with which I was at one. Yet unlike a Zen meditator who may have similar experiences in a state of tranquillity and low arousal I had accessed this domain in great agitation. As Albertus Magnus emphasised, a state of mental excess, in my case due to intense abstract thinking and extreme sensuality, may help open the door to magical and mystical experiences, and it did.

In these obscure journal writings I was probing in order to characterise a state, which I felt to be extant, of being outside time and space, beyond language, beyond social conventions, beyond all arbitrary rules. I was seeking 'the ground' out of which these are merely differentiates or exudates. Where 'I' therefore existed, in existing in the world at all, was not even inside my own head; it was in a realm or point between the zone of *potential* and the zone of *actuality*.

Had I been less aroused and agitated, if I had in everyday language 'kept my cool', I would have realised that I had discovered also a level of cognitive engineering that characterises not only the mystic but also *the actor*. There was no doubt that (like my grandfather and my mother, from whom I had probably inherited the capacity) I was an actor but on the community stage. I had been using the hardware of the neural networks of my brain to create something beyond myself. I was creating fictions and in creating fictions I was myself, even though the products were constructions. Where *I* lay was in the construction process between potentiality and actuality, between the organic ground and the communal social figure. Indeed the actor is *real* in the process of creation of his or her image. The actor's identity is in the *process*, not the product. Through our masks we are our most true. But somehow I could not see this. It was there for the taking, a genuinely original insight – that the mystic and the actor are psychologically related – but I let it slip through my fingers.

Instead my attributions, in my dilapidated state, had to be more spectacular than this, more self-inflatory. I was surely an agent of God, misunderstood, tormented, crucified yet redeemed and blissfully happy. My energy level rose, I hardly needed to eat. At night I was 'at one' with the stars, the universe and I were a unity. The beauty that is the cosmos was my beauty, in turn my beauty belonged to the world.

Now my inner vacuity, my sense of being 'nothing', became a positive advantage. Through this inner vacancy left by my 'murdered soul' came the spiritual, came God. Battered by the gossip of the world, betrayed by all, slandered, rejected, existing as 'a hole in space-time' or 'a wound in mind space' as I termed it, I was now this 'cylinder open at both ends', a tunnel or channel for the spiritual realm to enter and indeed to transform the world. From 'nothing and nobody' I became everything and everybody. A euphoric love pervaded me for the world and for the whole of humanity. I felt I had healing and forgiveness powers, that I sensed everyone's thoughts, that the unconscious of the world was known to me. My destiny was with God and in God. Everything that could possibly happen *had* now surely happened; *this* was my terminus, my terminus was Nirvana . . .

Despite realising how inadequate words were I longed to communicate my discovery. Eventually a kind of synthesis emerged in the form of an article entitled: 'Half man, half boat, the mind of the Borderline Normal' (Chadwick, 1979). This effort was useless. Within a day or so I realised that between the lines was the implicit communication: 'The Borderliner is good'. I had not been able to hold the transcendent middle ground state while writing about my experience. The realisation of this error came as a terrible blow, I sat in the park, with my head down, bitterly disappointed, even ashamed of myself. I had betrayed my lower, earthly, sensual nature. The article had been motivated by a wish for self-defence and self-justification. Even though I knew that the desire for self-justification can inspire much creative thought, I felt that I had been cowardly and pathetic. After this I ceased writing altogether. But my mental state had changed. And not only had it changed, I was soon to realise that it would never be the same again.

It is well known that the early stages of psychosis are often characterised by euphoria and by an enhancement of mental functioning (Breggin, 1991). Psychotic states also can develop from religious or mystical states (Lenz, 1979, 1983) and desperate (pre-psychotic) attempts at higher 'meaning seeking' can occur consequent on terrible emotional and social stress (Roberts, 1991). Clearly all of these phenomena are involved in the narrative above, which was indeed soon followed by outright psychosis. It may be that the Borderline mystical state, such as I have described it, is exceedingly difficult both to think and dwell within and very easily collapses into madness. It is perhaps the other side of madness. It is clearly impossible, however, adequately to reduce the above to biological language or to interpret it in terms of 'regression'. The experience is too rich and complex and makes reference to ontological states of affairs which deserve explaining rather than explaining away. However, it is fairly easy to see how people could come to see themselves as profoundly significant and spiritual if they were to access this state unreflectively – a state which, after all, if it could happen to me, could happen to anyone.

The significance of the mystical Borderline experience is the licence it gives us then to wonder. Have great religious figures of the past been here – but been able to hold the state? Does being able to maintain the state require colossal spiritual development? Are many people touched by this, but do few survive (Greenberg et al., 1992)? It could indeed be that the practitioners of the endeavours of spirituality and of psychophysics have much to say to each other. If the deepest level of reality is a semantic realm which orchestrates (at the observable level) both physical and mental events to fulfil an ever-unfolding purpose, then if one somehow approaches that 'ground', physical and mental events would indeed dovetail together, permitting psychokinesis and telepathy and the events could understandably be felt to be 'pregnant with meaning'. We have the possibility before us of accounting for a wide range of previously esoteric phenomena if we take such experiences as the above seriously.

The alternative conception to this is a neurological account in terms of aberrant brain functioning consequent on low food intake – possibly instantiated by my almost anorexic physical state. This of course arbitrarily dispenses with the reference of my account and essentially claims that all that is involved is a particular patterning of brain activity which is unusual and interesting in itself but of no other substantial significance. This of course is the typical reductionist's fallacy of confusing aetiology with value (Sacks, 1986). A particularly unusual mode of neural network functioning may indeed *permit* perception of what are perhaps best described as 'dimensions' of reality not accessible in easily consensually validated states of consciousness.

The critical issue which needs to be faced in order to defend the latter perspective is: can access to this realm prove to be theoretically and empirically productive? It has been fashionable among twentieth-century intellectuals to decry mystical states as theoretically useless. However, the work on the transduction of these states to delusional states (see Chapter 7) does put the experience to work in solving ongoing problems. Also my concern with the potential-to-actual conversion is in parallel with similar concerns about this issue in quantum physics (Laurikainen, 1988). The experience is also consistent with pantheistic beliefs in which God is instantiated in all things but that near-access to the zone of potential via a certain brain state does give direct experience of this Presence. The mistake is to attribute the experience to being 'chosen' when really the state is one of 'access'. Clearly the profound effects of experiences such as these (see Donaldson, 1993) suggest that they should be encouraged and discussion of them raised in educational contexts. This would surely be preferable to having them subjected to pre-emptive interpretation in terms of electrochemical activity alone. As a final comment, however, it is evident that in this realm of experience words are poor guides and given that body and mind have limits, we should be prepared to face the possibility that this 'access' is to territory beyond the capacity of any human fully to comprehend. On matters such as these, Thomas Hobbes was prudent:

> Words are wise men's counters, they do but reckon with them; but they are the money of fools.
>
> (*Leviathan* I)

Appendix II

'We're tough': on the paranoid psychology behind positivism and falsificationism*

Truth is independent of facts always.

Oscar Wilde (1854–1900)

This book frequently has dealt with the 'un-normality' of normal people. In this brief appendix I will highlight the actual implicit paranoia in the ideology of psychological science itself. Clearly if one works perennially with a paranoid ideology, however appropriate it might be for finding facts in the material world, its transfer to relating with humanity in life is liable to be negative.

I wish this short section to be self-contained, so I hope the reader will excuse very occasional reference to concepts already dealt with in earlier pages.

In 1936 A.J. Ayer published the then definitive statement in the English language of the logical positivist position: *Language, Truth and Logic* (Ayer, 2001/1936). The book was written apparently in a state of high passion (Rogers, 2001) yet I shall argue here that ironically it has been used by many people to actually dampen ideational ardour ever since, with such immediate challenges to excitedly delivered hunches and ideas as, 'How would you test that?', 'Define your terms more clearly!' and 'How would you prove that?' Logical positivism, I will claim, has become 'impatient positivism'. The system also has produced generations of positivistic psychologists – since the philosophy seems to have been taken on board by academic psychology more enthusiastically than by anybody else – who will never dare to let their imaginations roam anywhere that they cannot prove (itself crippling of creative work) and scientific psychologists generally who will never go any deeper than positivism will take them (itself a limitation on truth-seeking). In this section I shall therefore examine the psychological meanings of the positivist position and the Popperian parallel to it as I take

* This Appendix was first published in *The Journal of Critical Psychology, Counselling and Psychotherapy*, 2006, Volume 6, No. 2 (Summer), pp. 63–69.

it as granted that the psychological implications of philosophies are far from trivial.

REFLEXIVITY AND PARADOX

Unlike Karl Popper's (1959) falsificationist philosophy of science, which stresses the application of refutation bias (seeking to find out if one is wrong) rather than confirmation bias as a method of approaching 'better' more corroborated theories – a principle which in principle, and interestingly, could be laboratory tested, and has been (see later) – Ayer's philosophy is not reflexive, it does not apply to itself. To clarify: logical positivism, following the earlier leads of Wittgenstein and Russell, insists on rigorous definitional clarity and on propositions having to be based on the evidence of the senses to achieve the status of being 'meaningful' statements. On this basis evidence-based medicine is 'meaningful' for being so. The philosophy itself, however, cannot be 'tested' in this way. In a similar sense, mathematics, which has the measure of all things in the material world, cannot itself be measured. On a positivistic philosophy this would actually mean that mathematics does not exist.

Though Bannister and Fransella (1971) argue that a reflexive theory is a superior one, one cannot really *insist*, as Russell knew, that a theory, other than a theory of meaning itself, be reflexive. We are merely lucky if it is – as of course in psychology social constructionist theory and personal construct theory are but Skinner's radical behaviourist theory is not. Radical behaviourism doesn't explain how Skinner became a radical behaviourist. So: though a cooker may heat itself as well as the food within it, a pen cannot be expected to write along its own length nor a pair of scissors to cut itself. A theory or rationale (though not a person) as instrument can still be a good instrument yet lack reflexivity.

What is so paradoxical, however, is that Ayer's positivism, largely if not entirely derived at the time from the thinking of the Vienna Circle of Schlick, Carnap, Feigl, Neurath and others (see Valentine, 1992, for an outline), has infused itself into departments of academic psychology to this day when Ayer himself admitted later that the whole endeavour was almost entirely wrong (Straughan, 2005). Ayer became even more conflicted after a near-death experience in 1988 when he saw 'a Divine Being' (*Sunday Telegraph*, 25 February 2001; Straughan, 2005), something which seems to have caused a cryptic fracas within to the end of his life. Such is the conflict (also felt by Kant and David Hume) between theory and experience.

THE END OF HISTORY AND EXPERIENCE

Positivism and falsificationism have provided a philosophical road-map which basically guides us to think that the only valid or legitimate route to knowledge is via empirical (preferably laboratory) testing and re-testing of clearly defined and articulated propositions (Ayer, Schlick etc.) but that we can never be sure of this knowledge, only of its refutation (Popper).

Setting aside the outcry that fairly quickly developed in philosophy against these two rationales (e.g. Braithwaite, 1953; Lakatos, 1970; Laudan, 1977; Nagel, 1967; Polanyi, 1966), something which many psychologists seem completely to ignore, my purpose in this article is to argue that at foundational level both of them are intrinsically paranoid in tone and distortional of the way true knowledge could and should be sought. Furthermore they have locked psychology into a fragmented microtheoretic endeavour in which field evidence, cultural historical evidence, human experience and even 'far-reach' theorising itself – to say nothing of truly grand theorising – have all a secondary and marginal position.

The philosopher Stephen Toulmin was himself discontented by Popper's approach. He once said, 'Popper's own philosophy of science had this element of paranoia in it. Because what he used to teach us is that the nearest thing to a true theory is one that hasn't betrayed you yet. Any proposition is bound to let you down finally, but we cling on to the ones that haven't let us down yet' (Edmonds and Eidinow, 2002, p. 229). The general distrust in our own subject of anything that has not received two laboratory replications shows that Ayer has injected a similar degree of suspiciousness amongst us himself (how would one laboratory test Einstein's claim that imagination is more important than knowledge or Wilde's claim that life is simple but people are complex – and the right thing to do is the simple thing?).

In fairness to Ayer he was prepared to leave the problem of induction (the intrinsic uncertainty involved in inferring a general law from particular instances) unsolved, and induction, like the bias to confirmation-seeking that feeds it, depends in the last analysis on trust. Sadly although Ayer seemed to allow this, he then tried to minimise its necessity as much as possible – as if trust is something we should rid our procedures of at all costs. One can see what a pernicious ideology this is.

SUNSHINE VERSUS FROST

Of course, educationally, it is nonetheless convenient. It is much easier to train critical thinking ('What is the confounding variable here?') than it is to train people to think psychologically. One can structure an experimental design and statistics class a lot more easily than a class on divergent thinking, and teach IT skills a lot more easily than humanity, passion and imagination.

Ironically the words 'experiment' and 'experience' both derive from the same root: *expiriri* in Latin meaning 'try'. This is the core essence of our research lives. This drive comes from kindling something deep within. It has long been known that creativity itself (though often seeded in suffering) thrives in an atmosphere of acceptance, passion and enthusiasm for ideas (Barron, 1962, 1972; Martindale, 1975; Torrance *et al.*, 1958) rather than in one of 'knocking everything down' in the spirit of 'critical rigour' and 'incisive thought'. Indeed, who would ever want to do science if all they ever could achieve was certainty about what was *not* the case? Popper himself was an enemy of open-ended, wide and free-ranging ideation in his own life, being wryly dubbed by philosophers the writer not of *The Open Society and its Enemies* but of *The Open Society by One of its Enemies* (Edmonds and Eidinow, 2002, p. 139) while Ayer, as has already been hinted, wrote a cold water philosophy in a hot water state of mind. The overall effect of these theorists on psychology is that in the everyday nitty gritty of academic work the context of justification (testing, checking, refining, fine-tuning) has been allowed to psychologically intrude far too much into the context of discovery. The subject has been chilled, because of its ravenous hunger for scientific respectability, into a safe, conservative cynicism where, as so many journals demonstrate, any outré, lateral thinking or dramatically adventurous ideas are snubbed and treated with a sneering ridicule. How psychologists of such house-trained and standardised mentalities could have dared to conceive the subjectively strange ideas of the kind evolved not only in twentieth-century physics but in geology and art (and which reflect a lateral thinking style that might indeed be needed for us to get our minds around Consciousness) I do not know. While the subject poses as celebrating 'difference', when anything 'different' is presented to it its first response is to crush it.

FALSIFIABILITY IN TROUBLE

The empirical evidence on the use of a refutationist strategy does show that people can use disconfirming evidence when it is presented to them (Mynatt *et al.*, 1977) but the actual strategy of actively and deliberately 'seeking to be wrong' is difficult to elicit, participants have difficulty using it, difficulty understanding it, and as a sole strategy it is poor (Tweney *et al.*, 1981). Eysenck (1981) argued that a better strategy in general scientific work is to first seek confirmation and only subsequently refutation and theoretical modification. Mitroff (1974), in a classic study, found considerable evidence of confirmation bias in a qualitative study of NASA scientists although the great success of the Apollo project at least suggests that the strategy was successful.

Popper, as already intimated, was – despite his overt support for refutation and discreditation – himself a man who took criticism extraordinarily badly (see the remarkable section on this in Edmonds and Eidinow, 2002, Chapter 15) whilst at the same time having negligible insight into this trait in his character (p. 142). In all fairness to him, however, he may have been, perhaps like Nietzsche (see Köhler, 2002), writing as his Ideal Self rather than his Real Self. He was – after all – trying, for the most part, to destroy Fascism; he had been 'calibrated' in the 1930s and 1940s by a world where that was the dominant threat to peace. It is not surprising that he was rather relentless and uncompromising. But it was extremely sad that he became, in everyday ways, very like the aggressor he was trying to destroy. Not alas an uncommon phenomenon when one is thinking of that aggressor's paranoid ways so often and one has taken them into oneself to attack them (see Thomas, 2002 on this relational view of mind).

The context of discovery is a liberal permissive one though few departments in psychology reflect this in their ambience. Everything from dreams, hypnogogic images, mystical intuitions, thought experiments and fantasies (far away at times from what one can prove) may be necessary to get first rate ideas which can then be 'logicised' and tested. Edward de Bono's work in the 1960s and 1970s on relatively basic thinking strategies, designed to encourage thinking in children (e.g. De Bono, 1967), showed that one may have to go outside the boundaries of a problem so as to be able to find a solution to a dilemma within them. Indeed it could be said that if one has no interest in The Impossible one never knows what the boundaries are of The Possible. Apart from its evident motive to be as little like psychoanalysis as possible (see Chadwick, 2001a, p. 18) there may be other more cryptic drives at work in the crisp, cold, sharp realms of psychology's academia. Drives that cause such impatient inducements to move from ideational fervour to structured, testable proposition the moment a conception is out of somebody's mouth and into the discursive world.

THE TIGER AND THE FOX

One distinct possibility here is that we are dealing not with reason but with *intellectual machismo*. To put it pithily it is, as Katie Carr said in her book on surviving cancer, about the medical profession's attitude to cancer treatment (see Carr, 2004), basically 'Big willy talk'. This may seem facetious but really the implicit, and in some texts explicit, communication from the materialistic and atheistic hard science body of psychology is 'We're hard nosed . . . no loose, gullible, woolly thinking for us . . . we're tough'. The message concerning life and mind is, 'There's no grand meaning, no overall purpose, no afterlife, no soul, no God . . . but we can face all this and live with it . . . you can't, you're weak . . . now come on, tighten up your thinking, toughen up and join us'. The implicit statement 'We're tough' therefore heralds the statement 'We have the truth, the real truth'. But the question has bothered me for a long time: since when have people generally believed that tough people have the truth? Since when have tough people been particularly honest or accurate about anything? The fact is that tough people, in the general flow of life, come across more as aggressive, mistrustful, unempathic, insensitive, cold and unintuitive. What has all that got to do with being harbingers of truth? Ironically the empirical literature itself, as in Hans Eysenck's EPQ research (Eysenck and Eysenck, 1975, 1991), shows that in the P scale tough-mindedness and paranoia are factorially together. Once again empirical findings are uncomfortable for empiricists.

The hard liners' phobia of the intuitive, the qualitative and the holistic is not only paranoid intellectual machismo but, like all machismo, a stance that conceals a hidden fragility.

There is an old Chinese fable about 'The fox that benefited from the tiger's might'. This fable has other aspects to it but the essence of it (see Hsein-Yi and Yang, 1957) is that while the tiger could be seen by the forest creatures walking just behind him in the undergrowth, all would run away from the fox, who thereby derived his power not from himself but from what he signalled and was associated with. In psychology we have a similar situation. Practitioners know that while they ornament themselves with the emblems of everything that heralds and seems to 'mean' positivistic science then they at least have the tiger (let's say of experimental physics) there behind them in everything they say and write. I suggest instead that we renounce this apparent toughness and focus on knowledge (Latin *scientia*) in its widest sense to create a broader, fuller psychology and indeed approach to understanding generally. (See e.g. the refreshing move in this direction by Arends and Thackara (2001).) Sadly many people seem to think that if they stand out away from the tiger of 'Big Science' then they are, relatively speaking, on their own. They would have to fight and hunt without its protection. Alas, most investigators seem just a little too frightened to do this. (The Research Assessment Exercise, impaired funding chances and lack of promotional possibilities are powerful threats.) Clearly the tiger has many foxes, from evolutionary psychology, economics to sociology – and even some historians fancy their subject as a candidate fox. Most of these academics are quite simply used to having the tiger there behind them as a telling and commanding backdrop. He's been there so long, they don't appear to know how to live and work any other way. Seen for what it is, it's all rather . . . well . . . it really smacks of a basic lack of self-confidence. (For an invigorating antidote, however, to pre-emptive scientism of this kind and a beautiful blend of science and art see Hermelin, 2001.)

TRUTH VERSUS CLARITY

My criticisms of course are somewhat embarrassing. It is not my aim, however, to hurt or snub psychology itself. As Freud would understand, I love the subject and that's why, in my own limited way, I don't spare it. But, though I criticise standing in front of the tiger of physics to make the animals in the wood credit me with power, there is an important thought I would borrow from quantum physicist Niels Bohr (1958). He argued that in the search for what he used to call Deep Truth we have to face the dilemma of Truth/Clarity Uncertainty. If we want more clarity we have to settle for less truth; but if we want more truth we will have to suffer less clarity. One might have imagined the pre-Socratics, the Romantics and perhaps also the Chinese philosopher Lao-tzu saying the same thing. For psychologists with the appetite for verbal rigour of a Wittgenstein or an Austin, this is a solemn thought (for a more human portrayal of Wittgenstein than this see Hayes, 1989).

DEEP TRUTH TO DEEP MUSIC

In conclusion: if we are to ask such critical questions as 'What is the relationship between love and cognition?', 'What is the role of creativity in relationships?' and 'What *is* a mind that it can have spiritual thoughts and feelings?' or if we are to face up to Edward Hopper's statement, 'If you could say it in words there would be no need to paint' or W.H. Auden's 'A shilling life will give you all the facts', we are going to have to sacrifice snapshot measurement, rigid assessment frames and pin-point precision. To bring everything under the regulation of rational thought is, in any case, the attitude of an obsessive-compulsive. Psychologists in the fullest sense of the word have to be more than that. Life is bigger than reason. What, after all, does any therapist really have to do but grasp the poetry of their client's mind, the melody of their behaviour and the potential beauty of their evolving personality? It may indeed be, as Heaney (2002) has argued, that we reach the deepest strata of the Self not through words (or numbers) but by being resonant to the musical properties of what is being conveyed to us.

Bibliography

Abel, E.L. (1982) *Marihuana: The First Twelve Thousand Years*, Blacklick, OH: McGraw-Hill.

ABI (American Biographical Institute) (2007) John Forbes Nash, Jr, in *Great Minds of the 21st Century, 2006/2007 Edition*, Raleigh, NC: American Biographical Institute: ccxxxvi–ccxci.

Ah-mane, S. and Holloway, J. (2002) Drawing connections between us, *Mental Health Today*, March: 28–30.

Alanen, Y.O. (1997a) *Schizophrenia: Its Origins and Need-adapted Treatment*, London: Karnac Books.

—— (1997b) Vulnerability to schizophrenia and psychotherapeutic treatment of schizophrenic patients: towards an integrated view, *Psychiatry*, 60: 142–57.

Alexandrian, S. (1991) *Surrealist Art*, London: Thames and Hudson.

Alford, B.A. and Beck, A.T. (1997) *The Integrative Power of Cognitive Therapy*, New York: Guilford.

Alford, G.S., Fleece, L. and Rothblum, E. (1982) Hallucinatory-delusional verbalisations: modification in a chronic schizophrenic by self control and cognitive restructuring, *Behaviour Modification*, 6: 421–35.

Alvarez, A. (1971) *The Savage God: A Study of Suicide*, Harmondsworth: Penguin.

Anderson, F.S. (2007) *Bodies in Treatment: The Unspoken Dimension*, London: The Analytic Press.

Andrews, G. (1967) *The Book of Grass: An Anthology of Indian Hemp*, London: Peter Owen.

Anthony, W.A. (1993) Recovery from mental illness: the guiding vision of the mental health service system in the 1990s, *Psychosocial Rehabilitation Journal*, 16: 11–23.

Anthony, W. and Liberman, R.P. (1986) The practice of psychiatric rehabilitation: historical, conceptual and research base, *Schizophrenia Bulletin*, 12: 542–59.

Anthony, W.A., Rogers, E.S. and Farkas, M. (2003) Research on evidence-based practice: future directions in an era of recovery. *Community Mental Health Journal*, 39: 101–14.

Antoniou, J. (2007) Schizophrenia – what's in a name? *ISPS Newsletter*, June: 13.

APA (American Psychiatric Association) (1994) *Diagnostic and Statistical Manual of Mental Disorders, DSM IV*, Washington, DC: American Psychiatric Association.

Arends, B. and Thackara, D. (2001) *Experiment: Conversations in Art and Science*, London: Wellcome Trust.

Argyle, M. (1993) *The Psychology of Happiness*, London and New York: Routledge.

Aron, E.N. (1999) *The Highly Sensitive Person*, London: Thorsons.

Arranz, M.J., Munro, J., Birkett, J. *et al.* (2000) Pharmacogenetic predictions of clozapine response, *Lancet*, 355: 1615–16.

Atkinson, J.M., Coia, D.A., Harper Gilmore, W. and Harper, J.P. (1996) The impact of education groups for people with schizophrenia on social functioning and quality of life, *British Journal of Psychiatry*, 168: 199–204.

Attwood, C. (2007) Recovery: what does it mean? *Your Voice*, Autumn (September): 18–19.

Ayer, A.J. (2001/1936) *Language, Truth and Logic*, Harmondsworth: Penguin.

Baker-Brown, S. (2007) The pursuit of reality, *Your Voice* (Summer), 14.

Bannister, D. and Fransella, F. (1971) *Inquiring Man: The Theory of Personal Constructs*, London: Penguin.

Barker, P. and Buchanan-Barker, P. (2003) *Breakthrough: Spirituality and Mental Health*, London: Whurr.

Barron, F. (1962) The psychology of imagination, in S.J. Parnes and H.F. Harding (eds), *Source Book for Creative Thinking*, New York: Charles Scribner, Selection 19: 227–37.

—— (1972) The creative personality: akin to madness, *Psychology Today*, 6(2; July): 42–4 and 84–5.

Beatrice, J. (1985) A psychological comparison of heterosexuals, transvestites, preoperative transsexuals and postoperative transsexuals, *Journal of Nervous and Mental Disease*, 173(6): 358–65.

Bebbington, P.E. and Kuipers, E. (2003) Schizophrenia and psychosocial stresses, in S.R. Hirsch and D.R. Weinberger (eds), *Schizophrenia*, 2nd edn, Oxford: Blackwell Science, Chapter 31: 613–36.

Bebbington, P. and McGuffin, P. (eds) (1988) *Schizophrenia: The Major Issues*, London: Heinemann.

Beck, A.T. (1952) Successful outpatient psychotherapy of a chronic schizophrenic with a delusion based on borrowed guilt, *Psychiatry*, 15: 305–12.

—— (1976) *Cognitive Therapy and the Emotional Disorders*, New York: International Universities Press.

Becker, H.S. (1966) Marihuana: a sociological overview, in D. Solomon (ed.), *The Marihuana Papers*, Indianapolis, IN: Bobbs-Merrill, 65–102.

Bender, M. (1976) *Community Psychology*, London: Methuen.

Bennett, J. (1964) *Rationality – An Essay Towards Analysis*, London: Routledge and Kegan Paul.

Benor, D.J. (1990) Survey of spiritual healing research, *Complementary Medicine*, 4(3): 9–33.

—— (1993) *Healing Research: Holistic Energy Medicine and Spirituality, Volume 1: Research in Healing*, Deddington, Oxon: Helix Editions.

Bentall, R.P. (1994) Cognitive biases and abnormal beliefs: towards a model of persecutory delusions, in A.S. David and J.C. Cutting (eds), *The Neuropsychology of Schizophrenia*, Hove and Hillsdale, NJ: Lawrence Erlbaum Associates, Chapter 19: 337–60.

—— (2003a) *Madness Explained: Psychosis and Human Nature*, London: Allen Lane.

—— (2003b) Conference contribution, 'Schizophrenia: What works?' Nottingham, 8/9 May.

Bentall, R.P., Jackson, H.F. and Pilgrim, D. (1988) Abandoning the concept of 'schizophrenia': some implications of validity arguments for psychological research into psychotic phenomena, *British Journal of Clinical Psychology*, 27: 303–24.

Bergreen, L. (1998) *Louis Armstrong: An Extravagant Life*, London: Harper Collins.

Bernstein, D.P., Useda, D. and Siever, L.J. (1996) Paranoid personality disorder, in T.A. Widigal, A.J. Frances, H.A. Pincus, R. Ross, M.B. First and W.W. Davis (eds), *DSM IV Sourcebook*, Vol. 2, Washington, DC: American Psychiatric Association: 665–74.

Berrios, G. (1991) Delusions as 'wrong beliefs': a conceptual history, *British Journal of Psychiatry*, 159: 6–13.

Bilu, Y. and Witztum, E. (1994) Culturally sensitive therapy with ultra-orthodox patients: the strategic employment of religious idioms of distress, *Israel Journal of Psychiatry*, 31(3): 170–82.

Bion, W.R. (1954) Notes on the theory of schizophrenia, *International Journal of Psychoanalysis*, 35: 113–18.

—— (1955) Language and the schizophrenic, in M. Klein, P. Heimann and R. Money-Kyrle (eds), *New Directions in Psychoanalysis*, London: Tavistock.

—— (1956) Development of schizophrenic thought, *International Journal of Psychoanalysis*, 37: 344–6.

—— (1957) Differentiation of the psychotic from the non-psychotic personalities, *International Journal of Psychoanalysis*, 38: 266–75.

—— (1967) *Second Thoughts*, London: Heinemann.

Birchwood, M. (1995) Early intervention in psychotic relapse: cognitive approaches to detection and management, *Behaviour Change*, 12: 2–19.

—— (2000) The critical period for early intervention, in M. Birchwood, D. Fowler and C. Jackson (eds), *Early Intervention in Psychosis*, Chichester: Wiley, 28–63.

Birchwood, M., Smith, J. and Cochran, R. (1992) Specific and non-specific effects of educational intervention for families living with schizophrenia, *British Journal of Psychiatry*, 160: 806–14.

Birchwood, M., Meaden, A., Trower, P., Gilbert, P. and Plaistow, J. (2000) The power and omnipotence of voices: subordination and entrapment by voices and significant others, *Psychological Medicine*, 30: 337–44.

Birchwood, M., Meaden, A. Trower, P. and Gilbert, P. (2002) Shame, humiliation and entrapment in psychosis: a social rank theory approach to cognitive interventions with voices and delusions, in A.P. Morrison (ed.), *A Casebook of Cognitive Therapy for Psychosis*, Hove: Brunner-Routledge, Chapter 7: 108–31.

Blackmore, S.J. (1982) *Beyond the Body*, London: Heinemann.

—— (1987) Where am I? Perspectives in imagery and the out-of-body experience, *Journal of Mental Imagery*, 11: 53–66.

Bleuler, E. (1955/1911) *Dementia Praecox or the Group of Schizophrenias*, New York: International Universities Press.

Bleuler, M. (1978) *The Schizophrenic Disorders: Long Term Patient and Family Studies*, New Haven, CT: Yale University Press.

Bloch, A. (1979) *Murphy's Law and Other Reasons Why Things Go Wrong*, London: Magnum Books.

Boal, A. (1979) *Theatre of the Oppressed*, London: Pluto Press.

Bohr, N. (1958) *Atomic Physics and Human Knowledge*, New York: John Wiley.

Boisen, A.T. (1947) Onset in acute psychosis, *Psychiatry*, 10: 159–67.

—— (1952) Mystical identification in mental disorder, *Psychiatry*, 15: 287–97.

Bola, J.R. and Mosher, L.R. (2003) Treatment of acute psychosis without neuro-leptics: two-year outcomes from the Soteria project, *Journal of Nervous and Mental Disease*, 191: 219–29.

Bolton, G. (1999) *The Therapeutic Potential of Creative Writing: Writing Myself*, London and Philadelphia: Jessica Kingsley.

Boyle, M. (2002) *Schizophrenia: A Scientific Delusion?* London: Routledge.

Braithwaite, R.B. (1953) *Scientific Explanation*, Cambridge: Cambridge University Press.

Brand, J., Davis, G. and Wood, R. (1979) Experiments with Matthew Manning, *Journal of the Society for Psychical Research*, 15(782): 199–223.

Breggin, P. (1991) *Toxic Psychiatry: Drugs and ECT, the Truth and Better Alternatives*, London: Fontana.

Britt, D. (ed.) (1999) *Modern Art: Impressionism to Post-Modernism*, London: Thames and Hudson.

Brüne, M. (2004) Understanding the symptoms of 'schizophrenia' in evolutionary terms, *Behavioural and Brain Sciences*, 27(6): 857.

Buckley, P. (1981) Mystical experience and schizophrenia, *Schizophrenia Bulletin*, 7(3): 516–21.

Buckley, P. and Galanter, M. (1979) Mystical experience, spiritual knowledge and a contemporary ecstatic religion, *British Journal of Medical Psychology*, 52: 281–9.

Burke, T.P. (2004) *The Major Religions*, Oxford: Blackwell.

Busch, F.N. and Sandberg, L.S. (2007) *Psychotherapy and Medication*, London: The Analytic Press.

Butler, A.M. and Ford, B. (2003) *Postmodernism*, Harpenden, Herts: Pocket Essentials.

Butler, C. (2004) An awareness-raising tool addressing lesbian and gay lives, *Clinical Psychology*, 36 (April): 15–17.

Byatt, A.S. (2004) Soul searching, *The Guardian* (Review), Saturday, 14 February: 4–6.

Calvocoressi, R. (1984) *Magritte*, Oxford: Phaidon Press.

Cardno, A.G. and Gottesman, I.I. (2000) Twin studies of schizophrenia: from bow and arrow concordances to Star Wars MX and functional genomics, *American Journal of Medical Genetics*, 97: 12–17.

Carless, D. and Douglas, K. (2004) A golf programme for people with severe and enduring mental health problems, *Journal of Mental Health Promotion*, 3(4): 26–39.

Carless, D. and Douglas, K. (2007) Narrative, identity and mental health: how men with serious mental illness restory their lives through sport and exercise, *Psychology of Sport and Exercise*, doi: 10.1016/j.psychsport.2007.08.002.

Carless, D. and Sparkes, A.C. (2007) The physical activity experiences of men with serious mental illness: three short stories, *Psychology of Sport and Exercise*, doi.10.1016/j.psychsport.2007.03.008.

Carr, K. (2004) *It's Not like That Actually: A Memoir of Surviving Cancer – and Beyond*, London: Vermillion.

Carter-Morris, R. (2001) They think it's all over, *Nursing Times*, 97(15; April): 27–8.

Cepeda, C. (2006) *Psychotic Symptoms in Children and Adolescents: Assessment, Differential Diagnosis and Treatment*, London and New York: Routledge.

Chadwick, P.D.J. (2006) *Person-based cognitive therapy for distressing psychosis*, Chichester: Wiley.

Chadwick, P.D.J. and Lowe, C.F. (1990) Measurement and modification of delusional beliefs, *Journal of Consulting and Clinical Psychiatry*, 78(2): 225–32.

Chadwick, P.D.J., Birchwood, M. and Trower, P. (1996) *Cognitive Therapy for Delusions, Voices and Paranoia*, Chichester: Wiley.

Chadwick, P.K. (1975a) A psychological analysis of observation in geology, *Nature*, 256 (5518, 14 August): 570–3.

—— (1975b) Psychology of geological observations, *New Scientist*, 68, 18/25 December: 728–31, see also Correction, 22 January, 1976, 201.

—— (1976) Visual illusions in geology, *Nature*, 260: 397–401.

—— (1977) Scientists can have illusions too, *New Scientist*, 73(1045, 31 March): 768–71.

—— (1979) Half man, half boat, the mind of the Borderline Normal, unpublished manuscript.

—— (1982) 'Earth boundedness' in geological observation, *Geology Teaching*, 7(3; March): 16–22.

—— (1983) 'Peak preference' and waveform perception, *Perception*, 12: 255–67.

—— (1988) *A psychological study of paranoia and delusional thinking*, Doctorate Dissertation, Royal Holloway and Bedford New College, University of London.

—— (1992) *Borderline: A Psychological Study of Paranoia and Delusional Thinking*, London and New York: Routledge.

—— (1993) The stepladder to The Impossible: A first hand phenomenological account of a schizoaffective psychotic crisis, *Journal of Mental Illness*, 2: 239–50.

—— (1995a) The artist as psychologist, *The Psychologist* (Letters), 8(9; September): 391.

—— (1995b) *Understanding Paranoia: What Causes It, How It Feels and What to Do about It*, London: Thorson's Health Series/Harper Collins.

—— (1996) A meeting place for science, art and spirituality: the perception of reality in insane and 'supersane' states, *Network: The Scientific and Medical Network Review*, 60 (April): 3–8.

—— (1997a) *Schizophrenia – the Positive Perspective: In Search of Dignity for Schizophrenic People*, London and New York: Routledge.

—— (1997b) Recovery from psychosis: learning more from patients, *Journal of Mental Health*, 6(6): 577–88.

—— (1997c) Oscar Wilde: psychologist, *Changes*, 15(3; August): 163–74.

—— (1997d) Return to the meeting place for art, science and spirituality: mystical and psychotic perceptions of reality – some replies to correspondents, *Network: The Scientific and Medical Network Review*, 64 (August): 8–11.

—— (2000) Spiritual experience or religious psychosis? *Nursing Times*, 96(16; 20 April): 42–3.

—— (2001a) *Personality as Art: Artistic Approaches in Psychology*, Ross-on-Wye: PCCS Books.

—— (2001b) Psychotic consciousness, *International Journal of Social Psychiatry*, 47(1): 52–62.

—— (2001c) Sanity to supersanity to insanity: a personal journal, in I. Clarke (ed.), *Psychosis and Spirituality: Exploring the New Frontier*, London and Philadelphia: Whurr, Chapter 5: 75–89.

—— (2002a) How to become better after psychosis than you were before, *Open Mind*, 115 (May/June): 12–13.

—— (2002b) Spirituality and psychosis from the inside, *Journal of Critical Psychology, Counselling and Psychotherapy* (Special Issue: 'Taking Spirituality Seriously'), 2(4, Winter): 203–7.

—— (2002c) Understanding one man's schizophrenic experience, *Nursing Times*, 98(38; 17 September): 32–3.

—— (2003a) The artist's Diagnostic and Statistical Manual of Mental Disorders (DSM V), *Journal of Critical Psychology, Counselling and Psychotherapy*, 3(1; Spring): 45–7.

—— (2003b) The stream of psychotic consciousness, *Open Mind*, 124, (November/December): 22–3.

—— (2004a) Paranormal, spiritual and metaphysical aspects of madness: an essay on love and cognition, *The Paranormal Review*, 31 (July): 13–16.

—— (2004b) When once is too often, *Your Voice*, Winter: 8.

—— (2004c) The pen and the spirit: writing as a therapeutic adventure, *Open Mind*, 129 (September/October): 12.

—— (2004d) Beyond the machine metaphor: academic psychology as the study of mind and soul, *Journal of Critical Psychology, Counselling and Psychotherapy*, 4(4; Winter): 247–51.

—— (2005a) Oscar Wilde: the artist as psychologist, *The Wildean*, 27 (July): 2–11.

—— (2005b) Psychosis, psychokinesis, theta waves and subtle energies, *The Paranormal Review*, 34 (April): 13–16.

—— (2005c) The other side of delusions: magic, fiction making and personal growth, *Journal of Critical Psychology, Counselling and Psychotherapy*, 5(2; Summer): 85–8.

—— (2005d) How about THIS for a sackful of stigmas and diagnoses? *Your Voice* (Summer): 14.

—— (2006a) How social difficulties produce cognitive problems during the mediation of psychosis: a qualitative study, *International Journal of Social Psychiatry*, 52(5): 459–68.

—— (2006b) Oscar Wilde: the Playwright as psychologist, *The Wildean*, 28 (January): 17–23.

—— (2006c) Wilde's creative strategies, *The Wildean*, 29 (July): 28–39.

—— (2006d) If my parents had known, *Your Voice*, Winter: 8–9.

—— (2006e) Critical psychology via the short story: on the masculinity and heterosexuality thought police (MASHTOP), *Journal of Critical Psychology, Counselling and Psychotherapy*, 6(4, December): 200–209.

—— (2007a) Peer-professional first-person account: schizophrenia from the inside – phenomenology and the integration of causes and meanings, *Schizophrenia Bulletin*, 33(1): 166–73.

—— (2007b) On the dominance of male metaphors for thought in psychology, *Journal of Critical Psychology, Counselling and Psychotherapy*, 17(3; Autumn): 146–9.

—— (2007c) Freud meets Wilde: a playlet, *The Wildean*, 31 (July): 2–22.

—— (2007d) Laughing at a funeral: understanding the 'un-understandable' in psychosis, *Your Voice*, (Winter, February): 20–22.

—— (2008) Delusional thinking from the inside: paranoia and personal growth, in D. Freeman, R. Bentall and P. Garety (eds), *Persecutory Delusions – Assessment, Theory and Treatment*, Oxford: Oxford University Press.

Chadwick, P.K. and Hughes, E.M. (1980) Which way-up is upside-down? *Geology Teaching*, 5(3, September): 87–9.

Charles, H., Manoranjitham, S.D. and Jacob, K.S. (2007) Stigma and explanatory models among people with schizophrenia and their relatives in Vellore, South India, *International Journal of Social Psychiatry*, 53(4; July): 325–32.

Chiu, M.Y.L. and Chan, K.K.L. (2007) Community attitudes towards discriminatory practice against people with severe mental illness in Hong Kong, *International Journal of Social Psychiatry*, 53(2; March): 159–74.

Chrzanowski, G. (1977) The rational id and the irrational ego, in A. Heigl-Evers, H. Brazil and W. Schwidder (eds), *Das Irrationale in der Psychoanalyse – Theoretische und Klinische Aspekte*, Gottingen: Vandenhoek and Ruprecht: 90–98.

Claridge, G.S. (1967) *Personality and Arousal*, Oxford: Pergamon.

—— (1985) *Origins of Mental Illness*, Oxford: Blackwell.

—— (1988) Schizotypy and schizophrenia, in P. Bebbington and P. McGuffin (eds), *Schizophrenia: The Major Issues*, London: Heinemann.

—— (1990) Can a disease model of schizophrenia survive? In R.P. Bentall (ed.), *Reconstructing Schizophrenia*, London and New York: Routledge, Chapter 6: 157–83.

—— (1997) *Schizotypy: Implications for Illness and Health*, Oxford: Oxford University Press.

Claridge, G.S., Pryor, R. and Watkins, G. (1990) *Sounds from the Bell Jar: Ten Psychotic Authors*, London: Macmillan.

Clarke, I. (ed.) (2001) *Psychosis and Spirituality: Exploring the New Frontier*, London and Philadelphia: Whurr.

—— (2002) Is there anything there? The problem of spirituality considered, *Journal of Critical Psychology, Counselling and Psychotherapy*, 2: 261–66.

Cobb, A. and Roberts, M. (2007) Putting the soul back into psychiatry, *Open Mind*, 147 (September/October): 6–7.

Cohen, G. (1992) Comments on 'Towards a discursive psychology of remembering' by D. Edwards, J. Potter and D. Middleton, *The Psychologist*, 5(10): 449.

Collins, G.R. (1988) *Christian Counselling: A Comprehensive Guide*, Dallas, TX: Ward Inc.

Collins, J. and Selina, H. (2006) *Introducing Heidegger*, Cambridge: Icon Books.

Consroe, P. (1997) The perceived effects of smoked cannabis on patients with multiple sclerosis, *European Neurology*, 8(1): 44–8.

Cooley, C.N. (1902) *Human Nature and the Social Order*, New York: Charles Scribner's Sons.

Cornwell, J. (1999) Bard of prey, *The Sunday Times Magazine*, 3 October: 30–37.

Corr, P.J. (2006) *Understanding Biological Psychology*, Oxford: Blackwell Publishing.

Corrigan, P.W. (2004) *Beat the Stigma and Discrimination! Four Lessons for Mental Health Advocates*, Tinley Park: Recovery Press.

Coupland, N. and Coupland, J. (1990) Language and later life, in H. Giles and W.P. Robinson (eds), *Handbook of Language and Social Psychology*, Chichester: John Wiley and Sons.

Cox, D. and Cowling, P. (1989) *Are You Normal?* London: Tower Press.

Craig, T.K.J., Liberman, R.P., Browne, M., Robertson, M.J. and O'Flynn, D. (2003) Psychiatric rehabilitation, in S.R. Hirsch and D.R. Weinberger (eds), *Schizophrenia*, Oxford: Blackwell Science, Chapter 32: 637–56.

Crow, T.J. (1993) Sexual selection, Machiavellian intelligence and the origins of psychosis, *Lancet*, 342 (8871): 594–8.

—— (1995) A continuum of psychosis, one human gene, and not much else – the case for homogeneity, *Schizophrenia Research*, 17(2): 135–45.

—— (1997) Is schizophrenia the price Homo Sapiens pays for language? *Schizophrenia Research*, 28: 127–41.

—— (2004) Cerebral asymmetry and the lateralisation of language: core deficits in schizophrenia as pointers to the gene, *Current Opinion in Psychiatry*, 17: 96–106.

—— (2006) March 27, 1827 and what happened later – the impact of psychiatry on evolutionary theory, *Progress in Neuro-psychopharmacology and Biological Psychiatry*, 30: 785–96.

Crow, T.J., DeLisi, L.E. and Johnstone, E.C. (1989) Concordance by sex in sibling pairs with schizophrenia is paternally inherited: evidence for a pseudoautosomal locus, *British Journal of Psychiatry*, 155: 92–7.

Crystal, D. (2000) *The Cambridge Fact Finder (Fourth Edition)*, Cambridge: Cambridge University Press.

Cullberg, J. (2000) *Psykoser: ett humanistiskt och biologiskt perspectiv*, Stockholm: Natur och Kultur.

—— (2001) The parachute project: first episode psychosis – background and treatment, in P. Williams (ed.), *A Language for Psychosis – Psychoanalysis of Psychotic States*, London: Whurr: 115–25.

Curtis, T., Dellar, R., Leslie, E. and Watson, B. (2001) *Mad Pride: A Celebration of Mad Culture*, London: Handsell.

Csikszentmihalyi, M. (1992) *Flow: The Psychology of Happiness*, London: Rider Press.

Davies, B. (1995) *Past Life Regression with Transsexuals*, Presentation at the Psychotherapy and Spiritual Healing International Conference, Regents College, 10–11 April.

De Bono, E. (1967) *The Five-day Course in Thinking*, Harmondsworth: Penguin.

De Quincey, T. (1998) *Confessions of an English Opium-eater, and Other Writings*, Oxford: Oxford University Press. (First published 1822.)

Deikmann, A.J. (1966) Deautomatization and the mystic experience, *Psychiatry*, Vol. 29, reprinted in R. Ornstein (1986) *The Psychology of Consciousness*, Chapter 7, New York: Penguin.

—— (1977) Comment on the GAP report on mysticism, *Journal of Nervous and Mental Disease*, 165(3): 213–17.

Dickerson, F.B. (2000) Cognitive behavioural psychotherapy for schizophrenia: a review of recent empirical studies, *Schizophrenia Research*, 43: 71–90.

Dickerson, F., Sommerville, J., Origoni, A., Ringel, N. and Parente, F. (2002) Experiences of stigma among outpatients with schizophrenia, *Schizophrenia Bulletin*, 28: 143–55.

Dietrich, S., Matschinger, H. and Angermeyer, M.C. (2006) The relationship between biogenetic causal explanations and social distance toward people with mental disorders: results from a population survey in Germany, *International Journal of Social Psychiatry*, 52 (4; March): 164–74.

Dixon, N.F. (1981) *Preconscious Processing*, Chichester: Wiley.

Dobson, R. (2007) The oldest swingers: sex games of Stone Age exposed, *Sunday Times*, April 29th: 20.

Donaldson, M. (1993) *Human Minds: An Exploration*, Harmondsworth: Penguin.

Dostoyevsky, F. (1972/1864) *Notes from Underground/The Double (1846)*, Harmondsworth: Penguin.

Dryden, W. (1999) *How To Accept Yourself*, London: Sheldon Press.

Duchene, A., Graves, R.E. and Brugger, P. (1998) Schizotypal thinking and associative processing: a response commonality analysis of verbal fluency, *Journal of Psychiatry and Neuroscience*, 23: 56–60.

Edmonds, D. and Eidinow, J. (2002) *Wittgenstein's Poker: The Story of a Ten Minute Argument Between Two Great Philosophers*, London: Faber and Faber.

Edwards, D. (1989) Cognitive restructuring through guided imagery: lessons from gestalt therapy, in A. Freeman, K. Simon, H. Arkowitz and L. Bentler (eds), *Comprehensive Handbook of Cognitive Therapy*, New York: Plenum.

—— (1990) Cognitive therapy and the restructuring of early memories through guided imagery, *Journal of Cognitive Psychotherapy: An International Quarterly*, 4: 33–49.

Eisenman, R. (2003) Using marijuana: positive and negative experiences, *International Journal of Psychosocial Rehabilitation*, 8: 21–4.

Elger, D. (2006) *Dadaism*, London and Cologne: Taschen.

Ellenberger, H.F. (1994/1970) *The Discovery of the Unconscious: The History and Evolution of Dynamic Psychiatry*, London: Basic Books.

Ellis, A. (1962) *Reason and Emotion in Psychotherapy*, Secausus, NJ: Lyle Stuart.

Ellmann, R. (1982/1959) *James Joyce*, Oxford: Oxford University Press.

Erikson, E.H. (1950) *Childhood and Society*, Harmondsworth: Pelican.

Evans, J.L. (1997) Semantic activation and preconscious processing in schizophrenia and schizotypy, in G.S. Claridge (ed.), *Schizotypy: Implications for Illness and Health*, Oxford: Oxford University Press, Chapter 5: 80–97.

Eysenck, H.J. (1967) *The Biological Basis of Personality*, Springfield, IL: Charles C. Thomas.

—— (ed.) (1981) *A Model for Personality*, Berlin and Heidelberg: Springer Verlag.

—— (1995) *Genius: The Natural History of Creativity*, Cambridge: Cambridge University Press.

Eysenck, H.J. and Eysenck, S.B.G. (1975) *Manual of the Eysenck Personality Questionnaire* (Junior and Adult), Sevenoaks, Kent: Hodder and Stoughton.

—— (1976) *Psychoticism as a Dimension of Personality*, London: Hodder and Stoughton.

—— (1991) *Manual of the Eysenck Personality Scales (EPQ-R)*, London: Hodder and Stoughton.

Fachner, J. (2003) Jazz, improvisation and a social pharmacology of music, *Music Therapy Today* (online), 4(3) June.

Federn, P. (1934) The analysis of psychotics, *International Journal of Psychoanalysis*, 15: 209–15.

—— (1977) *Ego Psychology and the Psychoses*, London: Maresfield Reprints.

Fenigstein, A. (1984) Self-consciousness and the over-perception of Self as a target, *Journal of Personality and Social Psychology*, 47(4): 860–70.

Firth, S. (2004) Raymond Moody on theories of the paranormal, NDEs and the afterlife, *Network Review*, 85 (Summer): 28–9.

Fonaghy, P. and Target, M. (1997) Attachment and reflective function: their role in self-organisation, *Development and Psychopathology*, 9: 679–700.

Fowler, D., Garety, P. and Kuipers, E. (1995) *Cognitive Behaviour Therapy for Psychosis*, Chichester: Wiley.

Franck, D. (2002) *The Bohemians: The Birth of Modern Art, Paris 1900–1930*, London: Phoenix.

Frankl, V.E. (1959) *From Death Camp to Existentialism*, Boston: Beacon Press.

—— (1963) *Man's Search for Meaning*, New York: Washington Square Press.

—— (1969) *The Doctor and the Soul*, New York: Bantam Books.

Freeman, D., Freeman, J. and Garety, P. (2006) *Overcoming Paranoid and Suspicious Thoughts: A Self-help Guide Using Cognitive Behavioural Techniques*, London: Robinson.

Freeman, D. and Garety, P. (2004a) *Paranoia: The Psychology of Persecutory Delusions Maudsley Monographs*, 45, Hove and New York: Psychology Press.

—— (2004b) Bats among birds, *The Psychologist*, 17(11): 642–5.

Freeman, N.H., Sinha, C.G. and Stedman, J.A. (1982) All the cars – which cars? From word meaning to discourse analysis, in M. Beveridge (ed.), *Children Thinking Through Language*, London: Edward Arnold.

French, C.C. (1992) Factors underlying belief in the paranormal: do sheep and goats think differently?, *The Psychologist*, 5: 295–9.

Freud, S. (1911) *Psychoanalytic Notes on an Autobiographical Account of a Case of Paranoia (Dementia Paranoides) – The Case of Schreber*, Standard Edition 12, London: Hogarth Press: 3–82.

—— (1940) *An Outline of Psychoanalysis*, Standard Edition 23, London: Hogarth Press.

Fung, K.M.T., Tsang, H.W.H., Corrigan, P.W., Lam, C.S. and Cheung, W.-M. (2007) Measuring self-stigma of mental illness in China and its implications for recovery, *International Journal of Social Psychiatry*, 53(5; September): 408–18.

Furnham, A. and Igboaka, A. (2007) Young people's recognition and understanding of schizophrenia: a cross-cultural study of young people from Britain and Nigeria, *International Journal of Social Psychiatry*, 53(5; September): 430–46.

Gallant, M. (2005) My 'feelings of forgiveness', *Journal of Critical Psychology, Counselling and Psychotherapy*, 5(3; Winter): 132–44.

Galvin, S. (1989) Burnout: a cautionary tale, *Clinical Psychology Forum*, 24 (December): 8–10.

Garety, P. (1985) Delusions: problems in definition and measurement, *British Journal of Medical Psychology*, 58 (Part 1: March): 25–34.

Garety, P.A. and Freeman, D. (1999) Cognitive approaches to delusions: a critical review of theories and evidence, *British Journal of Clinical Psychology*, 38(2): 113–54.

Garety, P.A. and Hemsley, D.R. (1994) *Delusions: Investigations into the Psychology of Delusional Reasoning*, Maudsley Monographs No. 36, Institute of Psychiatry, Oxford: Oxford University Press.

Garety, P.A., Dunn, G., Fowler, D. and Kuipers, E. (1998) The evaluation of cognitive behavioural therapy for psychosis, in T. Wykes, N. Tarrier and S. Lewis (eds), *Outcome and Innovation in Psychological Treatment of Schizophrenia*, Chichester: Wiley: 101–18.

Gergen, K.J. (1985) The social constructionist movement in modern psychology, *American Psychologist*, 40: 266–75.

—— (1990) Therapeutic professions and the diffusion of deficit, *Journal of Mind and Behaviour*, 11: 353–67.

Gleick, J. (1994) *Chaos: Making a New Science*, London: Abacus.

Glover, G. (2001) Technician to the imagination, *Mental Health Today*, November: 12–13.

Goldberg, S.C., Schulz, S.C. and Schulz, P.M. (1986) Borderline and schizotypal personality disorders treated with low dose thiothixene vs placebo, *Archives of General Psychiatry*, 43: 680–6.

Goldstein, M., Rodnick, E., Evans, J., May, P. and Steinberg, M. (1978) Drug and family therapy in the aftercare of acute schizophrenics, *Archives of General Psychiatry*, 35: 1169–77.

Gottdiener, W.H. (2004) Psychodynamic psychotherapy for schizophrenia: empirical support, in J. Read, L.R. Mosher and R.P. Bentall (eds), *Models of Madness*, London and New York: Routledge, 307–18.

Grant, J. (2007) The participation of mental health service users in Ontario, Canada: a Canadian application of the Consumer Participating Questionnaire, *International Journal of Social Psychiatry*, 53(2, March): 148–58.

Gray, N.S., Fernandez, M., Williams, J., Ruddle, R.A. and Snowden, R.J. (2002) Which schizotypal dimensions abolish latent inhibition? *British Journal of Clinical Psychology*, 41(3; September): 271–84.

Green, M. (1996) What are the functional consequences of neuro-cognitive deficits in schizophrenia? *American Journal of Psychiatry*, 153: 321–30.

Green, M., Kern, R.S., Braff, D.L. and Mintz, J. (2000) Neurocognitive deficits and functional outcome in schizophrenia: Are we measuring 'the right stuff'? *Schizophrenia Bulletin*, 26: 119–36.

Green, R., Kavanagh, D. and Young, R. (2003) Being stoned: a review of self-reported cannabis effects, *Drug and Alcohol Review*, 22(4): 453–60.

Greenberg, D., Witztum, E. and Buchbinder, J.T. (1992) Mysticism and psychosis: the fate of Ben Zoma, *British Journal of Medical Psychology*, 65: 223–36.

Gregory, R.L. (1970) *The Intelligent Eye*, London: Weidenfeld and Nicolson.

Greyson, B. (1977) Telepathy in mental illness: deluge or delusion? *Journal of Nervous and Mental Disease*, 165: 184–200.

Guilford, J.P. (1959) *Personality*, New York: McGraw Hill.

Guishard-Pine, J. (2006) Can humanistic and existential therapies help the psychological problems of adolescents in the National Health Service? *Journal of Critical Psychology, Counselling and Psychotherapy*, 6 (1; Winter): 48–55.

Hafner, H. and an der Heiden, W. (2003) Course and outcome of schizophrenia, in S.R. Hirsch and D.R. Weinberger (eds), *Schizophrenia*, Oxford: Blackwell Science, Chapter 8: 101–41.

Halberstadt-Freud, H.C. (1991) *Freud, Proust, Perversion and Love*, Amsterdam: Swets and Zeitlinger.

Hallam, R.S. (2004) CBT and the arts, *Clinical Psychology*, 39 (July): 27–9.

Hammersley, R. and Leon, V. (2006) Patterns of cannabis use and positive and negative experiences of use amongst university students, *Addiction Research and Theory*, 14(2, April): 189–205.

Harding, C.M., Brooks, G.W., Ashikaga, T., Strauss, J.S. and Breier, A. (1987a) The Vermont Longitudinal Study of persons with severe mental illness, I: Methodology, study sample and overall status 32 years later, *American Journal of Psychiatry*, 144:718–26.

—— (1987b) The Vermont Longitudinal Study of persons with severe mental illness, II: Long term outcome of subjects who retrospectively met DSM III criteria for schizophrenia, *American Journal of Psychiatry*, 144: 727–35.

Harding, C.M., Zubin, J. and Strauss, J. (1988) Chronicity in Schizophrenia: fact, practical fact or artifact? *Hospital and Community Psychiatry*, 38: 477–86.

Harrison, G., Hopper, K., Craig, T., Laska, E., Siegel, J., Wanderling, J., Dube, K.C., Ganev, K., Giel, R., An der Heiden, W., Holmberg, S.K., Janca, A., Lee, P.W.H., Leon, C.A., Malhatra, S., Marsella, A.J., Nakane, Y., Sartorius, N., Shen, Y., Skoda, C., Thare, R., Tsirkin, S.J., Varma, V.K., Walsh, D. and Wiersma, D. (2001) Recovery from psychotic illness: a 15- and 25-year international follow-up study, *British Journal of Psychiatry*, 178: 506–17.

Harrow, M. and Jobe, T. (2007) Factors involved in outcome and recovery in schizophrenia patients not on antipsychotic medications: a 15-year multifollow-up study, *Journal of Nervous and Mental Disease*, 195: 406–14.

Hayes, J. (1989) Wittgenstein, religion, Freud and Ireland, *Irish Philosophical Journal*, 6: 191–249.

Heaney, S. (2002) *Finders Keepers: Selected Prose 1971–2001*, London: Faber.

Heidegger, M. (1962/1927) *Being and Time*, Transl. J. Macquarrie and E.S. Robinson, Oxford: Blackwell.

Heider, F. (1958) *The Psychology of Interpersonal Relations*, New York: Wiley.

Heishman, S.J., Arasteh, K. and Stitzer, M.L. (1997) Comparative effects of alcohol and marijuana on mood, memory and performance, *Pharmacology, Biochemistry and Behaviour*, 58(1): 93–101.

Heller, K. (1988) Research hypotheses for intervention with delusion-prone individuals, in T.F. Oltmanns and B.A. Maher (eds), *Delusional Beliefs*, New York: Wiley, Chapter 15.

Hemsley, D.R. (2005) The schizophrenic experience: taken out of context? *Schizophrenia Bulletin*, 31(1): 43–53.

Hermelin, B. (2001) *Bright Splinters of the Mind: A Personal Story of Research with Autistic Savants*, London: Jessica Kingsley.

Herrera, H. (2003) *Frida*, London: Bloomsbury.

Hewstone, M. (1983) *Attribution Theory: Social and Functional Perspectives*, Oxford: Basil Blackwell.

Hinshelwood, R.D. (2004) *Suffering Insanity: Psychoanalytic Essays on Psychosis*, East Sussex: Brunner-Routledge.

Hirsch, S.R. and Weinberger, D.R. (eds) (2003) *Schizophrenia*, 2nd edn, Oxford: Blackwell Science.

Hodges, R.D. and Scofield, A.H. (1995) Is spiritual healing a valid and effective therapy? *Journal of the Royal Society of Medicine*, 88 (April): 203–7.

Hogarty, G.E. and Anderson, C.M. (1986) Medication, family psychoeducation and social skills training: first year relapse results of a controlled study, *Psychopharmacology Bulletin*, 22: 860–2.

Hollander, A. (2002) *Sex and Suits: The Evolution of Modern Dress*, London: Claridge Press.

Horney, K. (1937) *The Neurotic Personality of Our Time*, New York: W.W. Norton.

Hsein-Yi, Y. and Yang, C. (1957) *Ancient Chinese Fables*, Peking: Foreign Languages Press.

Idemudia, S.E. (2003) Mental health and psychotherapy 'through' the eyes of culture: lessons for African psychotherapy, in *The Unifying Aspects of Culture*, Internet-Zeitschift für Kulturwissenschaften.

Ilan, A.B., Smith, M.E. and Gevins, A. (2004) Effects of marijuana on neurophysiological signals of working and episodic memory, *Psychopharmacology*, 176(2; November): 214–22.

Irwin, H.J. (1986) Perceptual perceptions of visual imagery in OBEs, dreams and reminiscence, *Journal of the Society for Psychical Research*, 53: 210–17.

—— (1993) Belief in the paranormal: a review of the empirical literature, *Journal of the American Society for Psychical Research*, 87(1; January): 22–31.

—— (2003) Paranormal beliefs and the maintenance of assumptive world views, *Journal of the Society for Psychical Research*, 67.1(870; January): 18–25.

Jackson, M. (1997) Benign schizotypy? The case of spiritual experience, in G.S. Claridge (ed.), *Schizotypy: Implications for Illness and Health*, Oxford: Oxford University Press, Chapter 11: 227–50.

Jackson, M. (2001) Psychotic and spiritual experience: a case study comparison, in I. Clarke (ed.), *Psychosis and Spirituality: Exploring the New Frontier*, London and Philadelphia: Whurr, Chapter 10: 165–90.

Jackson, M. and Claridge, G.S. (1991) Reliability and validity of a psychotic traits questionnaire (STQ), *British Journal of Clinical Psychology*, 30(4; November): 311–24.

James, A. (2002) The voice of reason, *Nursing Times*, 98(42; 15/21 October): 26–7.

James, W. (1936) *The Varieties of Religious Experience*, New York: Longman Green.

Jamison, K.R. (1993) *Touched with Fire: Manic-Depressive Illness and the Artistic Temperament*, New York: The Free Press.

Jaspers, K. (1963) *General Psychopathology*, Transl. J. Hoenig and M.W. Hamilton, Manchester: Manchester University Press.

Jenkins, J.H. and Barrett, R.J. (eds) (2004) *Schizophrenia, Culture and Subjectivity: The Edge of Inner Experience*, Cambridge: Cambridge University Press.

Johns, A. (2001) Psychiatric effects of cannabis, *British Journal of Psychiatry*, 178: 116–22.

Johnstone, L. and Dallos, R. (eds) (2006) *Formulation in Psychology and Psychotherapy: Making Sense of People's Problems*, London and New York: Routledge.

Jones, R.T. and Stone, G.C. (1970) Psychological studies of marijuana and alcohol in man, *Psychopharmacologia*, 18(1): 108–17.

Joy, J.E., Watson, J. and Benson, J.A. (eds) (1999) *Marijuana and Medicine*, Washington, DC: National Academic Press.

Jung, C.G. (1963) *Memories, Dreams, Reflections*, London: Collins.

—— (1969) *The Structure and Dynamics of the Psyche*, Collected Works, Vol. 8, London: Routledge and Kegan Paul.

—— (1970) *Civilisation in Transition*, Collected Works, Vol. 10, London: Routledge and Kegan Paul.

—— (1971/1930) *Ulysses:* A monologue, in *The Spirit in Men, Art and Literature*, London: Routledge and Kegan Paul.

—— (1985/1955) *Synchronicity: An Acausal Connecting Principle*, London: Ark.

Jung, C.G. and Pauli, W. (1955) *The Interpretation of Nature and the Psyche*, New York: Pantheon Books.

Kahneman, D., Slovic, P. and Tversky, A. (1982) *Judgement under Uncertainty: Heuristics and Biases*, Cambridge: Cambridge University Press.

Kaines, S. (2002) The bipolar originating consciousness, *Open Mind*, 114 (March/April): 10–11.

Kalidindi, S. and Murray, R. (2004) First genes of schizophrenia found, *Your Voice*, (Autumn): 6–9.

Kandinsky, V. (1982/1922) *Complete Writings on Art*, Vol. 2 (edited by Kenneth C. Lindsay and Peter Vergo), London: Faber and Faber.

Kandinsky, V. (2004/1912) *Concerning the Spiritual in Art*, Transl. Michael Sadler, R.A. Kessinger Publishing.

Kaney, S. and Bentall, R.P. (1989) Persecutory delusions and attributional style, *British Journal of Medical Psychology*, 62: 191–8.

Kaplan-Solms, K. and Solms, M. (2000) *Clinical Studies in Neuro-Psychoanalysis*, London: Karnac.

Karlsson, J.L. (1972) An Icelandic family study of schizophrenia, in A.R. Kaplan (ed.), *Genetic Factors in Schizophrenia*, Springfield, IL: Charles C. Thomas: 246–55.

Kaye, C. and Blee, T. (1997) *The Arts in Health Care: A Palette of Possibilities*, London and Bristol: Jessica Kingsley.

Keefe, J.A. and Magaro, P.A. (1980) Creativity and schizophrenia: an equivalence of cognitive processing, *Journal of Abnormal Psychology*, 89(3): 390–8.

Kelly, G. (1955) *The Psychology of Personal Constructs*, New York: W.W. Norton.

Kemp, D. (2000) A Platonic delusion: the identification of psychosis and mysticism, *Mental Health, Religion and Culture*, 3(2): 157–72.

Kernberg, O. (1986) Identification and its vicissitudes as observed in psychosis, *International Journal of Psychoanalysis*, 67: 147–59.

Kettenmann, A. (2002) *Kahlo*, Cologne: Taschen.

Kettle, M. (2006) The gulf between the arts and New Labour is growing wider, *The Guardian*, Saturday 20 May, 35.

Kinderman, P. (1994) Attentional bias, persecutory delusions and the self-concept, *British Journal of Medical Psychology*, 67: 53–66.

Kinderman, P. and Bentall, R.P. (1996) Self-discrepancies and persecutory delusions: evidence for a defensive model of paranoid ideation, *Journal of Abnormal Psychology*, 105: 106–14.

Kingdon, D.G. and Turkington, D. (1994) *Cognitive-Behavioural Therapy of Schizophrenia*, Hove: Lawrence Erlbaum Associates.

Kinsey, A.C., Pomeroy, W.B., Martin, C.E. and Gebhard, P.H. (1966/1953) *Sexual Behaviour in the Human Female*, New York: Pocket Books, first published August 1953 by W.B. Saunders.

Kissane, D. (2001) Demoralisation – a useful conceptualisation of existential distress for the elderly, *Australasian Journal on Ageing*, 20(3): 110–11.

Klerman, G. (1984) Ideology and science in the individual psychotherapy of schizophrenia, *Schizophrenia Bulletin*, 10: 608–12.

Kliewer, S.P. and Saulty, J. (2005) *Healthcare and Spirituality*, London: Radcliffe Publishing.

Kline, P. (1981) *Fact and Fantasy in Freudian Theory*, London: Methuen.

Knight, M. (1954) *William James*, London: Pelican.

Knight, T. (2004) You'd better believe it! *Open Mind*, 128 (July/August): 12–13.

Köhler, J. (2002) *Zarathustra's Secret: The Interior Life of Friedrich Nietzsche*, New Haven and London: Yale University Press.

Kuchta, D. (2002) *The Three Piece Suit and Modern Masculinity*, Berkeley, CA: California University Press.

Laing, R.D. (1990/1960) *The Divided Self*, London: Penguin (first published by Tavistock Publications).

—— (1990/1967) *The Politics of Experience and The Bird of Paradise*, London: Penguin.

—— (1970) *Knots*, New York: Pantheon Books.

Lakatos, I. (1970) Falsification and the methodology of scientific research pro-grammes, in I. Lakatos and A. Musgrave (eds), *Criticism and the Growth of Knowledge*, Cambridge: Cambridge University Press.

Landesman, C. (2003) It's only skin deep (Review of the film *Far from Heaven*), *Sunday Times* (Culture), 9 March: 8.

Lapidus, L.B. and Schmolling, P. (1975) Anxiety, arousal and schizophrenia: a theoretical integration, *Psychological Bulletin*, 32(5): 689–710.

La Russo, L. (1978) Sensitivity of paranoid patients to non-verbal cues, *Journal of Abnormal Psychology*, 87(5; October): 463–71.

Laudan, L. (1977) *Progress and its Problems*, Berkeley: University of California Press.

Laumon, B., Gadegbeku, B., Martin, J.L. and Biecheler, M.B. (2005) Cannabis intoxication and fatal road crashes in France: population based case-control study, *British Medical Journal*, 331: 1371.

Laurikainen, K.V. (1988) *Beyond the Atom: The Philosophical Thought of Wolfgang Pauli*, Berlin: Springer Verlag.

Lawn, S., Bathesby, M.W., Pols, R.G., Lawrence, J., Parry, T. and Urukalo, M. (2007) The mental health expert patient: findings from a pilot study of a generic chronic condition self-management programme for people with mental illness, *International Journal of Social Psychiatry*, 33(1): 63–74.

Learmonth, E. (2003) Creative healing, *Open Mind*, 120 (March/April): 19.

Lee, A.G. (1991) About the investigation technique of some unusual mental phenomena, *Parapsychology in the USSR*, 2: 34–8 (in Russian).

—— (1994) Extrasensory phenomena in the psychiatric clinic, *Parapsychology and Psychophysics*, 1: 53–6.

Leff, J.P. (1994) Commentary on four papers on psychiatry and religion, *Israel Journal of Psychiatry*, 31(3): 192–3.

Lehman, A.F. and Steinwachs, D.M. (1998) Translating research into practice: the Schizophrenic Patient Outcome Research Team (PORT) treatment recommendations *Schizophrenia Bulletin*, 24: 1–10.

Lemert, E.M. (1962) Paranoia and dynamics of exclusion, *Sociometry*, 25: 2–20.

Lenz, H. (1979) The element of the irrational at the beginning and during the course of delusion, *Confinia Psychiatrica*, 22: 183–90.

—— (1983) Belief and delusion: their common origin but different course of development, *Zygon*, 18 (2, June): 117–37.

Levin, T. (2006) Schizophrenia should be renamed to help educate patients and the public, *International Journal of Social Psychiatry*, 52(4): 324–31.

Liberman, R.P. (2002) Cognitive remediation, in H. Kashima, I.R.H. Falloon, M. Mizuro and M. Asai (eds), *Comprehensive Treatment of Schizophrenia*, Tokyo: Springer Verlag: 254–78.

Libet, B. (1993) *Neurophysiology of Consciousness: Selected Papers and New Essays*, Boston, MA: Birkhäuser.

Liddle, P.F. (1987) The symptoms of chronic schizophrenia: a re-examination of the positive-negative dichotomy, *British Journal of Psychiatry*, 151: 145–51.

Lines, D. (2006) *Spirituality in Counselling and Psychotherapy*, London: Sage.

Lines, R. (2005) Artistic gobbledegook, *The Sunday Times* (letters), 5 June: 18.

Lukoff, D. (1985) The diagnosis of mystical experience with psychotic features, *Journal of Transpersonal Psychology*, 17(2): 155–81.

McCreery, C. and Claridge, G.S. (1995) Out of the body experience and personality, *Journal of the Society for Psychical Research*, 60: 129–48.

McDowell, C. (2002) Why modern men think that less is more, *Sunday Times* (Culture), 30 June: 34–5.

Mace, C. (2007) *Mindfulness and Mental Health – Therapy Theory and Science*, London and New York: Routledge.

McGrath, A. and McGrath, J.C. (2007) *The Dawkins Delusion: Atheist Fundamentalism and the Denial of the Divine*, London: SPCK Publishing.

McHoul, A. and Rapley, M. (2000) Sacks and clinical psychology, *Clinical Psychology Forum*, 142 (August): 5–12.

McKenna, P. (2003) Debate on delusions, with R. Bentall, P.K. Chadwick and R. Persaud, BBC Radio 4, *All in the Mind*, Broadcast 5 August, 2003.

MacPherson, R., Jerrom, B. and Hughes, A. (1996) A controlled study of education about drug treatment in schizophrenia, *British Journal of Psychiatry*, 168 (June): 709–17.

Magee, B. (2001) *The Story of Philosophy*, London and New York: Dorling Kindersley.

Malevich, K. (1959) *The Non-objective World*, Chicago: Paul Theobald and Co.

—— (1968) *Essays on Art (1915–33) Volume 1*, London: Rapp and Whiting.

Marland, G. (2000) Cognitive deficits in schizophrenia, *Nursing Times*, 96(16): 43–4.

Marsh, R. and Leroux, P. (2002) The importance of failing, *Clinical Psychology*, 12 (April): 27–8.

Marshall, A. (2003) Peer support among clients: an underused resource? *Clinical Psychology*, 26 (June): 11–14.

Marshall, D. (2002) *Journal of an Urban Robinson Crusoe: London and Brighton*, Burgess Hill, West Sussex: Saxon Books.

Martindale, B.V., Mueser, K.T., Kuipers, E, Sensky, T. and Green, L. (2003) Psychological treatments for schizophrenia, in S.R. Hirsch and D.R. Weinberger (eds) *Schizophrenia*, 2nd edn, Oxford: Blackwell Science, Chapter 33: 657–87.

Martindale, C. (1975) What makes creative people different? *Psychology Today*, 9 (July): 44–50.

Martindale, C. and Armstrong, J. (1974) The relationship of creativity to cortical activation and its operant control, *Journal of Genetic Psychology*, 123: 329–35.

Martyn, D. (2002) *The Experiences and Views of Self-management of People with a Schizophrenia Diagnosis*, London: NSF Self-Management Project.

Maslow, A.H. (1968) *Toward a Psychology of Being*, Princeton, NJ: Van Nostrand.

—— (1971) *The Farther Reaches of Human Nature*, New York: Viking.

—— (1973) Self actualising and beyond, in G. Lindzey, C.S. Hall and M. Morosevitz (eds), *Theories of Personality: Primary Sources and Research*, New York: Wiley.

May, R. (2000) Routes to recovery from psychosis: the roots of a clinical psychologist, *Clinical Psychology Forum*, 146: 6–10.

—— (2006) Resisting the diagnostic gaze, *Journal of Critical Psychology, Counselling and Psychotherapy*, 6(3): 155–8.

Mayer-Gross, W. (1932) Die Klinik (der Schizophrenie). In O. Bumke (ed.), *Handbuch der Geisteskrankheiten, Band IX, Spezieller Teil V: Die Schizophrenie*, Berlin: Springer: 293–578.

Mayerhoff, D., Pelta, D, Valentino, C. and Chakos, M. (1991) Real-life basis for a patient's paranoia, *American Journal of Psychiatry*, 148: 682–3.

Meehl, P.E. (1962) Schizotaxia, schizotypy, schizophrenia, *American Psychologist*, 17: 827–38.

—— (1973) *Psychodiagnosis: Selected Papers*, Minneapolis: University of Minnesota Press.

Meissner, W.W. (1978) *The Paranoid Process*, New York: Aronson.

Meuris, J. (1992) *Magritte*, Cologne: Taschen.

Miell, D. and Dallos, R. (eds) (1996) *Social Interaction and Personal Relationships*, Milton Keynes: Open University Press.

Milton, J., Polmear, C. and Fabricius, J. (2004) *A Short Introduction to Psychoanalysis*, London: Sage.

Mitchell, S., Aron, L., Harris, A. and Suchet, M. (2007) *Relational Psychoanalysis* (3 Volumes), London: The Analytic Press.

Mitroff, I. (1974) *The Subjective Side of Science*, Amsterdam: Elsevier.

Molden, H.C. (1964) Therapeutic management of paranoid states, *Current Psychiatric Therapies*, 4: 108–12.

Moloney, P. and Kelly, P. (2003) Beck never lived in Birmingham: Why Cognitive Behaviour Therapy (CBT) may be a less useful treatment for psychological distress than is often assumed, *Journal of Critical Psychology, Counselling and Psychotherapy*, 3(4): 214–28.

Moor, J.H. and Tucker, G.J. (1979) Delusions: analysis and criteria, *Comprehensive Psychiatry*, 20(4): 388–93.

Moore, T.H.M., Zammit, S., Lingford-Hughes, A., Barnes, T.R.E., Jones, P.B., Burke, M. and Lewis, G. (2007) Cannabis use and risk of psychotic or affective mental health outcomes: a systematic review, *Lancet*, 370: 319–28.

Morrison, A.P. (ed.) (2002) *A Casebook of Cognitive Therapy for Psychosis*, Hove: Brunner-Routledge.

Morrison, A.P., Renton, J.C., Dunn, H., Williams, S. and Bentall, R.P. (2004) *Cognitive Therapy for Psychosis: A Formulation-based Approach*, Hove: Routledge.

Mosher, L.R. (2004) Non-hospital, non-drug interventions with first episode psychosis, in J. Read, L.R. Mosher and R.P. Bentall (eds), *Models of Madness*, London and New York: Routledge: 344–364.

Mosher, L.R. and Menn, A.Z. (1978) Community residential treatment for schizophrenia: two year follow up, *Hospital and Community Psychiatry*, 29: 715–23.

Mosher, L.R., Menn, A. and Matthews, S. (1975) Soteria: evaluation of a home-based treatment for schizophrenia, *American Journal of Orthopsychiatry*, 45: 455–67.

Mueser, K.T. and Berenbaum, H. (1990) Psychodynamic treatment of schizophrenia: is there a future? *Psychological Medicine*, 20: 253–62.

Murray, R. (2006) Discussion with Vivienne Parry for the programme, 'Am I Normal?' BBC Radio 4, Broadcast Tuesday, 21 November 2006.

Myhrman, A., Rantakallio, P., Isohanni, M., Jones, P. and Partanen, V. (1994) Unwantedness of a pregnancy and schizophrenia in the child, *British Journal of Psychiatry*, 169: 637–40.

Mynatt, C.R., Doherty, H.E. and Tweney, R.D. (1977) Consequences of confirmation and disconfirmation in a simulated research environment, *Quarterly Journal of Experimental Psychology*, 30: 395–406.

Nagel, E. (1967) What is true and what is false in science: Medawar and the anatomy of research, *Encounter*, 29: 68–70.

Namier, L. (1953) Human nature in politics, *The Listener*, 50 (1295) (24 December): 1078.

Neeleman, J. and King, M.B. (1993) Psychiatrists' religious attitudes in relation to their clinical practice, *Acta Psychiatrica Scandinavica*, 88: 420–4.

Neeleman, J. and Persaud, R. (1995) Why do psychiatrists neglect religion? *British Journal of Medical Psychology*, 68: 169–78.

Néret, G. (2002) *Malevich (1878–1935) and Suprematism*, London and Cologne: Taschen.

Nolen-Hoeksema, S. (1987) Sex differences in unipolar depression: evidence and theory, *Psychological Bulletin*, 101(2): 259–82.

O'Flynn, K., Gruzelier, J., Bergman, A. and Siever, L.J. (2003) The schizophrenia spectrum personality disorders, in S.R. Hirsch and D.R. Weinberger (eds), *Schizophrenia*, 2nd edn, Oxford: Blackwell Science, Chapter 7: 80–100.

Orford, J. (1992) *Community Psychology: Theory and Practice*, Chichester: Wiley.

Pagels, H.R. (1982) *The Cosmic Code: Quantum Physics as the Language of Nature*, London: Michael Joseph.

Palmer, J. (1971) Scoring in ESP tests as a function of belief in ESP, Part 1: the sheep-goat effect, *Journal of the American Society for Psychical Research*, 65(4; October): 373–407.

Pargament, K.I. (2007) *Spiritually Integrated Psychotherapy: Understanding and Assessing the Sacred*, London and New York: Routledge.

Peralta, V., Cuesta, M.J. and de Leon, J. (1991) Premorbid personality and positive and negative symptoms in schizophrenia, *Acta Psychiatrica Scandinavica*, 84: 336–9.

Perky, C.W. (1910) An experimental study of imagination. *American Journal of Psychology*, 21: 422–52.

Perls, F.S. (1969) *Gestalt Therapy Verbatim*, Lafayette, CA: Real People Press.

Persons, J.B. (1986) The advantages of studying psychological phenomena rather than psychiatric diagnoses, *American Psychologist*, 41: 1252–60.

Peters, E. (2001) Are delusions on a continuum? The case of religious and delusional beliefs, in I. Clarke (ed.), *Psychosis and Spirituality: Exploring the New Frontier*, London and Philadelphia: Whurr: 191–207.

Peters, E.R. Joseph, S. and Garety, P.A. (1999) The assessment of delusions in normal and psychotic populations: introducing the PDI (Peters *et al.* Delusions Inventory), *Schizophrenia Bulletin*, 25: 553–76.

Pettitt, S. (2007) What is it about Wagner? *Sunday Times (Culture)*, 5 August: 6–7.

Piaget, J. (1959) *The Language and Thought of the Child*, London: Routledge and Kegan Paul.

Pinfold, V., Toulmin, H., Thornicroft, G., Huxley, P., Farmer, P. and Graham, T. (2003) Reducing psychiatric stigma and discrimination: evaluation of educational interventions in UK secondary schools, *British Journal of Psychiatry*, 182: 342–6.

Pinfold, V., Byrne, P. and Toulmin, H. (2005) Challenging stigma and discrimination in communities: a focus group study identifying UK mental health service users' main campaign priorities, *International Journal of Social Psychiatry*, 51(2; June): 128–38.

Polanyi, M. (1966) *The Tacit Dimension*, London: Routledge and Kegan Paul.

Popper, K.R. (1959) *The Logic of Scientific Discovery*, London: Hutchinson.

Poreh, A.M., Whitman, D.R. and Ross, T.P. (1993) Creative thinking abilities and hemispheric asymmetry in schizotypal college students. *Current Psychology*, 12(4): 344–52.

Post, F. (1994) Creativity and psychopathology: a study of 291 world-famous men, *British Journal of Psychiatry*, 165: 22–34.

—— (1996) Verbal creativity, depression and alcoholism: an investigation of one hundred American and British writers, *British Journal of Psychiatry*, 168 (May): 545–55.

Pringle, A. (2004) Alive and kicking, *Open Mind*, 126 (March/April): 7.

Progoff, I. (1973) *Jung, Synchronicity and Human Destiny: Non-causal Dimensions of Human Experience*, New York: The Julian Press.

Rado, S. (1953) Dynamics and classification of disordered behaviour, *American Journal of Psychiatry*, 110: 406–14.

Ramon, S., Healy, B. and Renouf, N. (2007) Recovery from mental illness as an emergent concept and practice in Australia and the UK, *International Journal of Social Psychiatry*, 53(2, March): 108–22.

Read, J. (1997) Child abuse and psychosis: a literature review and implications for professional practice, *Professional Psychology: Research and Practice*, 28(5): 448–56.

Read, J., Agar, K., Argyle, N. and Aderhold, V. (2003) Sexual and physical abuse during childhood and adulthood as predictors of hallucinations, delusions and thought disorder, *Psychology and Psychotherapy: Theory, Research and Practice*, 76: 1–22.

Riley, B., Asherson, P. and McGuffin, P. (2003) Genetics and schizophrenia, in S.R. Hirsch and D.R. Weinberger (eds), *Schizophrenia*, 2nd edn, Oxford: Blackwell Science, Chapter 14: 251–76.

Robbins, M. (1993) *Experiences of Schizophrenia*, New York: Guilford.

Roberts, D. and Claridge, G.S. (1991) A genetic model compatible with a dimensional view of schizophrenia, *British Journal of Psychiatry*, 158: 451–6.

Roberts, G. (1991) Delusional belief systems and meaning: a preferred reality? *British Journal of Psychiatry*, 159 (suppl. 14): 19–28.

Robinson, M. (2006) *Kandinsky*, London: Flame Tree Publishing.

Rogers, A., Pilgrim, D. and Lacey, R. (1993) *Experiencing Psychiatry: Users' Views of Services*, London: Macmillan in association with Mind Publications.

Rogers, B. (2001) Introduction to A.J. Ayer (2001/1936) *Language, Truth and Logic*, Harmondsworth: Penguin.

Rogers, C.R. (1961) *On Becoming a Person*, Boston: Houghton Mifflin.

Rogo, D.S. (1990) *Beyond Reality: The Role Unseen Dimensions Play in Our Lives*, Wellingborough, Northants: The Aquarian Press.

Romme, M. and Escher, S. (1993) *Accepting Voices*, London: Mind Publications.

Rooney, E. (2003) The 'write' to be who I choose, *Open Mind*, 120 (March/April): 18.

Rosenfeld, H.A. (1965) *Psychotic States, A Psychoanalytical Approach*, London: Maresfield Reprints.

Rosenhan, D.L. (1973) On being sane in insane places, *Science*, 179: 250–8.

Rosenhan, D.L. and Seligman, M.E.P. (1995/1984) *Abnormal Psychology*, London, New York: W.W. Norton.

Rothko, M. (2004) *The Artist's Reality: Philosophies of Art*, New Haven, CT and London: Yale University Press.

Rotter, J.B. (1966) Generalised expectancies for internal versus external control of reinforcement, *Psychological Monographs*, 80: 1–27.

Rudden, M., Gilmore, M. and Frances, A. (1982) Delusions: when to confront the facts of life, *American Journal of Psychiatry*, 139(7): 929–32.

Ruse, M. (1990) *Homosexuality: A Philosophical Enquiry*, Oxford: Basil Blackwell.

Russell, R. (1994) Do you have a spiritual disorder? *The Psychologist*, 7(8): 384.

Ryle, A. (1990) *Cognitive Analytical Therapy*, Chichester: Wiley.

Sackheim, H.A. (1983) Self-deception, self-esteem and depression: the adaptive value of lying to oneself, in J. Masling (ed.), *Empirical Studies of Psychoanalytical Theories*, Hillsdale, NJ: Lawrence Erlbaum Associates, Chapter 4: 101–57.

Sacks, H. (1995/1992) *Lectures on Conversation*, Vols 1 and 2, Oxford: Blackwell.

Sacks, O. (1986) *The Man Who Mistook His Wife for a Hat*, London: Picador.

Sagan, C. (1977) *The Dragons of Eden. Speculations on the Evolution of Human Intelligence*, London: Hodder and Stoughton.

Sanders, P. (2007) Schizophrenia is not an illness – a response to van Blarikom, *Person-Centred and Experiential Psychotherapies*, 6(2): 112–28.

Sartre, J.P. (1956/1943) *Being and Nothingness: An Essay on Phenomenological Ontology*, Transl. H. Barnes. New York: New York Philosophical Library.

Sass, L.A. (1994) *Madness and Modernism: Insanity in the Light of Modern Art, Literature and Thought*, Cambridge, MA: Harvard University Press.

Scheidt, C.E., Waller, E., Schnock, C., Becker-Stoll, E., Zimmerman, P., Lucking, C.H. and Wirshing, M. (1999) Alexithymia and attachment representation in idiopathic spasmodic torticolis, *Journal of Nervous and Mental Disease*, 187: 47–52.

Schmeidler, G.R. and McConnell, R.A. (1958) *ESP and Personality Patterns*, New Haven, CT: Yale University Press.

Schmidtt, J. (2000) *Disciplined Minds: A Critical Look at Salaried Professionals and the Soul-Battering System that Shapes Their Lives*, New York: Rowan and Littlefields.

Schneider, K. (1959) *Clinical Psychopathology*, New York: Grune and Stratton.

Schore, A. (1994) *Affect Regulation and the Origin of the Self*, Hillsdale, NJ: Lawrence Erlbaum.

Schrödinger, E. (1955) *What is Life and Mind and Matter?* Cambridge: Cambridge University Press.

Schuldberg, D., French, C., Stone, B.L. and Haberle, J. (1988) Creativity and schizotypal traits: creativity test scores, perceptual aberration, magical ideation, and impulsive non-conformity. *Journal of Nervous and Mental Disease*, 176: 648–57.

Schwartz, R.H., Voth, E.A. and Sheridan, M.J. (1997) Marijuana to prevent nausea and vomiting in cancer patients: a survey of clinical oncologists, *Southern Medical Journal*, 90(2): 167–72.

Searles, H. (1963) Transference psychosis in the psychotherapy of chronic schizophrenia, *International Journal of Psychoanalysis*, 44: 249–81.

—— (1965) *Collected Papers on Schizophrenia and Related Subjects*, London: International Universities Press, Karnac Books.

—— (1979) *Countertransference and Related Subjects*, New York: International Universities Press.

Segal, H. (1973) *Introduction to the Work of Melanie Klein*, New York: Basic Books.

—— (2007) *Yesterday, Today and Tomorrow*, East Sussex: Routledge.

Sekuler, R. and Blake, R. (1985) *Perception*, New York: Knopf.

Sensky, T., Turkington, D., Kingdon, D., Scott, J.L., Scott, J., Siddle, R., O'Carrol, M. and Barnes, T.R.E. (2000) A randomised controlled trial of cognitive-behaviour therapy for persistent symptoms in schizophrenia resistant to medication, *Archives of General Psychiatry*, 57: 165–72.

Serban, G. and Siegel, S. (1984) Response of borderline and schizotypal patients to small doses of thiothixene and haloperidol, *American Journal of Psychiatry*, 141: 1455–8.

Shams, M. and Jackson, P.R. (1993) Religiosity as a predictor of well-being and moderator of the psychological impact of unemployment, *British Journal of Medical Psychology*, 66: 341–52.

Shloss, C.B. (2003) *Lucia Joyce: To Dance in the Wake*, London: Bloomsbury.

Short, R. (1994) *Dada and Surrealism*, London: Laurence King.

Sider, T. (2005) Travelling in A- and B- time, *The Monist*, 88 (3): 329–35.

Siever, L.J., Bernstein, D.P. and Silverman, J.M. (1996) Schizotypal personality disorder, in T.A. Widiger, A.J. Frances, H.A. Pincus, R. Ross, M.B. First and W.W. Davis (eds), *DSM IV Sourcebook*, Vol. 2, Washington, DC: American Psychiatric Association: 685–701.

Silver, A-L., Koehler, B. and Karon, B. (2004) Psychodynamic psychotherapy of schizophrenia: its history and development, in J. Read, L.R. Mosher and R.P. Bentall (eds), *Models of Madness*, London and New York: Routledge: 209–22.

Silverman, J. (1980) When schizophrenia helps. *Psychology Today*, September.

Simons, J., Correia, C.J., Carey, K.B. and Borsari, B.E. (1998) Validating a five-factor marijuana motives measure: relations with use, problems and alcohol motives, *Journal of Counselling Psychology*, 45: 265–73.

Singer, O. (2001) Biases towards individuals with psychiatric disabilities as related to community integration, *International Journal of Psychosocial Rehabilitation*, 6: 21–7.

Skinner, B.F. (1957) *Verbal Behaviour*, New York: Appleton-Century-Crofts.

Slater, L. (2004) *Opening Skinner's Box: Great Psychological Experiments of the 20th Century*, London: Bloomsbury.

Solms, M. (1995) Is the brain more real than the mind? *Psychoanalytic Psychotherapy*, 9: 107–20.

Soloff, P.H., George, A., Nathan, R.S. *et al.* (1986) Progress in pharmacotherapy of borderline disorders: a double-blind study of amitriptyline, haloperidol and placebo, *Archives of General Psychiatry*, 43: 691–7.

Song, L.Y., Chang, L.Y., Shih, C.Y., Lin, C.Y. and Yang, M.J. (2005) Community attitudes towards the mentally ill: the results of a national survey of the Taiwanese population, *International Journal of Social Psychiatry*, 51(2; June): 162–76.

Stanton-Jones, K. (1992) *An Introduction to Dance Movement Therapy in Psychiatry*, London and New York: Tavistock/Routledge.

Stefanis, N.C., Smyrnis, N., Avramopoulos, D., Evdokimidis, I., Ntzoufras, I. and Stefanis, C.N. (2004) Factorial composition of self-rated schizotypal traits among young males undergoing military training, *Schizophrenia Bulletin*, 30(2): 335–50.

Stern, D. (1985) *The Interpersonal World of the Infant*, New York: Basic Books.

Stevenson, A. (1998) *Bitter Fame: A Life of Sylvia Plath*, Harmondsworth: Penguin.

Stoller, R.J. (1969) Parental influences in male transsexualism, in R. Green and J. Money (eds), *Transsexualism and Sex Reassignment*, Baltimore: Johns Hopkins University Press.

—— (1975) *Perversion: The Erotic Form of Hatred*, New York: Dell Publishing Co.

Storr, A. (1958) *The Integrity of the Personality*, London: Penguin.

Straughan, R. (2005) On the relationship between theory and experience, *The Paranormal Review (letters)*, 33 (January): 33.

Strauss, J.S. (1969) Hallucinations and delusions as points on continua: rating scale evidence, *Archives of General Psychiatry*, 21: 581–6.

—— (1989) Subjective experiences of schizophrenia: toward a new dynamic psychiatry, II, *Schizophrenia Bulletin*, 15: 179–87.

—— (1994) The person with schizophrenia as a person, II. Approaches to the subjective and complex, *British Journal of Psychiatry*, 164: 103–7.

Sutherland, N.S. (1992) *Irrationality: The Enemy Within*, London: Constable.

Sweetman, D. (1995) *Paul Gaugin: A Complete Life*, London: Hodder and Stoughton.

Szigethy, E.M. and Schulz, S.C. (1997) Risperidone in comorbid borderline personality disorder and dysthymia, *Journal of Clinical Psychopharmacology*, 17: 326–7.

Tarrier, N. (ed.) (2006) *Case Formulation in Cognitive Behaviour Therapy: The Treatment of Challenging and Complex Cases*, London and New York: Routledge.

Tarrier, N., Barrowclough, C., Porceddu, K. and Fitzpatrick, E. (1994) The Salford Family Intervention Project: relapse rates of schizophrenia at 5 and 8 years, *British Journal of Psychiatry*, 165: 829–32.

Tart, C. (1971) *On Being Stoned: A Psychological Study of Marihuana Intoxication*, Palo Alto, CA: Science and Behaviour Books.

Taussig, N. (2002) My cure is better than yours, *Open Mind*, September/October: 10.

Thalbourne, M.A. (1994) Belief in the paranormal and its relationship to schizophrenia – relevant measures: a confirmatory study, *British Journal of Clinical Psychology*, 33(1; February): 78–80.

Thody, P. and Read, H. (2005) *Introducing Sartre*, Cambridge: Icon Books.

Thomas, K. (2002) The defensive Self: A psychodynamic perspective, in R. Stevens (ed.), *Understanding the Self*, Milton Keynes: Open University Press.

Thomson, M. (1989) *On Art and Therapy*, London: Virago Press.

Thornicroft, G. (2006) *Shunned: Discrimination Against People with Mental Illness*, Oxford: Oxford University Press.

Thorpe, C.D. (1964/1926) *The Mind of John Keats*, New York: Russell and Russell.

Tienari, P. (1991) Interaction between genetic vulnerability and family environment: the Finnish adoptive family study of schizophrenia, *Acta Psychiatrica Scandinavica*, 84: 460–465.

Tienari, P., Wynne, I.C., Moring, I. *et al.* (1994) The Finnish adoptive family study of schizophrenia: implications for family research, *British Journal of Psychiatry*, 164(23): 20–26.

Tolton, J.C. (2004) First person account: how insight poetry helped me to overcome my illness, *Schizophrenia Bulletin*, 30(2): 469–72.

Torrance, E.P., de Young, K.N., Ghei, S.N. and Michie, H.W. (1958) *Explorations in Creative Thinking: Some Characteristics of the More Creative Individuals*, Minneapolis: Bureau of Educational Research, University of Minnesota.

Toulmin, S. (1972) *Human Understanding*, Vol. 1, Oxford: Oxford University Press.

Turner, D.D. (2006) Universal vibration: exploring the link between music and one's life process, *Journal of Critical Psychology, Counselling and Psychotherapy*, 6(3): 159–69.

Tversky, A. and Kahneman, D. (1974) Judgement under uncertainty: heuristics and biases, *Science*, 185: 1124–31.

Tweney, R.D., Doherty, M.E. and Mynatt, C.R. (1981) *On Scientific Thinking*, New York: Columbia University Press.

Tyson, P. and Tyson, R.L. (1990) *Psychoanalytic Theories of Development: An Integra-tion*, New Haven, CT and London: Yale University Press.

Valentine, E.R. (1992) *Conceptual Issues in Psychology*, London and New York: Routledge.

van Deurzen-Smith, E. (1993) Existential therapy, in W. Dryden (ed.), *Individual Therapy: A Handbook*, Milton Keynes: Open University Press, 149–74.

Van Os, J. (2006) The diagnosis of 'schizophrenia', *Acta Psychiatrica Scandinavica Supplementum*, 431, 9.

Van Os, J., Hanssen, M., Bijl, R.V. and Rovell, A. (2000) Strauss (1969) revisited: A psychosis continuum in the normal population? *Schizophrenia Research*, 45: 11–20.

Venables, P.H. and Bailes, K. (1994) The structure of schizotypy, its relation to subdiagnoses of schizophrenia and to sex and age, *British Journal of Clinical Psychology*, 33(3, September): 277–94.

Voth, E.A. and Schwartz, R.H. (1997) Medicinal applications of delta-9-tetrahydrocannabinol and marijuana, *Annals of Internal Medicine*, 126(10): 791–8.

Waldberg, P. (1997) *Surrealism*, London: Thames and Hudson.

Waller, D. and Gilroy, A. (eds) (1992) *Art Therapy: A Handbook*, Buckingham and Philadelphia: Open University Press.

Warhol, A. (2007/1975) *The Philosophy of Andy Warhol (from A to B and Back Again)*, London and New York: Harvest.

Warren, R.M. (1970) Perceptual restoration of missing speech sounds, *Science*, 167: 392–3.

Wason, P.C. (1960) On the failure to eliminate hypotheses in a conceptual task, *Quar-terly Journal of Experimental Psychology*, 12: 129–40.

Waterfield, R. (2000) *The First Philosophers: The PreSocratics and the Sophists*, London and New York: Oxford University Press.

Watson, L. (1987) The love of satin, *The World of Transvestism*, 7(7): 47–50.

—— (1993) Secrets of silk and satin decadence, *The World of Transvestism*, 14(6): 28–32.

Watson, L. and Beaumont, D. (1989) Transvestism: towards the twenty-first century, *TV Scene*, 7 (February): 28–31.

Watts, F. and Dutton, K. (eds) (2006) *Why the Science and Religion Debate Matters*, Philadelphia and London: Templeton Foundation Press.

Watts, F.N., Powell, E.G. and Austin, S.V. (1973) The modification of abnormal beliefs, *British Journal of Medical Psychology*, 46: 359–63.

Webb, D. (2005) Bridging the spirituality gap, *Journal of Critical Psychology, Counsel-ling and Psychotherapy*, 5(4; Winter): 201–12.

Weber, A.L. (1992) *Social Psychology*, New York: Harper-Collins.

Webster, R. (1998) *Why Freud Was Wrong*, London: Harper Collins.

Weimer, W.B. (1979) *Notes on the Methodology of Scientific Research*, Hillsdale, NJ: Erlbaum.

Werry, J.S., McClellan, J.M., Andrews, L.K. and Ham, M. (1994) Clinical features and outcome of child and adolescent schizophrenia, *Schizophrenia Bulletin*, 20(4): 614–30.

West, W. (2000) *Psychotherapy and Spirituality: Crossing the Line Between Therapy and Religion*, London: Sage.

Wilde, S. (1987) *Affirmations*, Taos, NH: White Dover International.

Wilding, J. and Boaden, M. (2005) *God's Unfinished Business: The Evolution of Humanity*, London: Janus Publishing Co.

Williams, L.M. (1996) Cognitive inhibition and schizophrenic symptom subgroups, *Schizophrenia Bulletin*, 22(1): 139–51.

Williams, W.L. (1986) *The Spirit and the Flesh: Sexual Diversity in American Indian Culture*, Boston: Beacon Press.

Winnicott, D.W. (1960) Ego distortion in terms of true and false Self, in *The Maturational Processes and the Facilitating Environment* (1965), London: Hogarth Press.

—— (1965) *Through paediatrics to psychoanalysis*, London: Hogarth Press.

—— (1985/1960) *The Maturational Processes and the Facilitating Environment*, London: Hogarth Press.

Worthington, E.L. (ed.) (2005) *Handbook of Forgiveness*, London and New York: Routledge.

Wright, E. (1985) *History of the World: The Last Five Hundred Years*, Feltham, Middlesex: Newnes Books.

Wykes, T., Reeder, C., Corner, J., Williams, C. and Everitt, B. (1999) The effects of neurocognitive remediation on executive processing in patients with schizophrenia, *Schizophrenia Bulletin*, 25: 291–307.

Wykes, T. and Reeder, C. (2005) *Cognitive Remediation Therapy for Schizophrenia: Theory and Practice*, London and New York: Routledge.

Zaehner, R.C. (1957) *Mysticism: Sacred and Profane*, Oxford: Clarendon Press.

Zigler, E. and Glick, M. (1988) Is paranoid schizophrenia really camouflaged depression? *American Psychologist*, 43: 284–90.

Name Index

Subject Index